3 Sisters

3 Weeks

3 Countries

Dear Janette, Thanks for your support!

(STILL TALKING)

READERS' FAVORITE
FIVE STARS

Elizabeth
Moore Kraus

Best, Always Beth Moore Kraus

A HUMOROUS AND HEARTFELT MEMOIR

The names of the lovely people we met and are mentioned in this book as well as some specific details have been changed to in order to protect their privacy.

For Les and Rie,

My Sisters, My Friends, My Traveling Companions

Sister is probably the most competitive relationship

within the family,

But once the sisters are grown

It becomes the strongest relationship.

–Margaret Mead

Prologue

Right now? It doesn't matter that the scheduled time for arrival at Los Angeles International is not until 2:00 p.m. I still find myself waking up to a pre-dawn session of tossing and turning at 3:30 a.m. I am not overly surprised. With excitement and anticipation serving like a high-octane fuel for my busy brain, it is highly unlikely I will fall back to sleep. This being my reality, I begin to scooch myself up in bed in a stealthy manner in order to not disturb my husband, Dave, who I see is sleeping soundly to the rhythm of his snoring. I adjust myself into a comfortable upright position. I inhale deeply and quietly take in what lies ahead, our "sister trip," the one that starts today, August 1. It's when I exhale the questions pounce all at once:

Why is it that my mind goes down rabbit holes chasing after things I worry about even though I do not need to worry? Our sister trip is such a splendid idea (of course it is), so why is it when people hear of our plans, their voices are so full of surprise? Or shock? Yeah, that's a better word. Why is this so unbelievable for others but not for us?

Worries or not, here I am pre-flight, in this case extremely pre-flight, with my brain already in overdrive with concerns. It is not at all a surprise to me because I am a professional worrier, self-taught. So since I am wide awake with these predawn questions, there seems to be no better time than the present to untangle them and find out why they rustle me awake, demanding my attention at this ungodly hour. I am curious, though, as to why this couldn't have occurred during daylight hours? It's clear I was not consulted.

For the three Moore sisters, Les (Leslie), yours truly (I go by Liz or Diz, short for Elizabeth), and Rie (Laurie), we are not concerned about needing to exorcise a demon waiting to burst through the surface after years of submersion. The truth is, there is nothing long-simmering among us and this eliminates any jitters for these three weeks and five thousand miles away from our homes. So for us, it is not a question of why go but rather why not go? The answer to the latter question is easy: we are sisters who enjoy each other's company. Besides, we love each other. And with this, I am already thinking of our future trips.

If this trip is such a rousing success, why not start planning another? Slow it down, Liz. Apply the brakes. This is me getting ahead of myself, as I so often do.

We grew up in Southern California along with two brothers in a family-friendly neighborhood, our house being one of four facing each other on a very short cul-de-sac. Although the lives of the five Moore kids included some difficulties and challenges, none of us suffered punctures so sharp and so deep that they created life-long wounds. Being free of such scars is what has allowed Les, Rie, and me to appreciate our differences and likenesses: we are like individual stars, each bringing light to our sisters' constellation. This is why we can see this trip for what it is—a fun jaunt. I like the sound of this. And in the darkness of this early morning, I smile at what lies ahead of us.

But then, just like that, I return to my familiar pattern of worrying because even fun jaunts should include some kind of backup plan, right? Then there are the Moore sisters who approach this trip without any such plan. (And no, I am not suggesting us as role models).

The truth is we have been focusing on the thrill of the unknown while completely ignoring the known. I mean, what if one of us (I am thinking most likely Les or Rie) does something that sends us sideways? And by the way, when it comes to going sideways, let the record show the Moore sisters are highly capable of doing this, and at varying velocities. Sure, we are fun companions who are loving, empathetic, and semi-patient toward each other, yet we still lose our footing time and again because what sisters do not? But back to us possibly going sideways and if, no, when it occurs (because heaven knows it will), how do we handle it?

There is one thing I am sure we should not do: our usual stomping off. We share this propensity, so much so that I came up with a well-suited nickname specifically for us: "stomper-offers." And if I may be so bold, we are without a doubt some of the best "stomper-offers" due to our dedication to this craft. For us, it has long been our practice that the moment we decide we are done talking (okay, arguing with whomever), we turn away and stomp off. It is a brilliant tactic that rarely works, yet we continue to use it because it is part of our sisterhood manual, "The Moore Sisters Repertoire for Argumentative Skills." The thing is, though, stomping off could very much unbalance us and in turn become that one grain of rice that tips the scale against us, for good. From this visual alone my worrying level increases. And then, of course, I bring in other matters to stir up my mental mix even more.

It has been fifty-some years since we have shared this kind of dedicated time and living space. Oh, and what about how Les and Rie are firmly set in their ways? (I'm merely set in my ways).

At age sixty-seven, Les will be bringing with her three very entrenched life-long behaviors. First and foremost, as one who is easy to fool and tease, Les is often the loving target of her family; she is a remarkably good sport. Second, she keeps a very firm grip on her money. (We have no clue how this came to be.) And third, Les keeps an even tighter grip on her emotions and words. Both of her traveling companions are familiar with the nature of this older sister, how she prefers to hold back what she is thinking or feeling, yet she could surprise us on this trip. It could happen.

Next, there is yours truly, age sixty-six. I am the middle child of five as well as the middle sister. This makes me a middle-middle; sure, I have issues. However, beyond my issues (only a few, naturally), my most important job, and it is one I take very seriously, is to make my sisters laugh. My success rate is high. Besides that, I also have the strong propensity to either tend to or repair any kind of sticky sister situation requiring my expert handiwork, all according to my expert judgment, mind you. What could go wrong? Oh, but if it does, I will fix that too. Not that either sister requests me to do said fixing.

And then our youngest at age sixty-three is Rie. While most babies of a family are often taken care of, Rie is the antithesis of this: she is a caretaker. Part of what she does includes crafting different words to feed the soul as well as foods for feeding stomachs. And though her heart is quite often in the right place, she can struggle with boundaries. Oh, and this one is a wanderer. Anything bright and shiny has the power to tug at her attention and she is off. When this happens, and it does, and it will, her sisters share a knowing smile as we go in search of her.

As I remain sitting up in bed thinking about all of the above, I know there is no avoiding the whole matter of the oh-so-charming cord of stubbornness that runs through all three of us. Modeled to us by the very best, our mom, we apply this streak throughout all relationships, and often. Of course, wherever we go there we are, so stubbornness will be joining us on this three-week holiday as well. Splendid. This should work.

I am suddenly thinking I should give both sisters a call and ask how they feel about all of this, not about getting a phone call from me so very early in the morning, but coming up with some kind of plan for when one of us (again, mostly them) sends us sideways.

I see now it is almost 4:00 a.m. Look at me answering my questions, resolving matters, and all before daylight! Even so, I should give sleep another try as a very long day awaits. I am sure to be considerate of Dave, not that he will be the wiser, as I slide myself back into a prone position. I bunch up my pillow to create a soft nest-like space for my head and do my best to settle my busy brain. As I work at that, the sage advice of Ernest Hemingway makes a surprise pass through my thoughts: "Never go on trips with anyone you do not love." Easy enough for the Moore sisters. No worries where that is concerned.

1

A SISTER'S SIREN CALL

AMONGST THE THREE OF US, RIE, ALONG WITH HER HUSBAND TIM, HAS TRAVeled most extensively throughout different countries in Europe. Upon each return home, Rie would reach out to her sisters with the same appeal, trip after trip, year after year:

"The three of us need to take a trip of our own. What about next year?" Regrettably, over time, taking such a trip started to be further from our grasp. And as the years passed, Rie's siren calls had grown almost silent, but even so she never gave up trying to lure her sisters across the ocean with her travel song.

In 2018, Rie volunteered to host Thanksgiving. It was after turkey but before apple pie when Rie once again began her familiar siren call out to her two travel-resistant sisters. That's not an entirely true description of us: We had work schedules, commitments, and other demands on our lives. Subsequently, all combined made it impossible every time to tell Rie yes, which she understood; she did. She told us she did. But this year, Rie was clever with her siren song as it took on a different sound. She made sure it included a harmony of facts, a chorus of reasons, and it concluded on a crescendo of emotions.

"Listen, you two. Diz is retiring in May, and Les you are working part-time, besides you have the summer off. We are all in the financial position to afford a long trip. It's time. Let's make 2019 the year we finally take our sister's trip. I want us to have this happen. We are all in good health, so what better time? Come on you two, let's go!" She made sure we couldn't deny her invitation to travel, and after a few minutes, both Les and I spoke the one word Rie had been waiting patiently all those years to hear:

"Yes," we said, in near unison. Rie allowed herself to take it all in: "I'm so excited," she said, then tagged it with her personal guarantees: "You two are going to love it. We are going to have such a great time."

Rie immediately pitched Italy as a choice of destination. When she got around describing the Italian gelato, Les and I were as good as there but then I countered Italy with Ireland.

"I mean, we've just learned we are genetically linked to Ireland. Let's get acquainted with our family roots. Plus you've never been and we will all be on a level-playing field discovering this country together." Both sisters handed back a positive response (I sure hope this is a predictor for our trip together; I suggest and they agree). Rie then added, "I've always wanted to see Ireland too, and since we will already be there, why not go to Scotland? We've family roots there too." The three of us were like little school girls giggling as we imagined Ireland and Scotland unfolding in front of us. And then Les chimed in, "What about England? After all, Daddy's family is from there. Can't we visit all three countries? We are going to be near there too." Rie and I agreed to her idea. And with that, we realized how well we worked together in trip planning, and we were quite proud of ourselves for it.

"Wait," I said. "How long should we be gone?" To determine the length of time, we turned to our travel expert, Rie.

"It might be best to spend a week in each country, give or take a day here or there." We listened as she discerned how best to juggle our time. "We have to take into consideration travel time for air as well as rail. We also want to be able to explore each country. How about three weeks?" And once again, we agreed. (I imagined this same agreeable nature will be with us on our trip.)

"Three weeks works for me. Les?" She gave a positive nod. I was forced to pause here for a minute as I thought.

This trip and the three weeks are Rie's idea, but what about her alone time? This has always been very important to her, and I know it continues to be so. Should I worry, I mean just a little bit? But then again Rie is the seasoned traveler, her judgment is to be trusted, naturally. I then said aloud, "We've got the three weeks and three countries figured out, but now all we need is our when." It was as if I had blown a whistle for a race as we began calling out to each other various dates for travel. Different months and days were thrown around but after some good ol' sibling reciprocity, loose promises made for another time, we decided on August 1–21.

That's it then. The three Moore sisters have decided to head out on August 1st, 2019, for three weeks to three countries. With our plans now in place the hardest part of our trip must be over, all before our first bite of pie.

2

FROM A FAMILY TENT TO A SISTER TENT

As I BEGAN THE MENTAL PROCESS OF PREPARING FOR THIS JOURNEY, A FAMILIAR sense of exploration and adventure washed over me, one that reached back into the early days of childhood.

For the Moore family, our second home was a tent. The reason was we camped, often, year-round, made possible by Southern California weather. But even still, we encountered inclement weather and when we would our large family of seven was forced to scramble to reach inside of our tent. Whenever that was the case, the last one entering knew to pull the zipper down tightly to keep out the storm elements while our family and crucial camping equipment would be pinned together into a much too crowded space inside.

When camping was involved, as far as various weather conditions go, the wind was always the worst (it remains a big annoyance to the three sisters). Nevertheless, be it the mountains or the desert, the wind often served as a precursor of things to come. With a front-row seat, we would watch the stunning speed at which blue sky rolled up its puffy clouds and retreated in haste from the dark clouds rushing in, erasing all-natural light. But that was only the warm-up act for the main attraction. With the heavens as its stage, lightning performed a jagged sky dance, accompanied by booming thunder. Then as if on cue, the closing act—rain, my favorite part of Mother Nature's show. A good downpour is such an enjoyment for me, especially when it brings with it the earthy scent of petrichor, a unique and pleasant smell.

The combination of wind, lightning, thunder, and rain occurred more than a time or two while we camped. Known as a squall, it was something we always hoped our tent would withstand, particularly while we were all sequestered inside.

The Sierra Nevada Mountains, composed largely of granite and volcanic rock, are found in Central California, inland. This magnificent range hosts Yosemite on one side and Mammoth on the other, and the Moore family spent plenty of time camping in both locations. It's a particular time in Mammoth though that still stands out to me.

It was another late afternoon and as usual, Mom was at the two-burner Coleman stove cooking at one end of an affixed campground table. We were told to clean up for dinner, which meant using the tall water spigot adhered to a wooden post, shared with other campers. Before Mom could finish cooking, a thunderstorm crashed in, bringing with it rain and forcing us all to make a mad dash for the tent. On our way in, Mom grabbed the pots of food, Dad grabbed the stove, and a couple of us were quick to set up our small folding table to accommodate the reassembled cooking station. Mom now had to cook just inside the tent opening, and to avoid asphyxiation, the zipper remained up with one of the flaps of the tent off to the side. We learned years later that while in the middle of that mini-melee, Mom had been coming down with the flu. Her temperature had started to rise steadily, yet even with a fever, she continued cooking. And while she did, her kids huddled toward the middle of the tent, knowing to stay clear of the tent sides. As was common in the 1950s and 60s, our tent was made of a very thick canvas treated with an oil product that made it water-resistant, but not waterproof. This meant touching any part of the tent when it was raining would introduce a leak, or leaks, depending on how much we snuck touching the resistant material—a secret not kept for too long. What always started as the same lecture about resisting the temptation to tap our fingertips on the rain-drenched canvas would end up the same—with laughter. What else was there to do but laugh?

This time, as with each time, the Moore family rose above what challenged us when we camped because no matter where we pitched our tent it was always anchored by the strongest of tent stakes, our shared sense of humor and laughter.

For the Moore family, camping memories still hold a special place. As for my camping memories in particular? They are safely ensconced inside the framework of an imaginary tent in my mind, where I prefer to keep them. After spending more nights camping than I can count, I don't yearn to spend even one more night in a tent sleeping on an air mattress that refuses to hold its breath all night long. Yet the unique sound of a tent zipper going up or down, along with the heavily oil-scented canvas long baked under a warm sun are fond memories of the time spent camping in a tent. But would I want to experience it all first-hand once again? Absolutely not. Still, it only stands to reason that a tent serves as a touchstone, a point of reference, relatable to me and my siblings. And this is what leads me back to thinking about our trip.

I wonder what Les and Rie might think of a sister tent. After all, it is an object in which we all share a strong commonality, so it makes sense. What if, I mean just on the outside chance, we experience an emotional or verbal storm of our own making? Our sister tent can be this symbolic place where we know to wait it out as we huddle, regroup, and reclaim our humor and laughter. If it even comes to this. Not that it ever will. I don't see it happening because we are going to be just fine. Yes we are, just fine.

3

EVERY GROUP NEEDS A WORRIER

No MATTER THE BELIEF OF HOW STRONG THE RELATIONSHIP IS, THE HUMAN confluence of three siblings can be a bit tricky at times. Perhaps trickier when the siblings are sisters? I don't know. Truth be told, as it stands right now, the three of us get along. Yet as two, no matter the combination we often get along better. With three, sometimes one of us feels left out, and sometimes it is more than sometimes although we don't know why. We talk about it, unpack it, dissect it, accept it, repack it, and then just leave it for what we are: It's the conundrum of the three Moore sisters.

The good news is this is not a new revelation and for this reason alone it doesn't require further scrutiny prior to lift-off. Even better news is our sisterhood remains intact, albeit at different stages at different times. Good for us. Then again, coexisting for any length of time (I am saying a long weekend) often brings about a desire to break away for at least one of us. It might be sooner rather than later we pitch our sister tent? No. You know what? It's time I lay down The Worry Mantle. While I have always carried it for the family—the job was never posted; I just happened to be innately well-suited for it—I am going to head out on this trip worry-free, at least as much as possible. I am going to enjoy our sisterhood, a bond unique to us because we are three unique individuals.

Born nineteen months before me, Les preferred to be buried in a succession of books. Since early on, she has always kept most of her feelings to herself. Between her books and feelings, she was quiet, well at least when compared to me. When it came to our mom, she would tell Les to jump and she would because this daughter followed instructions; she never asked why. This didn't mean Les wanted to do as Mom directed; instead, Les has always been one to stick to the rules (don't change them mid-stream on her), and motivated to keep the peace until the bitter end and beyond that, if necessary. When our parents divorced, I was away at boarding school, so I missed a lot of the changes in our home. At only seventeen, Les was suddenly flung into the role of a surrogate Mom to our two youngest siblings who still remember how Les carried on, no complaining. Methodical by nature, no decision is made until it is fully reasoned in her mind; this made her a responsible seventeen-year-old. That said, it's fine to be cautious but when it comes to trying anything new, new is not Les' friend, starting with food, especially food.

What Les was, I was certainly not. I preferred being outdoors riding my bike, climbing trees, and such. At age thirteen, gangly and skinny-legged at 5'10", I saw myself a muted rainbow of beige when I wanted nothing more than to be like the vibrant colors of my popular, 5'6" older sister. It became clear that would never become a reality for me, so I took the opportunity to attend Thunderbird Adventist Academy, an out-of-state boarding school in Scottsdale, Arizona. It was here that I discovered a taste for self-confidence.

Mom referred to this daughter as busy. True. My curious mind? Always in perpetual motion, which might explain my impatience. Yes, that's me driving off while others are still talking about inventing the wheel. I take action. I can frustrate others with this tendency. I get it.

As for Rie, her early childhood included feeling slighted by her four older siblings, so she quietly played alone with her baby dolls as they proved to be the better siblings—never tattled. It was also during those early years that Rie perfected the art of being a silent observer. As a result, she grew to become a repository of words, which at times can be direct, blunt, and also poke and provoke. This can be good. This can be a challenge. This can be helpful. This is our little sister.

Four years younger than me, Rie was not even a part of my solar system. We grew up as extraordinary opposites. My fast? It struggled against her slow, and vice versa. Add to this how my tendency to hit the ground running was often sandpaper against her need to take time to consider and weigh options first. We did share Thunderbird Academy, though I had already graduated by the time she enrolled. Funny, even though I was her opposite sister, I was the one she called when she needed answers to various questions about life. And at that time, I knew just enough.

Lucky for us, by the time we all reached our forties, the Moore sisterhood started to enjoy the deepening of friendship. And now here we are in our sixties, exploring a whole new territory—traveling with each other. And with that, I require some reassurance from both sisters.

"Rie, are you sure you can go this length of time with sister togetherness?" (It's obvious I am not one hundred percent certain.) Immediately, she replied, "I will be just fine; I've traveled this long and even longer. "Besides I'll go to my room. Having a separate place to go off on my own always helps."

"Just to clarify," I say, "you know for certain you will be fine for this length of time even though you might require some alone time?" My questioning her is logical. Even so, I know not to belabor the point with sister number three, so I move on to sister number one. "Les?"

"Me too. Fine. Just fine."

"Les, I'm just reiterating here. You are telling me as well that if we are three weeks away from home, for your first long trip, you are certain you will be 'fine,' correct? I know you lean toward the same tendency to want alone time. How are you going to handle being three all of the time?"

"I'll be like Rie and go to my room. We don't need to be in the same space together all of the time, right?"

"No, no, we sure don't. That's for certain." And just like that, we solve any potential problem of too much togetherness. It's not going to happen because Les and Rie will each be hiding out in their respective bedrooms. Fine. Done. I am shredding my mental file of Middle Sister Worrying Too Much because according to my two deeply attuned sisters, we will all be fine. Fine. Just fine.

And then before we even depart, we aren't fine. In an all-out effort, Rie and I must do everything in our power to quell Les' growing fear of flying, specifically the very long flight to Ireland, mostly over the ocean. I jump into preventative mode before something becomes irreparably broken and I am unable to fix it. So I reassure her.

"Les, no matter how many times I have flown and how far, I still struggle. You need to plan on a distraction, such as lots of movies. And remember, we chose the night flight so we could sleep. You've got this." The truth is, like me, Les must figure out for herself a way to deal with these fears. She needs to tap into her innate strength and resilience, which unfortunately is shoved down by her powerful tendencies to be cautious. And then, in the midst of it all, we hear the good news: Les continues to pack.

This little hiccup serves as a reminder that even though our older sis has her limits, it usually takes a good long while for the problem to travel from stewing deep inside her to finally becoming visible to those around her. In other words, Rie and I need to be cognizant of Les so we prevent her from going sideways. Easy. We'll take turns. Easier.

4

AGREEING HAS NEVER BEEN EASIER

NOT A DECEMBER GOES BY THAT THE THREE OF US MISS WATCHING THE GOLD standard of holiday movies, "White Christmas." We do this together, or two of us, or alone. We've come to a point in our lives that when we get together, it's quite natural for us to break out singing our favorite song from the movie—the one about sisters who care so much for each other that nothing or nobody will separate them? Yes, those sisters. But they now have me thinking. Naturally. So I say to my sisters, "With this being our first venture together, what do you think of no one wandering off on her own?" I come to this for two reasons. The first is Les. She has little travel experience, and zero overseas. And number two? Rie, who appreciates alone time. This leads me to gently push my point just a smidge more.

"Think about it. We are investing a lot of money as well as time into this trip. So why not learn about traveling together as well as making this about us. At least for this first time?" We have no clue how else to reconcile everything about this journey at this point. We must wait for the end of each day to help us navigate the next. Yet until then? Right now this is the right decision for us. Granted it's not the right decision for everyone, much less for everyone to understand. Yet for the Moore sisters, it's a starting point.

Then I reiterate to both sisters, "Are we all good with this? It's not etched in concrete. This might help our mom not worry so much about losing all three of her daughters at once. We know this is what she is thinking. And then husbands might worry. I see it in this order: Greg, Dave, and then Tim. Don't you see it this way too?" We all laugh at this undeniable truth about our Mom and our husbands.

So we make our commitment to "no one wandering off" because it worked for the sisters in "White Christmas," and it will for us as well, the whole sticking-together-no-matter-what part.

And just when everything is moving in the right direction, pesky little snags start to demand our attention. It's time to FaceTime Les and Rie.

"Ladies, we are overlapping with information, ideas, and sights to see. There has got to be a better way. We're unproductively spinning our wheels." Les tells the one with all of the ideas, "Liz, do you have a better idea?" And just as quickly I do. "What if each sister picks a country she is responsible for? This includes securing lodging and transportation. Thoughts?" My sisters like it. Then I add, "And how about when it's our country we include a special location or two of interest for all of us to explore together?"

From Rie, "Let's do it. I'm starting to feel organized."

"Les, all good?"

"Yep."

"How about sweetening the pot?" (This is my brain never stopping.) "If it's your country we are visiting, the first choice of bedrooms goes to you. So because Ireland is my country, I get to pick which bedroom I want. Les in England, Rie in Scotland." (I believe my idea is rather brilliant. This is the same adjective Les and Rie use too. I think. I need to confirm this.) "Les, Rie. I'm seeing a wonderful pattern developing here: I make a suggestion, you both agree."

Rie protests with a laugh, "Don't be so sure of yourself, Diz!" I smile back at her and say, "It sure seemed as though I was on a roll."

Late July arrives quickly with the first of August coming straight at us. We are texting or calling about what we should or need to pack. Les gives a shot over the bow: she requires a bigger suitcase for a trip this long, so I offer to lend her one of my larger suitcases rather than her going out and buying a new one; that would involve Les having to part with some of her cash. A big fan of not spending money if she can help it, she likes the idea of borrowing my suitcase, Moreover, she claims both style and size suit her needs perfectly for this trip. It's common practice for the three of us to share.

I can't recall how far back it goes, the three of us exchanging goods. For such a long time, we have taken to sharing, trading, and giving whatever we come to realize fits the other better, looks better on the other, matches the style of another better, or are just through with it. Then again, there is always the exception. Our exception is pants. We don't exchange pants. We can't do pants because we each have our unique hip shape and leg length, starting with theirs that are high waters on me. But shoes? Sure. And handbags, jewelry, and even some home décor? Yes, no rules apply. Well, one rule. If we accept something from one sister only to realize it's not something that works, we aren't obliged to keep it. No hard feelings. Simply bag it up and ship it off to the next sister. That's pretty much it. So when Les mentions the need for a suitcase, it's the norm for us—shop the sister store first.

5

WHAT COULD POSSIBLY GO WRONG?

MY VERY LARGE OVER-PACKED SUITCASE (PERHAPS A BIT TOO LARGE FOR THREE weeks?) is waiting on the tile entryway of my home when the other two show up with their owners. These suitcases are smaller in size. Well, now, it appears as though Les has shifted over to the dark side of downsizing rather quickly. This is very interesting.

"So I see you ended up buying a different suitcase after all?"

"No, I'm borrowing this from Rie." I am thinking to myself—or do I say it aloud? I can't quite remember: "You'll regret your decision." I think I do speak it so they both hear. This sounds more like me, their mouthy middle sister.

In truth, the size of the suitcase doesn't matter. Despite all of our good intentions, I have no doubt each of us ends up finding enough room to pack some sister dynamics that easily mixes and matches with whatever we wear. And there is most likely some corner space left to cram in some justifiable self-defense, just to be on the safe side. And those small zipper pockets? Ideal for holding a smidge of heart-piercing verbal ammunition, I mean, on the off chance it will even be needed.

I'd like to believe this will not be the case.

I'd like to think this will not be the case.

I hope this will not be the case because if it is, it will pierce a hole in our sister tent.

We have twenty-one glorious days spread out before us, what could possibly go wrong?

Life is Either a Daring Adventure Or Nothing at All

--Helen Keller

PART ONE * IRELAND

6

DUBLIN'S WELCOMING COMMITTEE: A PUB AND A PANE

GREAT NEWS FOR LES. WE'VE LANDED SAFELY IN DUBLIN. I AM HOPING THIS will be a confidence booster for her when we fly from Ireland to England. I smile at her and say, "See. Now that wasn't too hard, was it?

"Oh, you mean aside from you and Rie sleeping through the medical emergency when an elderly man fell on the other side of me? No, it wasn't hard at all. I can't wait to see what happens on our flight home. I am so ready to get off this plane!"

While grabbing our carry-on, Rie and I calm Les down. Inside the terminal, we follow the arrows to Baggage Claim/Eileamh Bagaiste. The signs throughout the airport are in English and Gaelic and though the letters present a lyrical combination, we've no clue how to properly pronounce them but hoping to learn.

Luggage in hand, we head outside to where rows of cabbies are in line (a queue over here). Upon sight of the three of us and our luggage, the man who assigns cabs sends a van in our direction. Good call. All loaded up and ready to start on our adventures, we begin chatting away with our driver; ah, the lovely Irish brogue.

"What's the address, ladies?" My voice responds in one-fourth excitement and three-fourths nervousness as I give the address for our vacation rental.

Ireland is my assigned country, and with it being our first stop, I am hoping there are no snags with our reservations made online. Scrolling through countless websites for vacation rentals, I found this gem, well, at least according to the pictures it's a gem. I shared more than a few emails with the owner who came across as quite friendly, so I trust my instincts that he's trustworthy; it's a leap of faith. Even still, this is what trusting the Internet 5,000 miles away feels like for me—intimidating.

With each mile closer to our home for the next seven days, I grow that much more nauseated. No. A better description is a churning vortex in my gut—even while I am smiling and chatting away with the driver and my sisters. With my deepest fears refusing to let up, I begin to silently whisper an urgent prayer. And then I petition several prayers in a rapid succession, which I am sure works even more in my favor:

"Oh please, please, please dear God, let this not be a hole-in-the-wall." I am busy in prayer mode when our driver says something about our address: "Your place is in the Phibsborough neighborhood, a short walk to Dublin's City Center. Being out here should be a lot quieter if that's what you are looking for."

At this stage of our lives, this is fine by us. We'd rather all of our nights not be subjected to various levels of drunken reveries of locals and tourists alike. And with that, the driver pulls up to the curb. From my vantage point inside the taxi, our rental appears to be a good choice, and with that, I release a quiet sigh of relief. Oh, I also give thanks to the god who is in charge of online vacation rentals.

After our driver unloads our suitcases, we each tip him. Wanting to get this right, I've read up on the guidelines of tipping in Ireland. It's not at all mandatory, especially for cab drivers, yet if the customer appreciates the driver/ride then round off the fare to the nearest five or ten Euro. For example, the ride costs eight Euro, give the driver ten. Our driver expresses gratitude for our tip, and he gives us one in return: "See McGowans Pub across the street?" We turn toward the pub. It's pretty hard to miss. He continues, "Whenever you take a taxi just tell the driver you need to go to McGowans and they will know exactly where to take you. I promise every driver in Dublin knows how to get to McGowans."

Now that's a good tip.

With luggage in tow, we make our way in through the freshly painted decorative, black wrought-iron gate. Just inside the yard is the iconic red POST mailbox. It's only now, upon closer inspection, when the lack of curb appeal becomes apparent. There is no front yard, meaning no grass, plants, flowers, but for our viewing pleasure is a cement patch, about 10' × 10'. The outside of the house is built of mostly brown brick with the trim and windows painted white. The front door is black, and on either side sit black gallon pots, each containing a small, decorative tree of about two feet, much like the kind in front of fancy hotels although these two differ in one distinct way—both are dead. To be fair, one tree does have a teensy bit of green at its very tip; the poor thing is hanging on for dear life. As it appears right now, from this side of the sidewalk, I'm not too impressed with the outside, and it has me bracing for what the inside might be like.

"It's going to be alright. This is going to be just fine." This is me doing my best to reassure my two sisters, as well as myself.

We drag our suitcases and ourselves up the seven cement steps to the front door. (I have a long-running habit of counting steps, stairs.) We are weary from the flight, the nerves, the anticipation, and with all of that our exhaustion is now taking full advantage and slams hard into each of us. Even so, we work at remaining upright as Rie punches in the door code. The door opens and we spill into the narrow entryway. Large squares of black and white tiles greet us. I am encouraged. "See, the inside looks much better than the outside. I'll be honest here. I was a little nervous." Les agrees. We leave our luggage behind as we begin to explore the property.

The tiles give way to light blonde wood floors throughout. In the living room, we find a two small white tufted leather couches, a bookcase filled with knick-knacks, and a television and lamp in one of the corners. There is also a round glass coffee table with a rug underneath and a three-ring binder—rental information on top. I quickly thumb my way through, making a mental note of things we might want to know about later. Each page is in a plastic sleeve and while it keeps the pages clean renter-to-renter, they go between being slippery and sticking together, thanks to static. Oh well, the information is handy should we need it.

I open the curtains and the large window reveals our view. It begins with our cement yard, then the four-lane road (very quiet; not much traffic at all), and ends at McGowans Pub.

Established in 1860, the pub is a two-story, colorful establishment and it's not at all what we expect a pub to look like. In other words, it's not like what we see in California. Made mostly of light red bricks with wood on either side painted dark red, it also has copious amounts of hanging pots, everywhere, even all about the fire escape, and the flower pots are spilling over the brim in an explosion of colors made up of petunias, geraniums, lobelia, and more.

Rie is already making her way to the kitchen only to find a narrow hallway on the left reveals a tiny utility room. At the end of this short hall is an even tinier half bath or as it is called here a water closet. I can already see that my long legs will prove a challenge for me should I have to use this space. I make a slow turn and find one of the tiniest sinks ever. My guess is the holding capacity for this sink might be two cups of liquid, though I could be exaggerating, but not by much. So be it, but again it's apparent space is at a premium in this converted closet now bathroom/ mop and broom space.

We enter the kitchen, focusing on the appliances and note how everything is updated. But it's the elephant in the room, well, in this case an over-sized dining room set, that can't be ignored. It gobbles up almost all of the free space necessary for maneuvering. I speak the obvious.

"Oh boy! It looks like we will be taking turns. One can be prepping, one can use the stovetop, and the other... hum... I guess just sit and wait your turn."

Too tired to see any other option at this time, we continue our self-guided tour. To the right of the kitchen we see another door that opens to steps leading down to a back door, which opens up to a very small patch of very green grass, and a clothesline. "All good here. Especially clean. Let's head up to the second floor."

I count ten steps made of the same wood as the lower floor. We were not expecting an elevator. Pausing at the landing before completing the next set of steps, I say, "You know, having to haul our luggage up all of these stairs will only make us appreciate the elevator in England." To which Rie adds, "And my place has an elevator too!"

"So then we are double-appreciative of these stairs." Although we are ready to unwind, our spirits are high as we carry our bags up the remaining nine steps.

We are happy to find the upstairs space is carpeted. This makes it a much friendlier greeting for when our feet hit the floor first thing each morning. Because Ireland is my country, I pick my room first while leaving Les and Rie to decide which of the two rooms suits each other best. I chose the bedroom on the right; it has a queen bed as do the other rooms. With no en-suite bathroom, we will all be sharing this one bathroom; it will be fine. With both a tub (short) and a shower (narrow), it for certain rivals the utility closet downstairs.

As soon as I plop my carry-on bag and purse on my bed, I immediately turn to pull back the floor-to-ceiling thick fabric curtains away from the one window in this room. My room faces west leaving it feeling a bit stuffy and warm due to the lingering afternoon sun, so I am happy to see a long, tall window rather than a short and narrow one. I take a brief moment to appreciate my view, but before I do anything else opening the window is my first priority. I'll study the backyard more once this is done. And then I become distracted, which for me is so easy for me to do.

I notice that beyond the yard is an alley. And on the other side of the alley is another neighborhood where I am instantly drawn to the charm of a neighbor's clothesline filled with various pieces of clothing, sheets, and towels. I take note of how the laundry is not sticking to the assigned boring task of just hanging there, waiting to dry. Instead, it appears to be sashaying about thanks to the little breeze pushing it all around. It's all so rather charming. It mesmerizes me. It transports me back to a much earlier time. As my eyes lazily follow the clothesline from right to left, I easily imagine Mom with clothespins in her pockets, and always a couple in her mouth, as she goes about the task of hanging up the huge pile of her family's damp laundry. My memory also triggers the fresh scent of clean clothes, towels, and sheets, stiff from the fresh air and sun. No dryer softener fabrics in those days. Wait a minute. Is that man sitting in a lawn chair looking in my window? I do a double-take around me. Yeah, that's what he is doing alright. With that I find myself contorting my body (albeit in a very unfamiliar way), away from the window. Let me add that it's a stunning surprise how I am still able to bend as such and at my age. Without question, this will most likely hurt later.

I catch my breath as I slowly move back for a sneak peek from behind one of the curtains—no man there. *Your mind is overtired and in overdrive. Calm down, Liz.*

Gone. Good. No sign of the man. Back to my task at hand: I must open this window because I need to get some air circulating in this warm room. I feel as though I am suffocating if I don't have a flow of air, so I must make this work. It's all about constant air movement, which at my age is not overrated. Upon closer inspection of this window, I now see what I am up against—a window configuration unfamiliar to me. The lower part of the upper window is screwed into the upper part of the lower window. All I need to do is loosen this rather odd wood screw (think of an ice cream cone with the end of the cone burrowing very tightly into the wood), and for the life of me, I cannot make it budge. And from where I am standing, I can't get a grasp on the damn thing. All I need to do is loosen the screw—how hard can this be—to open this window. But how to do this? Better leverage should do the trick.

I consider the ample width of the window sill and see how it's simply a matter of launching my body up and onto the sill in order to stand above the screw. Excellent plan. How to get me up there though? I am looking around my room and see a vanity chair, of which I am quite certain is not intended for the use that I have in mind, yet I need an open window. I walk myself through the steps that seem to make perfect sense, at this moment: "Okay, the vanity chair is in place between the sill and bed. Standing on the bed, I'll stretch my right foot over from the end of the bed and onto the vanity chair (again, not made for this purpose). Make sure I don't use my full weight, then swing my left leg off the bed onto the sill. Grab some part (any part) of the window frame then bring the right leg up to the sill, and viola! I'll be fine!"

And before I know it, I am suddenly a mid-sixties Olive Oyl, Popeye's girlfriend, trying her best to incorporate some graceful movement from the foot of the bed to the sill. And just like that here I am, standing above the screw. I immediately get to work only to realize my leverage does not make one bit of difference because the screw is still not budging. And yes, I do call this inanimate object a stupid screw, and yes, as a matter of fact, this somehow helps. Oh wait, this should help too. My nosey backyard neighbor is back once again, firmly ensconced in his patio chair. Lucky him. He is right on time for the second installment of a very loose Irish adaptation of Hitchcock's "Rear Window," although I don't die, injured perhaps, but no suspicious death. So anyway, my neighbor, who I've decided to christen Mr. Pane, sits in his front-row seat once again, staring laser-focused into my window. Well, I think he is. It sure seems to me that he is. My assumption launches me back onto the bed, and again I am flabbergasted that I don't break, twist, or sprain anything this time either. I shout out, "Les, Rie, hurry up. Come to my room." When they come racing in I say "Get on the bed you two. Keep your heads down. Are you able to sneak over to the window to see if a man is staring into my room?" And before I can reiterate "sneak," they are both obvious as they see for themselves. Les reports back, "Yea, there is a man over there. What about him?"

"Is he looking in my window?" I ask.

She turns back in full view of him, very un-stealth-like. Any sneaking is now out of the question, which sends us into giggles on the bed as I explain Mr. Pane and his name. "All I want to do is to open the darn window, and in the middle of my efforts, Mr. Pane over there takes in the show, of course," as I jab a frustrated finger toward the closed window. And with this, Les decides to solve my window problem.

"I've got this, Sis. I don't care about your Mr. Pane."

"Right, Les, so he's mine now?" So be it. I just want the window opened. This sister in particular has always been blessed with remarkable upper arm strength. I can't begin to count all of the school lunch periods Les would take on one boy after another who challenged her to arm wrestling. They kept trying while she kept winning. So now I am almost certain she can loosen this screw. Electing to remain standing on the floor, Les reaches for the screw. She fails. (Without a doubt, old age is robbing her of arm strength.)

"What's wrong, Sis?" I tease. Then I challenge Rie. "Are you willing to give it a try?" She is. She too fails. Once again, the three of us are back on the bed rolling in giggles. Oh sure, it's funny yet my window remains tightly screwed shut.

I have no choice but to call the management office concerning our lack of strength. The voice on the other end reassures me assistance is on the way. And who should appear but a skinny, scrawny girl in her very early twenties. I turn to both sisters and whisper from the side of my mouth so only they hear, "How is she going to help?" As she goes toward the window she shares, "This happens all of the time. A lot of guests aren't familiar with this type of window configuration and this particular kind of screw." And just as she is about to jump up onto the window sill (without the assistance of either bed or vanity chair; show off), I shout out a warning about Mr. Pane. Even so, Ms. Young-Skinny-Scrawny assistant is not put off at all by him (he is back there but no longer staring in), and just like that, and with the greatest of ease, she unscrews that pesky little screw. Naturally, yet thanks to our Herculean efforts just before her arrival. Who cares. Done. I am happy. I've got fresh air flowing into my room now and this is all that matters. Mr. Pane be damned. Then again, maybe he is just enjoying his backyard but can't avoid watching the distant pantomime in the window across the alley. It had to be a hilarious sight to see from his point of view. I am giving him the benefit of doubt.

"Is there anything else you ladies need? Any questions I might answer? If you need anything at all, just call the number on the first page in the informational binder. Did you happen to see it in the living room? That will be your best resource. And as you can see, we are quick to respond."

The truth is Ms. Young-Skinny-Scrawny is stronger than the three of us put together and she is also quite helpful and pleasant. I am going to give her the benefit of doubt as well. I'm on vacation, after all.

During my window escapade, my two sisters have been settling into their separate rooms. How fortunate that Les and Rie have such a delightful view of the lovely McGowans in all of its blooming glory. And it's so very quiet too. I am now wondering if I might have chosen my room too quickly. Oh well. Then again, I have my Mr. Pane and they don't, so there's that to consider.

Bedrooms picked, windows opened, and our unpacking now pretty much complete, one of the two sisters shouts out to the other two, "Hey, it's time to start foraging for food. Is anyone else hungry? Besides, we also need some groceries for later."

It looks like our second wind has kicked in. Just like that, we throw our purses over our shoulders and see what the neighborhood looks like beyond Phibsborough Road. We settle on pizza because it's an easy walking distance from our place; a no-brainer. Our waitress takes our order when we notice she hesitates then asks, "Where are you visiting from?" The waitress hears in unison, "California."

She responds to "California" with true delight: "I want to visit there someday. I love your accent." We shake our heads at our silly waitress though we smile at her then encourage her to visit. After she leaves, we all look at each other quite puzzled. Les says (now spoken in her newly discovered California accent), "What accent? Californians don't have accents. That's so funny."

Before our trip, we decide if asked where we are visiting from we will say California. The first being California is so very far west of Ireland. The second reason is it just feels better as the world is becoming quite small, and opinions, well, everyone has one, two, three, or more. So for now, we want to leave behind all things political because we are on vacation.

Done with lunch, we make finding a grocery store our next order of business. We all consult our phones.

"The closest one to us is Cost Cutter," I say. "Sound good?" It's agreed upon because we are very much like the next person who appreciates the cutting of costs, in particular our sister Les. Then I add. "When you two are ready, let's head over there. And according to the map, it's a short walk from the restaurant and not too far of a distance from our place. It looks like an easy enough walk."

Entering Cost Cutter, we take a moment to determine the lay of the land. In other words, gaining a perspective regarding the whole courtesy issue of the proper direction for aisle traffic. Then again it doesn't seem applicable here. Instead, chaos sets us back on our heels.

"What is this?" One of us verbalizes as the other two are thinking the same thing. And all the while our eyes are scanning back and forth as we try in all earnest to make sense of this three-ring Cost Cutter circus. Frankly, we are quite unsure which ring to direct the focus of our attention. There is food on shelves (expected) as well as in boxes on the floor (unexpected). Now we understand why it is Cost Cutter. We also note there is neither rhyme nor reason for anything here but at least we can grasp how to shop in this store, so we foolishly believe.

"Listen," Rie advises, "We need groceries and therefore we have no other choice but to figure this all out."

She's right. And as we stand there observing the other shoppers, it becomes quite apparent that there is no time allotted for considering, contemplating: *Hmmm... do I want a loaf of this type of wheat bread, or ...* Nope. Gone. Eager customers all, they quickly grab what they need and are off on their next item. Okay. Fine. Now we get it.

We agree upon the familiar and trustworthy Divide and Conquer method. Ripping our list into thirds, the three of us jump into the grocery shopping melee with the rest of the customers. As soon as one of us come across an item from our list we can capture (because it does take on a feel as though we are hunting for our food), we resort to throwing our voices (yes, read this to mean 'shouting') to each other over the aisles. This is just us fitting in with the locals. Later, I will write in my journal: "*Wild. Wooly. Loud. What a crowd at Cost Cutter.*"

For this first go-round, our list is not all that long, so our chance of success is good. And the next time we shop for groceries? Our success is even greater because we shop elsewhere.

Elizabeth Moore Kraus

Having what we need, for now, we regroup near the check-out queue. There are several and it appears they have a specific designation. With that, the three of us look at each other. I offer up what we are all feeling. "This doesn't feel comfortable. Which line should we choose? Do either of you want to guess?" But I pick a line as we all do our best to act nonchalant. It pays off. The woman behind the counter scans our groceries and gives us the total, in Euros, naturally. We hesitate as we gather our financial wits about us, all the while we feel pressure coming off the shopping contingency closing in behind us. And there we are, the mature Moore sisters looking like three little school girls with coins in open palms when the kind cashier helps us out so we can get on our way—immediately. We cannot exit through the electronic sliding doors fast enough.

Having escaped Cost Cutter with our lives, it seems to us, we each carry two bags of our hard-fought-for groceries. Funny, the map app failed to include this direction being uphill. As a means to distract ourselves, we begin chatting about this and that when a cold, cutting wind shows up. (Have I mentioned already how the three of us don't have one positive thing to say about wind?) Well, anyway, the wind is making an all-out effort to push us backward, yet forward we go. And then to our unexpected delight, from the heavens comes a light yet steady drizzle. Pretty darn dreary and now damp as well, I can't help but comment. "So, Les and Rie. Any thoughts, comments about our warm welcome to Ireland?" We are exhausted so we laugh as we continue to trudge along, each in a whining mode of our own when a gentleman (he looks nice enough) joins us. He must be a local, I assume. Our drowned kitten appearances must strike him as pitiful. (When we get home and look in the mirror, we see it for ourselves.)

"Ladies, do you need some assistance?" Of course, it shows on our faces.

I respond, "We know where we need to go, but we just aren't sure the fastest way to get there."

"What's the address?" Which I give without hesitations. (Perfect, he is going to send his henchmen over later to murder us, not that he looks like a man who has henchmen.)

"I know a shortcut. Follow me."

Sounds good to us. And just like that, the three Moore sisters fail, completely, at heeding the years of parental advice about strangers and never talking with them. Furthermore, as we chat away with this particular stranger, we blithely follow him down an alley without any hesitation whatsoever. So much for the life lessons from Little Red Riding Hood. The whole stay on the path and don't talk with any wolf advice? We not only talk with a wolf but follow him as well. Oh, we are going to rock this vacation. That is if we don't go missing before we even get to explore Ireland.

We are lucky this time. We'll be more careful next time. Not that there will be a "next time." It's worth mentioning though how this one time, the wolf, I mean the man has our interest at heart. We end up back on our street all in one piece and with our place just two houses away. When we enter, we make sure the door is bolted shut. Such a nice man.

We head to the kitchen, unload groceries, and then drag our weary selves up those nineteen steps. It feels like a very difficult mountaineer climb at this point, yet we each make it to our rooms. I immediately head for the window, which is still open a bit; no screens. As we heard earlier today from our window whisperer, "There are no screens here. The rule of thumb is once bugs come inside it's time to close the windows." I pull back the curtains, open the window further, and I take in the coolness of this lovely Irish weather. The breeze has now become strong enough to push what is now a steady rainfall into a strong slant.

I can't help but notice the same clothesline across the alley and it remains full of clothes. With the stronger wind, it's as though the towels and sheets are chasing the pairs of jeans while in an attempt to run away, unsuccessfully. My heart goes out to the person who has hung their laundry out to dry only to have it as wet as when in the rinse cycle. The funny thing about this is as each day passes, and throughout Ireland, clothes remain on the line, rain or shine. I come to appreciate how the Irish have come to take full advantage of nature's rinse and dry cycle.

The three of us are very tired after our long flight and this long day. I am ready for sleep but not until I write the first entry in my travel journal.

I enjoy keeping some kind of written record of my travels. One journal might have pages filled with in-depth entries, another journal merely a jotting down of thoughts that provide an overview of the day; one journal is filled with daily entries to my granddaughter. No matter how they start, each becomes a unique souvenir of its own.

Who knows what my writing will reflect for these three weeks as I travel with these two. I imagine if Les or Rie were writing in journals of their own (Rie sometimes does), no doubt both would write about the joys of traveling with me. When I shout this across the hall, they respond by laughing. Just to clarify the meaning of their laughter, I ask them, "I should take this as a 'no'?" With this, three very tired sisters want to stop our laughter but we seem too tired to do even this. Saying my goodnight to each sis, I add, "I'll see you two in the morning." And then again, perhaps I should have been more specific about what time in the morning.

I sleep solidly until 3:30 a.m. only to awake to some noise coming from across the hall. As I focus my eyes, I am certain I see both Les and Rie leaning out of their open bedroom windows—still in their pajamas. Then again, I need to try to focus better in these pre-dawn hours of the morning. Perhaps I am not fully awake? This is just too odd.

Eyes still trying to open, I find my way to Rie's room.

"What in the world are you doing leaning out the window, Sis? Is it raining? Are you watching it rain? What the heck is going on?" While I ask these questions, my brain continues to reconcile with what is so fascinating. And then we turn to see Les join us then mumbles, "Well, I guess

I'm not getting any sleep. What's with all of the noise across the street?" By the time she finishes asking her question, I am now fully cognizant of what is going on. Then again, as much as one can be at pre-dawn.

"Wow! McGowans. Who knew, right? No wonder you two are awake." Even under a heavy drizzle, there must be at least some thirty inebriated customers milling about outside talking and laughing. Unbelievable. And they are loud. Drunk loud!

What's more unbelievable is that the three of us continue to stand here taking it all in at this ungodly hour in the morning. Such a scenario is uncommon in our daily lives, starting with hanging out a window at 3:30 in the morning, and in our pajamas. Still, we remain spellbound. Enough to add color commentary: "Aren't those big guys the bouncers? And shouldn't they be bouncing the patrons out of there? It looks like they are having just as much fun as everyone else. This is so crazy yet entertaining."

"I sure hope it's for this one night only," Les says. We all confer it's most likely. In the middle of our conversation, cabs pull up one after another to whisk away the inebriated. They shout their goodbyes from the top of their drunken lungs as if they might not ever see their drinking buddy ever again. For us, this is mesmerizing theatre playing out in real-time under yellow street lamps and the drizzle of rain.

By the way, we were wrong. This same revelry takes place the next night and on into a holiday weekend. So much for the wisdom of our cab driver when he assured us how being out here should be a lot quieter. At one point during the weekend, Rie can't take the loud noise any longer (window shut, curtains drawn), and in the wee hours I hear a whisper, "Diz, please. I'm begging. Can I crawl into your bed? The noise won't stop, and I'm so exhausted." I let her take up some space in my bed so she can get some much-needed rest. Even in the darkness of this hour, it's easy to see: Right now, I am her favorite sis.

7

MORE THAN WHAT MEETS THE EYE

DESPITE BEING AWAKE WITH THE DRUNKEN McGOWANS CROWD FROM 3:30–
4:30 a.m., we are up and semi-ready to go around 6:30 a.m., minus a
hangover. With our kitchen rotation schedule (that just fell into place),
we start to take turns making our breakfast, and when I am ready to sit
down, this monstrous table makes it a bit of a challenge. Frustrated, I
say, "Why would the owner choose this dining set for this space? It takes
up most of the real estate in the kitchen." As soon as I finish asking my
question (to which the three of us don't have an answer), I give the beast
a big shove, pushing it against a wall; the wood floors help make this
possible. Even if I can't open an Irish window configuration, I can give a
big heave-ho to afford us more kitchen space. "There. Done. I took care
of that! Now we all can eat comfortably as well as have a few more inches
to reach the appliances."

As I am about to take my first bite, my eye catches a small sign I
have failed to notice until now: Do NOT move the table! You will be fined
and/or lose your deposit!

Just great. We immediately start looking around for any hidden
cameras, none found, and then decide what's done is done. We leave it
while eating and when done, move it back. The rebels that we are, we go

through this same nonsense every day with this big beast while wise to always move it back before leaving for the day just in case the manager comes in to check on things. We will deal with the consequences later. Thank goodness the consequences never come.

With the start of the morning now fully underway, we are ready to make our first full day in Ireland one of exploring Dublin. As we gather up our things in the entryway and proceed to step across the threshold of the front door, I stop and ask, "Tell me what you think. Before we venture out each day we take a 'sister selfie?' I am thinking it will be a fun way to document our trip." And with that here the three of us stand in front of our Irish home, taking our first of twenty sister selfies. We come to enjoy our new sister selfie tradition. Well, there is that one time, but I am getting ahead of myself.

The first order of the day? Walking to the nearest stop for the Hop-On/Hop-Off bus. This is one of the better ways to get the lay of the land. We hop off at the Temple Bar District (even more hanging flower pots yet too many tourists). After a quick look-see, we stroll down enchanting cobblestone streets until we reach the Medieval Dublin Castle, which dates back to 1204.

It's a good day to wander around Dublin, allowing our bodies to adjust to the time change and any jet lag. Two days in, and I must say we are doing quite splendid together. This has me rethinking my whole worry catalog.

Even with "worry" out of the way, I am feeling crappy. The only reason I am is that my hair feels crappy. One day it's great and suddenly the next, not so much. I share my frustration. Rie suggests, "Find somebody here to cut it for you, Diz."

I like her idea, so I Google hair stylist near me then make a few calls. The salon Ultimate Hair has an 11:30 a.m. available. This shop has two things that matter to me: One, excellent reviews. Two, it's within walking distance from our place. This will do just fine. And then just fine quickly disappears as we become somewhat confused in the maze of narrow warrens filled with a variety of shops. The salon is in some far-off corner, but I make it on time.

I admit that I feel a sense of relief seeing how the salon looks much like what I would find at home. I guess on some level it gives me confidence in the hairdresser—modern salon, modern skills. While I settle in with my chatty and delightful stylist, Les and Rie head out on store reconnaissance duty for post-haircut shopping.

Returning about a half-hour later, they sit down and happily join in the bantering I am enjoying with my stylists, other stylists, the receptionist, and one other client. (It's what I do.)

"You are planning to visit Galway, right?" my stylist asks, pausing between cuts. I am laughing to myself while looking back into the mirror at my stylist, *I best give the right answer because the next snip of her scissors can go either way.*

"It's not on the list," is my embarrassed reply. Upon hearing my response, they all start telling at once how visiting Galway is a must.

"You will be so glad that you do." I say out to Les and Rie, "Ladies. It's coming from locals."

Both sisters agree. We also agree my hair looks better, which in part might be because we promise to visit Galway. I guess we will never know.

I am already thinking about how I will write about this experience in my journal. The three of us agree spending time at Ultimate Hair becomes one of those experiences that begins singular in purpose only to organically grow into something one quite does not expect. What springs to mind is a very watered-down version of The Butterfly Effect, a theory based upon a small change in one experience that has the power to result in large differences in another experience. So this small experience today should result in something greater, later. All theory, of course. Yet, I feel it will make better sense later. Again, this is my mind that never rests.

It's time to check out some of the shops pre-approved by Rie. Amongst the three of us, our little sis is the best shopper, I'm a close second, and then Les. Amid any hunt such as this, Rie is the one who lingers over the smallest of details. What Les and I will pass over, Rie sees what the two of us cannot envision.

It feels comfortable being here with my sisters. Once upon a time, Rie and I found ourselves much too willing to go our separate ways; we tried so very hard to do so.

After living out of state for a few years, in the early '90s, Dave and I, along with our son, Brent-Stig, moved back to Southern California. Living closer to my two sisters once again, I saw this as an opportunity for us to spend time together. Unfortunately, too quickly, we realized how we were in a constant flux that had one of us feeling left out. We were friends in training yet we struggled mightily. A sister-tent? Not even a part of our lexicon during that time.

Dave and I took Rie and her husband Tim up on their invitation: move on to their extensive property because they weren't moving there for sometime. We were not meant to be there for too long of a period, it just gradually became that way because Rie and Tim were rarely there. They eventually came to live there, after all the property belonged to them.

Due to the topography, we ended up living next door to each other, very next door to each other. Say ten steps? This worked well for more than several years. It did. And then it didn't. And although it felt as though it started to crash in on us at one particular moment, it didn't. Our whole falling apart came in the form of many little breaks and snaps, here and there, not even worth considering, so we brushed them aside. Until it became uncomfortable ignoring them because they had become one cumulative monstrosity.

Rie was now three months pregnant with her second child and her son was turning three, so Les and her family were visiting for the birthday weekend. As the weekend was wrapping up, Rie and I went from a deep, individual implosion to vomiting out an explosion of words, feelings, and personal truths. Rie was straining against her frustration toward me in a voice raised to varying octave levels, each word transmitted specifically at me.

"You have no business comparing my marriage to yours!" Because I was doing this. Tim traveled a great distance for his job. When he arrived home, it seemed he didn't acknowledge Rie. Said another way, Tim never greeted Rie as Dave would me if he were in Tim's shoes. I perceived this as Tim ignoring Rie, which of course was none of my business.

And then Rie continued to come at me with even more words. "Tim and I are not you and Dave. I don't need your advice! Quit butting in!" I thought I was being protective of my little sister when she had never asked for my protection in the first place. It was all on me. My fault.

It was only much later when I deconstructed her words that I could see they were fair and honest. But during that time, not so much. I took it on as a personal attack, naturally, and because I did I made sure I struck back at her with words that would be sure to create a verbal wound she would feel for quite some time.

"Everything we thought it could be, well it's not! I'm tired of living here next to you. I'm tired of you." She followed up with words heaved in my direction, strong and equally cutting. She stood with her legs apart which gave her a strong stance, allowing her to shove at me her last breath of anger, "No one is keeping you here! You are free to move." She was right. Her permission was not required. And with that last declaration, I already was making plans to move my family when Les interrupted. She tried her best to step in as referee for her sisters' verbal match.

"Really you two? Come on. Let's not let this get out of hand. Just cool down."

Rie did not appear to be interested in hearing what Les had to say. I know I wasn't. So I ignored her and placed myself back in the middle of the ring as I issued one last verbal blow: "Forget you!" I yell, "We are moving. And the sooner the better. I'm done with you!" I gathered up my rage, collected all of my tears, and I rushed over to my home, the one that now felt as though it were just right outside her door rather than the distance of ten steps.

Once inside my house, filled with a rush of emotional adrenaline, I began to pack as Dave observed but did not speak; wise man. Nonetheless, I shouted words at him although not meant for him. "This is what becoming too familiar looks like. Sisters shouldn't live so close to each other, well not these two sisters. Never again."

As I continued to pack in a flurry, I came across the hundreds of photos I had taken while living on their mountain top. I flung them into a small box. They rested there, unprotected. Let them. While I was at it, just for good measure, I recklessly tossed in my sister voice as well. I had no more words for Rie.

Unable to help change the trajectory of her two sisters, Les and her husband left for their home not knowing if any of those they left behind on the mountain top would be able to negotiate peace for themselves.

I decided to stop all I was doing in haste and take a deep breath. That was when I noticed through my window Rie off by herself. She was crying. Those words we spewed at each other? How was it that we twisted them all into some kind of personal justification? But that was what we both did. It was wrong. And in the middle of this wrong? We had dug for ourselves quite a chasm that neither seemed too interested in bridging even if it meant meeting halfway with the other.

Do you know how difficult it is to avoid a sister when there are only six people in residence, and practically living on top of one another? It's tricky. It's uncomfortable. It was the same for Rie and by the end of the week she made her way over to my front door. Because of her, we found

45

the words to help us around our stubborn selves. And then her news, "I lost the baby. My anger wanted to blame you, but my heart knew better." We both started to cry. I held her. I rocked her. I listened to her as she sobbed over this heart-wrenching loss. And a few years later, I was there for her second miscarriage, and again for her third. Each time my heart was breaking so very hard for her. Each time I held her. Because this is what a sister does. And because I love her so.

As we sat there in our shared sobs, I heard her say, "Diz, you know you don't have to move, right?" I do love the heart of my little sis.

"I know. But it will be best for all of us." We moved a few months later.

Since that horrific storm, another like it has never hovered over our sister tent. And though it is years in the past, it is our shared story. This history makes us who we are now—sisters who believe we are able to mend any tear, rip, or gash on our sister tent.

We hop off at Trinity College, established in 1592 by Queen Elizabeth I, for public viewing of the Book of Kells. Started as early as 563, these "illuminated manuscripts" record the Gospel in the New Testament of the Christian Bible. And as soon as we enter the room, it takes on the aura of a sacred space. All voices become hushed whispers.

These compelling manuscripts are not only physical evidence of deep and abiding faith but also display the meticulous work and arduous labor of the Irish Monks living on the isle of Iona, Scotland. The Monks chose vellum (treated calfskin) as their canvas and for their ink and paint a blending of various raw plant and mineral base pigments; the vibrancy of color remains intact. The artist's renditions? Simply stunning. I leave this exhibit thinking it must surely humble even the most cynic of visitors.

From here, we go to the second floor to where we enter the Long Room in the Old Library. Built between 1712 and 1732, at 213 feet in length, its name is applicable. With a ceiling of arches made of dark wood, this must be one of the most beautiful libraries in the world. Here visitors stand amongst rows upon rows of floor-to-ceiling shelves of books—around 200,000—original copies. The end caps for each row host a marble bust of either a renowned great writer or philosopher of the ages, such as Aristotle, Milton, and Shakespeare.

All of these books share this resplendent space with the "Proclamation of the Irish Republic." These words are what led to the 1916 Easter Rising, Irish Independence. The seven signatures at the bottom are the names of brave leaders of the rising who would later face execution.

Next to this national treasure is another, Brian Boru's harp. This instrument is Ireland's oldest, having survived since the fifteenth century. A national symbol for this country, it represents their love for music, something I connect with. I too have a deep and abiding love for music; I consider music to be my mother tongue.

Daddy was a singer who also had a chorale he created, directed, and sang with. Mom kept her musical talents honed on the stand-up Bass Violin performing for years with the Riverside Symphony Orchestra. Both parents passed on to their children a love of music, from the sacred to the secular although most often heard was their shared favorite, classical. This early exposure had me speaking music before I formed words. With classical music as our lullabies, mom said when I was just nineteen months old I would wake in the morning, be standing in my crib, and make a rhythmic opened-mouth hum (sounding a bit like uhuh) completing the same piece I had fallen asleep to the night before.

To this day, music remains a constant companion in my home, my car, and my head. I enjoy all genres of music, from Rock to Blues, Classical to Gospel, and everything in between. For me, it's not just the music in the foreground. It's also all of the instruments and singers in the background too. As well, the story behind the music is just as fascinating to me. I was pleased when my son told me, "Ma, it's because of you I read the liner notes on the album or CD I'm listening to so I can learn more about the artist, the music." I love hearing this.

As we leave the Trinity campus, we pass a Hop-On/Hop-Off stop and instead walk fifteen minutes toward two of Dublin's medieval cathedrals. Both represent amazing architecture, yet both are quite different from each other.

The first one we visit is the older of the two. Almost 1,000 years old, it was originally built by Sitric, King of the Dublin Norsemen and it later became the Liberties of Christ Church Cathedral. Due to a very long line, we choose to move on to Saint Patrick's Cathedral, the largest in Ireland. This is the eighteenth century in all of its grandeur. In the mid-1800s, Sir Benjamin Lee Guinness (yes, that Guinness—of family beer fame), footed the bill for the major reconstruction that makes this cathedral what it remains to be today, absolutely breathtaking with much to see. As we are settling in with our self-guided tour we hear the call that the cathedral doors will be closing in five minutes. We are disappointed, but we have no choice. Then again the exhaustion is getting to all three of us.

"We are done walking. I'm hailing a cab." I get no complaints from either Les or Rie. And just like that one pulls up. We get in and find ourselves in the presence of a funny and kind driver.

"Hello ladies, I'm Liam. Where can I take you?"

In unison: "McGowans."

"Okay, what's the address?"

Well now, that's an odd question and it immediately confuses the three of us. In our other cab rides, we give the name of the flowery pub across the street from us and the driver knows our exact location. It works every time, just as our driver from the airport advises. But he didn't figure on Liam because here we are questioning ourselves aloud.

"McGowans?" All the while he is looking at us as if we each have three heads. So what happened to our magic word? We explain it's a pub in the Phibsborough neighborhood. He knows the neighborhood, yet the name of the pub doesn't ring a bell. When we begin to explain our confusion over the fact that he does not know about McGowans, he starts to chuckle then goes on to share, "I'm probably the only Irish taxi driver who doesn't drink." Ah yes. Now, here is a conversation just waiting to happen. The three of us start sharing at once how growing up as Seventh Day Adventists (SDA) abstinence from alcohol and tobacco are two of the tenets of the church. We share with Liam what our ninety-year old mother would be telling him right now if she were here: "I have never had one drop of alcohol in my life." We end up chatting and laughing the entire way. And then just like that we are across the street from our place–directly in front of McGowans. I am quite certain this is a sign from the pub gods. If not, I am making it one.

"It's high time we meet our neighbor, McGowans. It's my treat. And it's time you two taste some Jameson Irish Whiskey. (Mom is going to be so proud of me when she hears this.) "Follow me, ladies," I say. "Up to the bar we go." I get them settled in and turn to the bartender. "Three shots of Jameson, please." I am throwing them directly into the deep end of the pool. They should take at least one sip from the shot glass. "Okay, bottoms up. Let's go."

Rie is on the fence about it. She drinks wine yet is willing to give the whiskey a taste. Les doesn't drink, which is fine. So here I go, gently pushing her into trying something new, gently persuading her to take just a little taste. (What is a middle sister for but to invite trouble into her life?) Rie does pretty well while Les, on the other hand? Her expression after one tiny (very tiny) sip is priceless. And she is done. This is all that she can muster. Fair enough. At least she is a good enough sport to give it a try.

"Are you two done because I see some left in your glasses?" Rie reassures me,

"I'll finish it up. Just give me a minute."

Les says, "Thanks. I'm done."

So I must be the one who sacrifices herself and I finish off her shot.

We sit for a while longer before we cross the four-lane road over to our place. It's a fun end to this day though we feel bone-weary. There is a good reason for this. We are breaking into a solid rhythm of walking—lots of walking. Today? It's 12,876 steps. In other words, 5.5 miles. It's all becoming an adjustment to our feet and our bodies.

Tonight, we all go to our rooms early, and by the time my head hits the pillow, I am asleep. And if at 3:30 a.m. McGowans is filled with revelers who spill out onto the sidewalk, I am none the wiser.

8

A BIG BUS TOUR: THROWING CAUTION TO THE WIND

IT TURNS OUT TO BE A GOOD THING WE ARE NOT STAYING IN DOWNTOWN Dublin as it forces us to walk more. Before it is all over, we will make the seventeen-minute walk into downtown several times. Although for us it's always more like twenty to twenty-five minutes. Rie and I will come to lead, waiting for Les who never leads. We hold out for hope at one point she will. It will happen. We have faith. Not complete. Not total, but darn it, we want to believe in our older sis.

Finding our way to Dublin's city center is aided by the famous 390-foot high spire, the "Spire of Dublin,' also known as the "Monument of Light," planted in the middle of O'Connell Street. Realizing all roads lead to this spire, we use this as our navigational star for the rest of the time we are in Dublin. Even if we are not physically next to it, it helps to see the spire from either a distance or on any map we reference, a starting point, if you will.

Today, we need the spire to guide us to the train station. We are planning to visit Belfast in a couple of days, and we are hearing the train fills quickly, so we follow the advice of locals and buy our tickets ahead of time. As we are making our way to the station our sunny Dublin morning skies become quite dark, quite quickly and quite rapidly the rain dumps on us. Instantly. Hard. We grab our umbrellas just in time for the sun to show up again. Really? It's as though the weather is taking great pleasure in teasing us with a game of Guess What I'm Going to Give You Next?

With train tickets to Belfast now in our possession, we make a U-turn, get ourselves across over the River Liffey using the Ha'Penny footbridge (its name derived from years earlier the toll of halfpence to cross), and then head for the City Center. It's time to enjoy what lies beyond Dublin's city limits, and we are going to experience it on a bus tour.

Unfamiliar with bus tours? Think of it as an emotional sliding scale in a constant back and forth movement that ranges anywhere from "This is so amazing" to "Oh my word, what were we thinking?" and everything in between. We learn this too late though. Our tickets are purchased and it's time we board the excursion bus (it seats about sixty). The three of us elect to sit in the front, which ends up being a good decision because of our tour guide, Jack. With a full head of gray hair, glasses, and a beard a few days out from his most recent shave, his demeanor alone brings about instant trust. (Or do the three of us simply trust any man in Ireland? Yes. This sounds like us, yet we don't give Jack our address; we are making progress.)

Our tour bus pushes beyond the bustling city streets that are filling up too quickly with too many tourists. By 8:30 a.m., we finally reach calm country roads where copious amounts of sheep create the image of white polka dots on the greenest of fields.

Jack takes his microphone in hand and with his opening line we deduce rather quickly he belongs on stage performing stand-up rather than being on a tour bus with a gaggle of largely unappreciative tourists. The Moore sisters are not part of the "largely unappreciative tourist group." No, we speak Jack's language of puns and jokes and find ourselves instantly laughing at his punchlines in his merry-filled narrations. Jack's straight man is Connor, our young driver, who somehow maneuvers this beast of a bus along some very narrow roads, which, from our seats, appear one-way. Then traffic from the opposite direction comes toward us. After this occurs a few times, we are no longer amazed, or terrified. Maybe it's because we are sitting in front, or just paying attention, but the Moore sisters are enjoying Jack's comedic timing and the tour, so far. Then again, I am prone to speaking too soon.

Our first stop is Glendalough, County Wicklow. Jack informs all who care to listen that this National Forest was once a glacial valley. It is also where we find Seven Churches, a historical landmark with countless ancient graves and markers. We are encouraged to seek out the gravesite of Francis Kehoe who died in 1768 at age 102, which is quite remarkable when life expectancy at that time was thirty-five.

Before disembarking, Jack makes it very clear to all, (then again the use of "all" might be seen as both hasty and presumptuous) that our stop here is for a specific amount of time. He stresses the allotted time quite emphatically, including finger tapping on his watch. He follows this up by emphasizing (hum, but does he emphasize this enough?) we are to return to the bus at a specific time, which he repeats more than a few times. Let's say five times. The same message. In various ways. *(Okay, Jack, we get it. Let's go.)* He polishes off his instructions by incorporating his upper limbs, as if a flight attendant, while adding with even greater clarity, (then again, great enough?) that upon returning to our bus exactly where we will find it: "See over there, the big cluster of all the tour buses?" (I believe we all look as he instructs us to do so.) "Our bus will be over there." (Using a finger he points in the specific direction.) He then finishes up with "Please keep track of your time because you don't want everyone waiting for you."

All the while I'm thinking to myself, *Can't we just leave them?* In truth, with all of the specific directions, and the repeating of the specific directions in more than a few ways, I can't imagine us having to wait for anyone.

Les, Rie, and I begin to explore this first stop. The various shades of green found everywhere—from the hills to the trees and the lush under-growth—dazzles us. As Southern California girls, sadly, the color brown has become the perpetual color of our landscape, so to our parched eyes this Irish green is a wonderful reprieve.

Our feet lead us to an extensive gathering of ancient headstones. Celtic crosses abound, symbolizing a powerful intertwining of faith, legend, and superstition. An old small stone church stands here as well. All is securely hemmed in by the deep blue water of Glendalough Lake.

We catch up with Jack and some others at The Round Tower, the crown jewel of this location. At almost 1,000 years old, it still keeps faithful watch over all who take their eternal rest in its long-reaching shadow. One hundred feet in height and with six floors, it has a few window openings yet only near the top. It's the odd entrance that confounds us all. At eleven feet up from the ground, there is no easy access; Jack clears up the confusion.

"This is how the inhabitants remained safe. When an alarm sounded, the keeper of the ladder would make sure it was family or friend, not foe, who wanted to gain entrance. Once it was determined safe, the ladder was lowered to permit entrance, otherwise the ladder was kept securely inside. Okay, now for a show of hands of those who are starting to think how to incorporate this kind of construction in your home?" For some, no doubt it deserves consideration.

We wander around a bit more on our own before heading back to the bus. When we do, we find it in the exact location as Jack stated. Easy enough.

Then again, what is "easy enough" for most of us is not for one couple. They somehow come to forget both time and location. I hate to wait for late, yet wait we all must. And then Connor spots our lost couple.

Jack disembarks the bus and heads toward those people, both good little soldiers standing exactly where they are not to be standing. And then it's watching Jack that becomes a real comedy skit in itself. We observe from afar his flinging of arms in exaggerated pantomime, fingers pointing toward the bus in numerous ways. It is hilarious to us. Odd. The couple isn't even smiling.

So much for Jack's repetition of instructions + exaggeration with finger-pointing and tapping on the face of his watch. Now as this lost pair makes their way into the bus, they are sure to express their discontent for all to hear. "We were standing exactly where the bus was earlier." The newly formed chatty and laughing group of Jack, Connor, Rie, Les, and yours truly are shaking our heads at their words. Whatever. Next stop, Kilkenny.

As the big bus bounces merrily along the ever narrow roads, Jack points out some never-ending rock walls. Standing eight to ten feet in height, about three feet wide, they run in very close parallel to the winding road.

Known as Penny Walls, it was during the potato famine countless starving men earned a penny a day building these rock walls; backbreaking work for a starving man. Borrowing from Robert Frost's "Mending Wall," these walls are not built to wall anything out or anyone in, nor to make good neighbors. They were built solely for the worker to afford food for his family.

Pulling into Kilkenny, we find ourselves in yet another lovely Irish village with its own enchanting castle. Before disembarking, Jack stands up and gives the same spiel, complete with flailing arms and finger-tapping on his watch as well as finger-pointing. Of course, we now fully understand why he was so adamant at the first stop. We can only hope for the best at Kilkenny.

Before I go any further, let me just go ahead and ruin the ending for you: His attempt to make clear his expectations will fail once again. My. Word.

Though built in 1195, Kilkenny Castle is homey, down-to-earth. Perhaps it is the various rooms with captivating wallpaper instead of only cold stone walls that make a strong argument for why it feels welcoming. It's a lovely place to meander.

Once we finish up with our meandering, the three of us cross the street to Castle Road to reach Kilkenny Design Centre, once the royal stables. This Centre serves two purposes: shopping and eating. Both happen to be on our To-Do List.

The ground floor is for shopping, largely handcrafted goods. We find intricately woven baskets (I do love baskets, but I have more than enough already), sweaters to blankets made of Irish wool (beautiful, yet a bit too itchy for me), and Kilkenny Crystal along with the local Castle Arch Pottery. (Lovely; I'll break it before I get it home.) Everything draws admiration from even a non-shopper (I don't fall into this category). Then of course for those who appreciate jewelry (I fall into this category), with most of it integrating the Celtic cross.

Shopping over, we reach the Food Hall on the second floor. It's cafeteria-style, which for two reasons makes me more than happy. First, I do much better when I have more than a few choices. Second, I am very visual.

With our food trays in hand, a Food Hall employee directs where we must stand in line, which is a problem for me. It places me at the opposite end from the most important food group: dessert. With several people already ahead of us, this leaves me pondering. How do I go about jumping ahead, politely, mind you, of everyone else in order to fill my plate with dessert and then work my way backward? This kind of thinking is not new to me.

For me, the best part of going to church? The potlucks after Sabbath church service. My plan of attack? It never changed: I always started with desserts (yes, plural) first and then ended with the main courses. I don't know why Mom allowed this, how I filled my plate and then my stomach first with desserts. But Mom would only shake her head at me then turn away. It was a mutual understanding that worked for years in my favor. Les and Rie? These two always followed protocol when it came to the flow of a potluck line.

And now while here, in Kilkenny, both sisters still follow the right direction. Me? I decide not to embarrass my two sisters (or myself) and instead practice a modicum of maturity by remaining steadfast in line, ignoring my naughty little girl's inner voice to do otherwise.

Maturity pays off as the food here proves worth the wait. Starting with bread options, from beautiful dark bread to Irish Flatbread, a staple known as Soda bread (baking soda, salt, flour, and buttermilk). The main dishes highlight typical Irish fare, cabbage with boiled potatoes, an array of meat choices, including the ubiquitous lamb. And yes, the desserts make it difficult to choose. I settle on a piece of apple pie because I'm curious why it has layers like a cake, but after a few bites, I decide to stick to my grandmother's apple pie recipe, minus any layers.

Upon finishing our meal, we are ready to explore the town. We have time enough for a quick walkabout along some of the charming cobblestone streets of Kilkenny when all too soon it is time to get back to the bus and head for Dublin.

The three of us once again ensconce ourselves in the front seats, continuing conversations with Jack and Connor. When we arrive back in Dublin it's 5:30 p.m., which equates to a ten-hour day, so far. No doubt we got our money's worth, but we are ready to be done with the day.

Upon disembarking, Jack joins us for a selfie. I share how I want to hear some traditional Irish music yet so far I am having no luck. It's important to me that while in Ireland I experience live, traditional music.

Does he have any suggestions? He grabs some paper out of his pocket and writes down a few names while emphasizing, "The Cobblestone. It's the best around. Go there. You'll be glad you did."

So let's recap this day so far: It has been a very, very long day covering many miles in a tour bus filled with strangers. We have already put in a lot of steps. (It will be 15,951 once the day is done, and by the way, this rounds off to about 7.3 miles.) No big deal, although our feet howl otherwise in protest. We are so ready to get a bite to eat. We are so ready to get home. We are so not walking home. So we hail a taxi.

As we enter our place, the thought of climbing those stairs at the end of this day seems much too difficult. Even so, up we go because a nice warm shower awaits as well as our comfy beds. Sharing the bathroom means it is not going to be soon enough that I get to crawl into my bed, but finally each Moore sister is in her bed. We begin to shout from our rooms various memories about the day, which has us erupting in laughter. And then the next thing I know, it's morning.

9

TO LET: ONE CAN'T BEGIN TO IMAGINE

OUR FEET WILL BE GETTING A BIT OF REPRIEVE TODAY. WE ARE TAKING THE two-hour bus ride from Dublin to Galway. But first, with our rental on the south side of the River Liffey, we need to get ourselves back to the Ha'Penny Bridge to cross over to the north side, which, and according to yesterday's guide Jack, is the poor side of town.

Feeling quite confident and refreshed, we all agree there is no need for a taxi and we walk instead to the bridge. It ends up being a direct route. Easy to remember, seems to me, but even so, the thought does cross my mind that putting some bread crumbs along the sidewalk might be a good idea. This is just me considering if I should worry or not. No. I am not going to worry. We are on vacation and I am going to practice the art of being worry-free. (*Hmmm...Should I worry about trying to be worry-free?*)

Now on our merry way, we start laughing about Jack's tour dialogue the other day when he explained the difference between the north and the south of Dublin. I happened to capture it on video, and now as we listen to it again while we are walking, we laugh just as hard as when we hear it the first time:

"We will soon be crossing over the River Liffey. It's what divides the City of Dublin. The north side and south side. This is the north side of the city. We will shortly be going to the south side. It is said, you know, that on the south side of this city the people who live there are people with big cars, great professionals, no mortgage arrears. And a house in Spain. People of high quality. That's the south side. My name is Jack, and I live on the north side of the river."

Every day, I drink a copious amount of water, and while I know better than to drink so much before we head off for our several blocks walk to the bus station, I still do. Upon seeing the flowing water of the River Liffey, I quickly realize I need to be on the lookout for a public restroom and let my sisters know I could use their assistance. As soon as we reach the sidewalk that runs parallel to the river, I am beginning to lengthen my stride and increase my pace all the while gearing into my desperate search when I hear from Les, "I see one. See that sign down there?"

"No, where?" I ask in both excitement and panic.

"Down the end of the sidewalk. See? It says toilet!" Yes, I am starting to get that frantic feeling, so I begin running toward the sign Les is pointing to. And regardless of not seeing her "Toilet" sign, I trust what she is telling me, so I continue running in the direction she is pointing.

All the while I am going as fast as I am able to, doing my best in the meantime to squeeze my legs together as tightly as I can. I need to make it there. I get to the sign. I stop. I am looking all around. I am not seeing the public bathroom Les is seeing. I shout out, "Les, where? I don't see it anywhere." She shakes her head in frustration while jabbing a finger upward,

"Right there! You are standing under the sign for heaven's sake!" I have now shifted over to desperate mode. I then look up and read the sign. Forgetting about anyone around us, I yell back at her, "Les! Les! It's To Let! To lease a space. Not toilet!"

By now Les and Rie have caught up to me because they too need to use the To Let. And with that, the three of us launch ourselves into hysterics, which I have absolutely no business doing.

But lucky me. Irish skies are smiling at this moment as I somehow notice between my laughing tears the CityLink Bus Station across the bridge, the same station we need to catch our bus to Galway.

"I've got to get over there, now! I'll see you two there," I say while running away from them and toward the station. I leave them where they are standing trying to think about what just happened. In the meantime, I begin to thread my way through the crowd of pedestrians on the bridge, making a full-out effort to be as polite as possible. Reaching the other side, I must wait for cars to pass before sprinting across the street to make my final mad dash into the station.

"Hi! I will be purchasing a ticket to Galway, but first, where is your toilet?" I plead to the girl behind the glassed-in ticket counter. She points. I run. So close. Such risks should not be taken at my age.

Exiting the 'To Let,' I see that Les and Rie are waiting in line. After, we begin laughing again, yet I now feel rather comfortable joining them as well. I think I need to revisit trusting Les. Then again it's just this one time, so I'll give her a free pass.

A cold wind has started to come off the river, so we stay inside to wait. We have arrived a bit early; the bus will arrive a bit late. In the meantime, we make ourselves comfortable. As Les and Rie start to play Wordscape on their phones, I look around and notice joining us on the hard, bright yellow, pre-formed plastic chairs is an older woman being tended to by a younger woman much younger than she, probably in her thirties. We smile at each other and soon strike up a conversation (she seems to me like she wants to chat). I introduce myself, then them to me, "This is my mom Maeve. I'm Aisling."

I ask her, "Are you two headed to Galway as well?"

"Mom is, not me. She has been visiting with us in Dublin for the past few days and is now returning home to Galway." Then volunteers with what seems to be such an off-handed comment. "My brother, her only son, lives right next door to her. Not that this matters."

I think to myself, *interesting words to share with a stranger, and it seems to me that her brother's behavior matters to her. It also seems she's wanting to get this off her chest. I happen to be available.* Aisling's words are strong enough to turn Les and Rie's attention toward the conversation. After I introduce both to Aisling and her mom, I mention, "It must be so nice for you and your mom with your brother living next door. It's less of a worry for you and more of a help for your mom."

And with this, Aisling launches into an explanation of how this is not the case at all. "Yes, well just because he lives next door should not lead you to believe he is at all helpful to her." This is rather hard to understand, Aisling's brother not being reliable, or for that matter understanding any son who has his mother as his neighbor especially immediately next door not being helpful.

Aisling continues to share how she is the one who must make the two and half-hour drive each way every few weeks just to do her mother's laundry, grocery shopping, and so on because the son won't do it.

"It's as though he is much too precious to do any of this for her. What? It's automatically my job just because I'm the daughter?"

Hearing Aisling sends my thoughts racing back to Hazel Gaynor's book 'The Lighthouse Keeper's Daughter.' A passage in Gaynor's book is a combination of words that both sting and strike with such a force that at the time I am reading them I take a photo of the passage on my cell phone:

"...to feel a prick of jealousy as I observe her, knowing she will never look at me that way. Daughters never hold their mother's affection the way their sons do. Daughters are dutiful, dependable, and disposable.

Sons are brave and admirable, essential to the continuation of the family line."

If there is a son in the home, a daughter or daughters can most likely relate to this "prick of jealousy." Aisling understands. I understand as does Les and Rie. And here, this morning in this Dublin CityLink Bus Station are three American daughters sitting across from this one Irish daughter in a deep, common understanding of which we nod our heads in agreement. I go on to reassure Aisling, "We get it. Truly we do." Aisling continues, "As daughters, don't you feel it is expected of us? And truthfully, it doesn't matter what I do, I am and always will be the leftover."

What word did she just say? I then repeat it back to her. "Leftover?" Her use of "leftover" jabs hard into the three of us Moore sisters as we have yet to hear this word used in this context, in such a powerful manner. And yet "leftover" unpacks a lot of truth for Les, Rie, and me, Janice's daughters, as much as it does for Maeve's daughter, who reiterates, "Daughters are leftovers as far as I'm concerned," and yet as this daughter speaks of her hurt, the mother just sits there. She does not deny. She does not correct. She does not speak.

This mother's silence is meant to silence her daughter and even while the younger speaks her truth, her words are deftly submerged—left to drown by the older.

The bus arrives. We reassure Aisling we will have her mom sit with one of us, taking care of her as daughters do. It's the least we can do for Aisling.

Rie, the comforter and caretaker, sits next to Maeve and teaches her how to play Wordscape for the two-hour ride. The bus drives head-on into a powerful rain squall, which I am enjoying, and as I look out the window, I can't help but perseverate on the conversation with Aisling, the relationship with her mom and brother. One thing is for certain: if either of our brothers lived next to Mom they would be more than helpful to her. That being said, there is no denying Doug and Brad continue to hold a very special place in Mom's heart. From this though Mom's response is always the same, "Come on now. I love all of my kids." Yes, yes, she does love all her kids. Yet just not the same. Her daughters have come to accept this.

When it came to affection, Mom was always more comfortable showing than saying. She sewed many dresses for her daughters, she cooked and baked only healthy meals, she made sure our clothes were clean, and so much more. A remarkable Mom indeed, yet part of her parenting included the incorporation of critical words. But to know Mom was to know her parents. and these two perfected their craft of criticism on their strong-willed third daughter. Our grandfather was a man of 5'4". Except for one brother at 5'11", the rest of his family was short in stature. Grandfather met a 5'6" beautiful young woman from Trinidad, Colorado; at age sixteen, she was crowned Miss Star of Trinidad. They married soon after and six kids followed (mom was number five), all 5'6" and under. Except for Mom. At 5'10", this tall daughter possessed the height her father so much wanted for himself; as though life is fair.

Years later, our mom gathered up the same harsh words that nearly crushed her and in turn, with the greatest of generosity, dished them out to her children. It seemed the only way for her because she knew no different, yet now her adult children understand and recognize the source of her words. And because I am very strong-willed, much like Mom, I grew up believing I was her main target; a child's interpretation.

"You are always underfoot." Yes. Yes, I was. I just wanted to help. Then these words followed: "Lizzie, go away." I interpreted it to mean I was to go far away. So I did. At age thirteen I went away to school in Montemorelos, Mexico (that's a story for another book). First my heart left her, and then I grabbed the rest of me. And whenever I returned I would hear, "The house is always so much quieter when you aren't here." I understood these words to mean she preferred my absence. It was only much later I came to understand she meant the house was too quiet and that she missed me. She knew what she meant when she spoke these words, yet she didn't know how to rearrange them to make the sentence sound gentler to my ears.

The older I became the more I decided to no longer leave pieces of me behind for her words to touch. And then I found a way to renegotiate our constant mother–daughter tug-of-war. I started calling her by her first name, Jan, which somehow served to diffuse us. It's better. And now, on this bus ride to Galway, a smile crosses my face thinking about Jan, about her three daughters.

It's only now that I notice the blue skies. A road sign announces we are about to arrive in Galway. The two-hour bus ride passes by quickly with so much to think about. I am ready to get out and explore. We learn on the bus that Les is low on Euros, so our first stop has to be at The Bank of Ireland.

We can't go in because this latest downpour has flooded the bank. We find this all rather peculiar in a land of rain. They expect and prepare for such downpours, yes? It doesn't appear to be the case in Galway. A bank employee tells us that we need to go to Dunnes (think multi-floor department store), where there is a money exchange window on the third floor. Sounds easy enough for us to handle. This is until we begin making our way to the store and then the third floor where we must serpentine through voluminous amounts of merchandise hanging on all different kinds of racks. All the while, we remain in search of the elusive teller. We finally locate her far back in a corner. Thick glass surrounds the teller who has an even thicker accent. Les must lean in to best understand her. And when Les gets the exchange rate, she is not sure she hears correctly. And with that, Les learns how much more it costs to exchange money on the third floor of a department store.

"Well, that didn't seem like a fair exchange. One thing for sure, that wasn't cheap. I won't make that mistake again." Euros now tucked safely away (very safely away), we are ready to begin our acquaintance with Galway. Before coming here we read this village offers authentic Irish yarn. We promise to return from this trip with some for our mom, and I promise the same for two of my girlfriends.

Every day on our walkabout in parts of Dublin and beyond, we pop into various yarn shops asking specifically about Irish wool yarn. What we find instead is mostly yarn from Turkey and elsewhere—all spun by machines. Until Galway. And our research leads us to what appears to be Irish wool yarn Nirvana: Knitwits & Crafty Stitchers.

I must stop right here and make something very clear: I am neither "knitwit" nor "crafty stitcher." I guess if I wanted to be, but I don't. That being said, my sisters are, so this store is perfect for them. Truthfully though, Rie just loves being in a store, any store, even this store. Then again, her talent as a seamstress is amazing.

Her costume credits include sewing from the simple and mundane to the stunning and extravagant for various schools, colleges, universities, and community plays.

And for non-knit-wit, uncrafty me? There is no other way to put this: I am in yarn and fabric store purgatory. I do give it a good try (perhaps I could try harder?) although my attention span here is that of a gnat. I struggle to maintain what little focus I have. Then again, I do have two girlfriends for whom I promise yarn. I want to get this right, so I make a sort of all-out effort trying to make sense of it all: size, width, weight, and the etcetera, as it applies to yarn. Fascinating, I am sure, but not to me. So as I wander about, I try making sense of what it is specifically I need to purchase for my girlfriends.

Coming to my rescue is a sales associate. A cheerful one she is, I am sure she is drawn to the "I could use some assistance" look on my face. And before I am even able to complete the purpose of my quest Ms. Knitwit and Crafty is venturing off into a deep and detailed diatribe from which I find myself drifting away into a trance as she yammers on about yarn.

Snapping out of my trance, I rejoin her once again. I try my darndest to emit enthusiasm that might come close to matching hers. I then remember just how well two girlfriends know me; both were wise enough to put pen to paper regarding their yarn wishes. I hand over to Ms. Perky my notes that speak her language because she is, after all, a yarn translator. Now speaking the same language (sort of), she takes me to where I need to be.

In all honesty, I am happy to purchase some Irish wool yarn for my girlfriends. In the meantime, Les and Rie find various colors of yarn they believe Mom will like, which we all chip in and purchase for her.

Once outdoors, I can breathe again. I am looking forward to the rest of the day and what Galway will bring. We almost stayed here for our time in Ireland rather than Dublin, and then we did a compare and contrast finding Dublin offered a larger variety of things to see and do. Dublin is large with many older areas mixed with the modern. Galway on the other hand is much smaller, a lot of charm.

We end up spending most of our time in the Latin Quarter, named as such because Galway once did a lot of trade with Portugal and Spain. In fact, over the years many Spaniards made the move across the sea to Galway—choosing rain over the sun. The Latin Quarter presents old architecture lined up along cobblestone streets that are narrow, twisting, and turning. We come across Irish dancers performing here and there as well as street musicians. It's in John F. Kennedy Park where I met a real charmer. An elderly gentleman, who I would guess is in his late seventies, early eighties, is playing his saxophone. He is wearing a white shirt with a wide red and black tie, which has the design of a saxophone on it. Over his shirt he is wearing a white wool cable knit sweater with wooden toggle buttons and then a suit jacket on top of this. It's his face though that draws me in. Under his checkered newsboy cap, his eyebrows are bushy, his complexion ruddy, and his mustache and beard wiry, both blowing every which way. When I approach him to drop money in his tin, I smile at him and he returns the favor. I tell him how much I enjoy his playing. And then he speaks. Yup, no clue at all what he is saying as his Irish brogue is strong. So I return the favor with my (alleged) California accent and ask to take his photo (he seems to understand me just fine), and after I take a couple he tells me something sweet, I imagine, so I drop more Euros into his tin.

10

GALWAY: THE PRESENT AND THE PAST

IRELAND SEES THIS SEASIDE FISHING VILLAGE OF GALWAY AS THEIR "CULTURAL Heart." We go to a part of town known as The Docks; it does not disappoint. Making our way down a narrow cobblestone road that hosts a parade of shops, my attention is drawn to a wall with a very old wooden sign. It includes the design of two Claddagh rings on each corner of the bottom half.

THOMAS DILLON / EST 1750

CLADDAGH GOLD.

ORIGINAL MAKERS OF THE CLADDAGH RING

THIS ESTABLISHMENT IS DEDICATED TO

FAIR PLAY AND A SQUARE DEAL

NO MAN SHOULD EXPECT LESS

NOR BE GIVEN MORE

The old village of Claddagh (an Cladach, Irish for "shore"), now gone, is where this unique ring originates. It includes a set of hands (friendship) that hold between the fingertips a heart (love) and a crown (loyalty) that sits on top of the heart.

Standing in front of this sign, I find myself missing my granddaughter, Pie (my nickname for her, or Miss Pie). It's a natural connection to be thinking of her because for years she performed the art of Irish dance, honing her skills at Claddagh School of Irish Dance in our hometown in California. And the owner of the studio? A Galway native. I know, right? This world.

It's Pie who has me reflecting on this world. Without a doubt, it's the many twists and turns I experience over the years, starting with her, or, rather, ending with her, that has me thinking about how I appreciate my life and the choices I made, beginning with her daddy, my son Brent-Stig.

Except for family and close friends, I've kept this part of my life private. Now that I am in the early years of the third stage of life, what does it matter now? So here it is: I married the first boy who professed his love for me. I divorced him four years later, which left me as a struggling single mom in her early twenties. Then there are all of those in-the-middle details. All of which I have no regrets. Never. Ever.

I followed in my mother's rebellious footsteps. I married someone she didn't want me to marry, although I was twenty-one, four years older than when she married Daddy whom her mom didn't want her to marry. Yes, there is a pattern here.

Up to a few hours before my wedding, oh wait. I would be remiss if I didn't unpack my family begets before going any farther. Think of it as the secular version of begets in the sacred Book of Genesis. But mine? A much twisted matrilineal begets:

Tillie is my mom's mom. Tillie is in love with a boy. Her mother does not approve. Her mother finds someone else for Tillie to marry. Tillie does as her mother tells her to do, always.

Janice is my mom. Janice is in love with a boy. Her mother does not approve. Telling Janice he is not suitable (whatever), and she is not to marry him. Janice ignores Tillie. Janice marries Leonard (our dad). This will show Tillie.

Leslie is my sister. Janice knows Leslie is in love with a boy. Janice does not approve. She finds someone else for Leslie to marry. Leslie does as her mother tells her to do, always.

I am Elizabeth. I am in love with a boy. Janice does not approve. Janice gives reasons why not to marry him (whatever). Liz ignores Janice. Liz marries the young man. This will show Janice.

Laurie (Rie) is my sister. Janice knows Laurie is in love with a boy. Janice does not approve. Janice gives reasons why not to marry him (whatever). Laurie ignores Janice. Rie marries the young man. This will show Janice.

And this whole mother begetting on the next generation of children? Leslie, Elizabeth, and Laurie make sure it stops with us.

Now, back to my wedding day. On the morning of my wedding, I hear from mom, "I have a terrible headache. I can't make it. I am sorry." She ended up attending after all. Daddy barely made it through singing his solo, "Sunrise, Sunset." And with that, I married the boy. Even though about a half-hour earlier when we saw each other (Bad luck? Perhaps.), he spoke no words that resembled anything like, "Liz, you are a beautiful bride." (Because I was, dammit!) And then my Daddy, ever so intuitive (a gift he bestowed upon me), asked just before he walked me down the aisle, "Are you sure about this, Lilibet?" (Lilibet, his nickname for me)

"No. No, I am not."

"We can call it off if this is what you want."

"No," to which I took my first step toward the front of the church and my future husband. I reasoned no one else would love me, even if it was as little as my young groom did, so down the aisle I went.

He didn't want to marry me—or anyone right then. But I wanted to marry him—right then. He struggled deeply. No worries. I decided I was capable of doing all the heavy lifting for us. But while taking my vows in my borrowed wedding gown, I had no idea what this would come to mean for my future.

Two years married, we are both twenty-three years old, and my doctor confirmed what I suspected: I was pregnant. On my way home, I imagined the many ways my husband would respond upon hearing this news. But when I delivered it, I heard words from him that went off-script. They did not correspond at all to what I expected: "I kind of prefer just the two of us." This was interesting information at this particular time. Then again, we never did discuss our plans for children. How silly! Why would we have done something like that, right? And then he followed up with probably his most honest words he ever spoke to me, "Until I am ready, I want you to get an abortion, I don't want to share you with a baby." I. Am. Gasping. For Air.

"You can't possibly mean what you are saying. And you don't want to share me with a baby?"

My head was spinning from his hurtful words. What was I supposed to do with them? With us? With our unborn baby? And it was at that moment I began redirecting all of my heart toward my baby and away from my husband. I knew I would be faced with some scary choices about the future for myself and my baby even though what and where those choices would be I didn't know at that time. In the meantime, it was hell for me to put up this charade, pretending we were happy together, and happy about the baby (one of us was).

There was only one person with whom I shared this shift in my heart and marriage, my trusted confidante, Les. It was my big sis who helped me survive this painful period. She was also pregnant at the time, with her second, and our delivery dates were just two weeks apart. Time spent with Les shopping for clothes for our ever-expanding bellies helped me a great deal. It was one time in particular, both of our bellies were burgeoning with only a month or so to go when I gave Les a call.

"I am running out of tops but with only a few weeks left I can see spending only a little on new tops. What if we went in together? Each buys a couple then we can trade-off, making it look like we have more?"

"That's a great idea. How about K-Mart? It won't be so expensive."

We met up at the store and started to go through the selection, each finding a few we had both agreed upon. Who knew getting a dressing room would be the tricky part? We waited for rooms to become available. Finally, one was free, so I waved Les over to me.

"There is one room only, but we can get in there together. We can fit in, come on. Besides, it will be easier to try on the clothes in the same room, and it will be fun." We proceeded to take off and try on different tops, and no matter which way we turned and twisted, that small changing room had our bellies bumping into each other. This had us laughing so hard it brought a Sales Associate to the outside of the dressing room.

"Ladies. What's going on in there? Is everything alright?"

For this moment for me, yes, everything was alright.

My young husband succeeded in jobs, he failed in jobs. Up and down. And then the lies soon followed. Or they were always there, and I just chose to ignore them? Most likely. Highly likely. But I listened with high hopes when he told me,

"I am going to start city college. I saw a counselor and I've already registered for a couple of classes. In fact, one starts tomorrow night, after work." Yes. Finally, he had a goal, progress. For him, making any kind of goal was much like nailing Jell-O to a tree.

And when the night of his first-class arrived one of us was quite excited (it wasn't him). "I have some food for you to take." And with that, from across the kitchen, I sent him a sincere smile while behind my back, all fingers crossed, "Good luck. You've got this. I am looking forward to hearing about your classes when you get home." He closed the door and walked out. I patted my expanding belly, speaking words of reassurance. "We might just have a future as a family after all. It might work." Such a silly girl. Maybe I should try harder for my pregnant self and my college-bound husband even though my ever-growing belly only created more distance and a deeper chasm between us.

As I got myself settled in for a quiet evening, someone approached the front door. I was surprised to see my husband.

"What's happened? Why are you home so soon? Did the car break down?"

"No. I need to tell you something."

"Now? You'll be late for your class. What is it?"

"Uh, well, I never did register for classes." I reached for the nearest chair to provide support for my weak legs.

"But why, what, your appointment with a counselor? You told me the schedule for the classes you signed up for. I am trying to understand." But I am ignored and my questions go unanswered. Then, "It's not what I want to do. You got excited so, well." And there I stood. Hearing once again how he had so cleverly layered one lie upon another.

"What are we going to do now?" I asked in the greatest of whispered hesitancy.

"I'll find a job. We'll be fine." And then we were not fine, not at all.

Some time passed, and I was due to deliver at any time. One evening I'm trying to get comfortable with my big belly as I'm watching television when my husband enters the room in nice clothes.

"What's going on? It's not your night to work."

"I am heading out to a party at a buddy's house. This is the number if you need anything." I'm thinking. *Wait. What?* I wish I had been brave enough at that young age to say what I was thinking. *If I need anything? I mean what could I possibly need? Hmm. Let me think. Hold on. Give me a second. I'm sure it will come to me. Oh, I know. How about my husband staying with me because I am scared to give birth, which is imminent?* And then it was as though I had an out-of-body experience as I watched myself plead in a high-pitched voice filled with jags, cuts, and sharp edges. "You can't stay here with me? I am terrified about giving birth. Why would you do this? I know you don't want this baby, but I'm scared." How nice it would have been to have my husband with me even if he didn't give a rat's ass. Which he didn't. I guess I should have emphasized "scared" a bit more for him. Instead, he left me feeling frightened with only a number to call; so thoughtful. And of course later that night I had to call the number at his buddy's house. (This is pre-cell phone days.)

"Hi. This is Liz. I need my husband home, now. Please. I am going into labor."

The person on the other end of the line yelled out my husband's name, and when I heard his voice I was so relieved. But my ardent plea fell on his deaf ears.

"I'll be home later. I am not coming home right now. You'll be fine." He spoke with such clear deliberation that each word felt meticulously shoved deep into my ears. Done with everything us, I hung up on him. Then I dropped to my knees and let out a primal scream in order to release my pain, sadness, and heartbreak yet at the same time acknowledged my inner-strength, too long marginalized and ignored. I stood up a stronger woman and while holding my belly I spoke with determination. "The fool has no idea that each time he pushes me away or ignores me, I only grow stronger. More independent. More determined." What little emotional life was left between us, I now made sure all that he had broken was scattered throughout our house. There was nowhere he couldn't step without walking on the broken shards of who we once were. Let him feel the same pain I had been feeling for so long. He could avoid me, but now he could no longer avoid getting cut on those shards he created, and he just might, someday, come to feel and perhaps see the emotional pain he inflicted on me.

It was a very pregnant Les who took me to the hospital the next morning. She stayed with me until my baby's father arrived. And still Les kept my sad secret for me, away from my parents, especially Mom. I didn't want her to be so very right about my husband. Because she was.

Now home with my baby boy, it was soon after the thunder made of hurt and broken dreams roared so loudly in our house that it cracked the foundation, the walls collapsed. There was no saving any part of us. I gathered up my infant son, and we started life on our own. I came to feel and breathe life as a single working mom. As for my young husband? He was not ready to live a responsible family life, so I became the responsible one. And I became happier as well as stronger.

Many years later, I received an email from my former husband asking if he could meet up with me and our son. Arrangements were made. Dave, who had adopted Brent as a five-year-old and raised him as his own, welcomed my former husband into our home. Formalities out of the way, the three of us moved to the backyard patio for a chat, leaving Dave and Brent's girlfriend at that time in the house to wait.

Brent-Stig, then a junior at the University of California, Santa Barbara, pulled up his chair very close to mine. He was sending a clear message to the man sitting across from us that he was here for his mom. We were facing a man neither of us had seen for over twenty years. I went first. "Before we begin, I have a question for you."

"Alright. Go for it." I broke the ice with this question:

"Did you tell me to get an abortion when I told you I was pregnant?" It wasn't that I wanted to skewer him, but it was instead his proclivity of altering the truth. I needed to know if after all of these years this grown man could finally speak honest words to me and to Brent-Stig, because it was what mattered.

"Yes. Yes, I did."

I exhaled.

"Okay. Thanks for telling the truth. Now we are open to talking."

If he had lied, I was going to end any conversation; rather, it was never going to begin. And then before we knew it, an hour had passed. Polite handshakes signaled our time was over. Afterward, I walked this man who was now basically a stranger to me to his car. As we stood for a moment on the driveway, my brain began playing a movie at high speed of when I met him, my first love, in high school, and our time together. And now, as I was about to say my goodbye to him, he said rather softly, "Liz, you need to know I still love you. I have never stopped loving you. I just needed to tell you this." I could see the pain in his eyes. I recognized it as the same pain lodged in my eyes all those years ago although now long healed over.

"You what?" I asked in utter surprise. I never expected this from him. "Why are you telling me this, and now? What am I supposed to do with this information? Tell you, 'Hold on, I'll just run in the house, grab a bag and leave with you?' You don't love me. You don't even know me. I am a fifty-year-old woman now. I am not at all the young girl who once loved you so deeply those many years ago. You love an idea of me, but me? No, no you don't."

He protested. "You don't understand. I blew it. I get it. Please."

"Please? And understand what? That you've changed your mind after all of these years? You are much too late with your declaration of your love for me. But please know this: I will forever love you because it's what brought me where I am today. I have Brent-Stig because of you. But my love is one of gratitude, not the one you are professing for me. I wish you all the best. Honestly, I do, but I've got to get back into the house," and with that, I turned away and didn't look back. I never saw him again. Brent-Stig never saw or heard from his father again despite hearing the words, "Please forgive me. I've changed. I want another chance to be in your life." But it was fine because he had been forgiven long before that day he came to visit. Sadly, he died years later.

So regrets? Not one bit. Instead, gratitude for what life was then and how it gave way to one better for me. A life that has led me to this Claddagh sign in Galway reflecting on the power of the past as I stand in the present thinking about my Miss Pie. This world, right?

Les, Rie, and I now make our way against the tide of tourists, turning toward the water inlet. Here stands a Spanish Arch, constructed in 1584, and 435 years later it now serves to frame a photo of the three of us. From here, we see the River Corrib, which points us in the direction toward the Atlantic Ocean, an uncommon sight for us Moore girls who grew up spending the summers of our childhood swimming in the warmer waters of the Pacific Ocean in Southern California, mostly at Corona del Mar State Beach.

But right now in Galway, the raindrops begin and they bring with them a cold wind. (Oh yeah, a Moore sister favorite!) That's our cue to head back to town. But as we make our way back along the Corrib River, we pause on the high bluff above the inlet and appreciate the numerous beautiful swans and other waterfowl. Then the pesky wind kicks it up a notch. It has become so strong it's as if we can reach out and touch birds as they try their best to fly into the headwind. For one seagull within arms' reach, it seems, all I need to do is to reach out and give it a gentle push from behind because it is going nowhere fast; flapping his wings seems to serve no purpose at all.

While we just scratch the surface of the history of this seaside city, it's time to catch the bus back to Dublin.

On the return bus ride, I look out my window and enjoy witnessing the sky rapidly transitioning from sunshine into various deep shades of gray to black. The darkness of the sky works its magic on landscape and sheep alike. In fact, the wool worn by the countless sheep appears to be an even brighter white because the rolling pastures where they graze are all a brilliant shade of green. I now understand (and see) why Ireland is known as the Emerald Isle. Taking a photo, I post it with the caption, "I've never seen such a deep and rich green before. Even the color green must be jealous of this brilliant emerald green of Ireland."

As our bus advances toward Dublin, the rain begins. It stops just as quickly. As I turn my glance to the front of the bus, a very distinct double-rainbow appears, framing the large front window of our bus. I excitedly point it out to Les and Rie, and we are like happy little girls oohing and aahing over a sight we now rarely see at home.

11

DOES AN INTERNAL GPS RUST OVER THE YEARS?

BY THE TIME WE RETURN TO DUBLIN, IT'S ALMOST 6:00 P.M., BUT THE SUN IS still fairly high in the summer sky. As per our usual now, we are ready to get off the bus. We are ready to get a bite to eat. We are ready to get 'home.'

"I notice we have already put in 10,000 steps so far today. It's time to hail a cab," I say. To which Les responds, "But we'll save money (Rie and I couldn't care less about this right now, thank you very much.) if we walk back to our rental." Adding, "It's not that far."

Let's just stop right here. When it comes to directions and distance, we trust Les explicitly. This is a trust with very deep familial roots.

Mom and Dad delighted in the innate navigational skills of their young daughter, Leslie Anne. So much so they often followed her directional advice.

"Go that way." Or, "Now go that way" with a tiny pointed finger and a little voice that guided the driver, all the while as she stood up in the back seat of the car (yes, while it was moving, and no, there were no seatbelts). And even now, we will hear from Les, "No, go that way. Turn there." With Les and directions, be it just once to the other side of town, city, or state, she always found her way home. Always. No matter the length of time; I am talking years. She amazed many with this talent. Her mind, it seems to me, is like a steel trap. It's as though she was born with some kind of internal GPS. It's important to share this talent about our older sis because it defines the years of trust we all have in her uncanny ability to always find the way back home.

Now back to "It's Not That Far." Rie and I are listening to Les. She repeats, "Come on, our walk back won't be that far! Why pay for a taxi?" True, it isn't that far. Even truer is we know our sis. She doesn't want to spend money on a taxi. The fact is we did make the walk with ease this morning, so Rie and I are now going along with the notion of walking, of course, dagnabbit, even at this point though we are both very pro-taxi. Les then adds as we step onto the Ha'penny Bridge, "And we turn left on the other side." We believe Les' sense of direction even as we are crossing over the bridge to the south side, on our very tired feet.

Les further then points out to us: "See those big trees up there? We will turn right there." And with these final directions is when Rie suddenly disagrees, adamantly. Still, all the while the three of us continue walking in the direction Les assures us is correct. (We never seem to stop to discuss directions. No, for some reason we just keep walking. We need to stop doing this. By the way, on this trip, we don't. Ever.)

"No! You are wrong, sis," Rie protests for the second time. I am suddenly torn. Which one to trust? I mean, she's going up against Les' years of proven history, after all. Yet Rie's voice exudes both confidence and determination. I am starting to lean toward Rie. I mean after all, Les did mislead me when it came to To Let. And then, Les interrupts my mental see-saw with the most stubborn of words, "I am right. You'll see." Ah yes, there it is. That stubborn streak. Here it is popping up sooner rather than later. I don't shake my head in surprise. But still, even with the stubborn streak in full operational mode and while in the middle of this directional disagreement, this does not stop the three of us from walking toward the large group of trees in the distance. What a trio. But then it's so odd. As we trudge toward the trees, they continue to recede. And this is where it all goes wrong. Not at first. Let's just say Les' innate compass does not seem to have a true north in this part of the world. Or put another way, is that steel trap of hers becoming rusty with age? And when do we come to realize this is the wrong way? Too many steps in, this is when. It's also when I stop this nonsense.

"It's time to make a U-turn. That was not the right direction; let's get our bearings." It seems they agree because in a synchronized fashion we all turn around, toward town. Along the way are many signs falsely advertising a toilet, of which we are not in desperation to find at this moment, thank goodness. Of course, we roar once again with laughter all the while shaking our heads. Leslie Anne. Mercy me. And then an alternative way home catches my attention.

"Look up there. Train tracks. Let's go there to see if there is a train that will get us closer to home, and sooner." They follow me as we attempt a brisk walk toward the tracks. All the while, I am trying to bring up a Map App on my cell phone, but the service in this particular area is proving to be very spotty. This isn't helping our cause.

How is it that this morning we take a direct route to the bus station yet now we can't seem to find this same direct route to get back home? (I should have left a trail of breadcrumbs after all. Darn me. Why didn't I worry this time?) How did this become so confusing? It's all because our older sister, once a navigational savant, has lost her GPS abilities. I'm going to ask for directions, and though Les is not too happy I want to do this (perhaps disappointment in her GPS going haywire), Rie is happy I want to do this. I make clear to both, "I am not going to participate any further in this recreation of the whole Biblical epoch of being lost in the desert." And just like that, a miracle. I like to call it that. As if appearing out of a burning sun mirage (not so much burning sun here), I see two young dads appear pushing strollers and walking their little ones. It's time to mention McGowans.

"Always mention McGowans and anyone will tell you how to get back to your place" works every time, well, there is Liam.

An immediate vote has me being the one to approach the men; such a surprise! Les and Rie serve as my backup, and for what I am not too certain. As I begin walking toward these two young men, I can't help but wonder why this whole getting lost with a sister (in this case two) has a familiar feel to it? Ah yes, there was that one time when I asked strangers for directions yet in a much worse predicament than I am right now, and no sister backup, nowhere in sight. Not that it would have mattered then either.

A good twenty-five years ago, Rie and I decided to meet at the Garment District in downtown Los Angeles for some shopping; great deals are always to be had. At this time, I was living about two-and-a-half hours north and Rie about two hours south of the District. She had driven herself there several times over, and me? A handful of times but with Dave driving. And I'll just admit it right now, no, I was not paying any attention.

The day I was to meet Rie, I drove myself. I pointed my car south on the 101, then to the 110, and then the 105. And then I am lost in Los Angeles. Pre-cell and pre-Google days, I could only do the next best thing, which was to pull off the freeway and find a gas station to point me back in the right direction.

It was only after I had pulled into the closest station I could find I took full stock of where I was: Watts. Home of the 1965 race riots that claimed thirty-four lives. Even in the middle '80s, it still was not the place where a young white woman, alone, was typically seen. As I sat in my car for a few minutes, I decided to do what Mom always told her kids: "Pull yourself up by your bootstraps. Figure it out." So I did both: Bootstraps and figured it out. As I exited my car, I pulled myself up to my full height as a way to project confidence (this is me convincing myself as well) and walked with my back as straight as possible (okay, my legs felt like rubber), and entered the cashier's office. And as soon as I did? I was surrounded by several young black men who stopped and turned to look at me. As one might guess, they were surprised to see me standing there. I then took a second to first reassure myself, *You've got this. They're no threat to you. Just be funny and relax. Reassure them:*

"Hey, guys, how are you doing? Are any of you willing to guess which one of us is lost?" I got a few laughs, then a few more. I felt my body start to relax a little. "So listen, I am meeting my sister at the Garment District in about fifteen minutes from now, and the last thing I told her was not to get lost, because she always gets lost. Joke's on me, right?"

Whew, I now had the attention of my audience. They were laughing. They were kind and friendly toward me; of course, why not? And then as if on cue, more than a few of them started to point every which way to direct me to where I needed to be. "Okay, men, which one do I listen to? Help me here."

And they settled on one guy and that was that. I looked each of them in the eye and smiled. "I appreciate you all. I am not so sure I want to share with my sister how I got so lost today, but after meeting you guys I won't keep this from her. You've all been great. See ya. No, probably not." (We all knew I wouldn't be returning to Watts any time soon just to pop in to say "Hi.") Their laughter and goodbyes were a gentle breeze on my back as I returned to my car. My gait was different from when I first approached the shop. I am quite certain I strolled. And though I got some stares from customers who had since pulled in for gas, I wanted to say to them, "It's cool. I'm with the guys in the shop."

Back on the freeway, I realized how I was able to talk with almost anyone. It helped to be respectful and apply a little humor. A true turning point for me, it became a life experience I forever carry around in my pocket. I am grateful for those young men and the shared experience.

So here in Dublin, as in Los Angeles, I approach unsuspecting men and ask for directions. "Hey guys, how are you doing? Any one of you willing to guess which three of us might be lost?" They both laugh. This is a good sign. "I am hoping you might point us in the direction of McGowans?" When they hear where we need to get to, they shake their heads. This isn't a good sign. They know this pub all right, yet hate telling me just how far out of our way we are. This is such great news, Les. Not really and in fact, we learn we are at the very least a good twenty-two-minutes out of our way—add this to our already long walk. In other words, we are now a strong mile and a half away from home, making it how many more steps ahead of us? Need I mention again that we are pretty road-weary right now? Well, I am mentioning it because we are.

Before Rie and I concoct a fool-proof plan for the best way to leave Les in Ireland, permanently, the guys skip right over my need for directions and ask, "What's your accent?"

We are hearing quite often about our Californian accent, which, again, we do not hear, and right now discussing it is furthest from my mind. What my mind is doing instead is achingly begging, *Please! We just want to get home. It's all we want. There's no accent to hear, by the way. Just point us in the right direction, will ya?* And then I calm down and respond, "California." I can tell by their expression this blows their mind until I add, "Southern California, all born and raised." I turn around and point to my two-person sister backup crew, who now are so bravely standing with the rest of us. And yes, I feel so much safer with them so close. In the meantime, these two young men are barely able to contain themselves upon hearing "Southern California." We get it. The magic and illusion of Hollywood, movie stars, Disneyland, and whatever else feeds the imagination of those hoping to visit someday. And then too it is where we are all standing right now: so very, very far away from Southern California, a bit over 5,000 miles. The distance only adds to the enchantment and a desire to visit. As they start peppering us with their questions, I look over at my sisters and can see how we are all forgetting for a few brief minutes how we are sinking into the soles of our shoes from exhaustion.

Forgetting their little ones, these two adult men start talking over each other in their high-pitched excitement. "We hope to take our kids to Disneyland someday. Have you ever been?" one wonders. I look over at Les and Rie. It's their cue to jump in, anytime.

"Yes, many times over. I am a huge fan," Rie replies because she is indeed a huge fan. She loves the magic of Disney. Always enjoying all things Disneyland, it is this beloved Auntie who many years earlier first introduces her kindergarten-age nephews and niece to The Happiest Place on Earth. Les then volunteers, "I live about an hour from Disneyland as a matter of fact," and when they hear this they can only shake their heads in disbelief. It's as if only something rather mystical allows one to live so very close to the Disney magic.

At this moment, when these three sisters just want to be back across the street from McGowans, it is rather magical in itself to be standing in front of these two dads and take in their joy. It's at this moment we witness the power of Tinker Bell's pixie dust from these many miles away.

And while I'm smiling back at them? I'm thinking, *Now back to us, please.*

They finally offer up the solution to get on the next train at the stop, which is east (according to MY internal compass), about 100 yards down the track.

"It's going in the direction you need to be going. Plus, they rarely check for tickets." We all thank them for their assistance. It's only once they are out of earshot range do we look at each other and start to belly laugh like the tired, silly girls we are at this moment. We know what kind of luck we have and we are not getting on the rail without a ticket.

As we are laughing, the next train quietly glides up to stop. We instantly stop laughing. It's clear each of us is mentally weighing running to catch this train, tickets be damned.

And just as quickly it glides away. Standing in the same spot, we once again start to laugh. We are overly tired; this is for certain. While this is Les' fault, because it is, it is fun to tease her about her compass being haywire when we need it the most. We still trust her... Uhm... sort of. Let's see how the rest of the trip plays out.

And once again our trudge toward home begins—in our all-new direction. Why not hail a cab? We can't find one where we are presently lost, uh, I mean, are standing. Trust me, Rie and I keep watching for one, more specifically one that carries two passengers only—her and me. And again, our phone apps are still not cooperating at all.

I announce to them both, "I am getting mighty thirsty, and I am not talking about the water I have been carrying. Oh, and Les, by the way, I need a To Let." Both sisters require a To Let as well. And are equally thirsty.

Lucky for us there is a pub on almost every corner. Irish fun fact: In this country of 70,200+ square miles made up of streets and roads, both broad and narrow, they house over 10,000 pubs for a population of a little over 6 million. My point being? There is plenty enough to share. And just like that, there is a corner pub. We pop in. It has my name all over it simply because it's a pub and because it is right in front of us.

We want, no, let me start over...we are in true need of their bathroom. Stepping inside we take in the long, narrow lay-out of this bar. Fortunately for us, opposite the entrance is a circular booth of faux red leather in a corner, and it's empty. We claim it as our own; it makes for a quick and easy entrance/exit. We do, after all, need to find our way back home sometime today.

Sliding into the booth, we decide the best way to use the bathroom is to order something to drink. Exhaustion is piling upon us, both physically and mentally, yet we quickly ascertain it's up to us to place our order at the bar. In other words, this requires one of us to approach the bar. We all look at each other. It doesn't take being a mind reader to know I will be the one making the long walk past the tables filled with mostly male patrons enjoying their after-work pints. Not that I see myself as a head-turner; rather, it's a long walk past tables filled with men. *Time to act confident, Liz.*

"Fine, I'll be the brave one," I confirm in a teasing voice.

When Les was in her twenties her first husband deserted her and their two little kids. He also absconded with what little was left of the once brave voice of our sister. He chipped away at it for years and it was during this subverted process we witnessed Les transition from voice to voicelessness.

And Rie? Although from an early age she believed observing and keeping silent were her safer choices, she later found value in her voice during her early college years. She expressed with ease her point of view and opinions. Then when she married her high school sweetheart, he honed in on her strengths and in a full-on assault weakened them. He took full advantage by reassuring her that what she had to say was not what he wanted to hear. So she tried out some new words for him to hear, "I am done. I am leaving." The husband tried even harder to steal away the quiet voice of this sister. She weighed, she considered. She left him. She returned to him. More importantly in that see-saw stage of her life Rie was determined not to make a mistake. And then when she saw it was a mistake to stay, she left. Leaving in haste, she forgot to shove into her suitcase her confidence, which was left unclaimed for a good long while.

When I would become too vocal in public, my first husband would begin to squeeze my knee. This was his method of telling me I needed to be quiet and that I had embarrassed him. I needed to know my place. I thought love was to deny myself. And then I decided he was wrong. After that, with every knee squeeze, I became more vocal. He was not going to silence me. And then came the time when I knew better. I refused to hand my voice over to him and took it with me when I went away.

The three of us Moore sisters still shake our heads at our first picks for husbands; we all chose better the second time around as we became stronger and better women. Yet still, here at the pub, who is going to the bar and order drinks and then ask about the To Let, I mean bathroom? Not a hard guess.

I come out to see our drinks waiting at the bar. I pay the tab, yet then pause a few minutes to take in my surroundings. The bartender lingers somewhat after collecting my cash and starts a conversation with me. And just like that, I am starting to lean in just a bit too far over the old wood bar toward this young, tall, a bit too slim for my taste but, hey, friendly and handsome bartender. And why should I leave? He is young, I am old. He is very friendly, part of his job description (doing great, by the way). I am a friendly customer, so I linger to listen to the lilt of his strong Irish accent while he attempts to guess mine, the one I do not have. This right now? It all feels much better than wandering around semi-lost with my two sisters.

Right. I have my sisters with me. Back to focusing on the task at hand. I walk toward them with their drinks while giving directions to the bathroom—it's not a straight shot by any means. Just like the one we were hoping to return us to McGowans, Les. Once we are all back at the booth together, we drink up fast, not wanting to sit long. Let's just get home.

And so we begin again. Perhaps it is not necessary. Never mind. It is necessary to mention just how grumpy the three of us are becoming with each step. We are entering dangerous territory as we plod along, so we are sure to tread lightly with one another. We don't need to unbalance ourselves at this moment. Fortunately, we all seem to sense this and slip into a mode of silent walking. Even I know to keep my voice to myself. To give both sisters this quiet time.

I check my watch. It's 6:45 p.m. We still have a few more hours of daylight. As we round yet another corner, I hear live music. Very loud Irish music. It's emitting from a bar. Not just any bar, but The Cobblestone. Look what we stumble upon. This lost one is found, and no one, not even my weary, semi-grumpy self and sisters alike will stop me from going inside, which I do with great haste. I quickly order myself a glass of Jameson, lean against the bar, and take in the music.

Leave.

Me.

Here.

Enjoying my drink and the music, I chuckle to myself just how surreal it is to be me right now. Thanks to the countless sermons, SDA youth knew bars were nothing but trouble. And then there was me who was always curious to know exactly what kind of trouble. It was Les who first found trouble, not me.

During high school, Les and her boyfriend were on a date when his gold Plymouth Barracuda broke down. The closest place for a payphone was a bowling alley. These two crazy kids went inside to call for assistance. (What were they thinking, right? People drink and smoke there.) The next day at school, both were directed to report to the Principal's office. Immediately. "I have heard you two were smoking. You can't deny it because I can smell it. Give me your letterman's jacket, young man." (Good ol' wool. It absorbs everything, even from an evil bowling alley.) These two young people needed to be disciplined. They needed to learn a lesson. But they were spared, fortunately for them, because daddy was the music teacher at the same school.

"This is all a misunderstanding. I can vouch that his car broke down and they had no choice but to call for help from a bowling alley." The Principal let them off without punishment, whatever that was going to be.

And now, here in The Cobblestone? This kind of trouble is working for me. I am here for my glass of Jameson and the music. Performing live are about eight musicians sitting in a circle. I say "about" because these musicians, I come to quickly realize, are playing a version of musical chairs; musicians come and go at their choosing, so it appears to me. The instruments range from the familiar—violins, banjoes, guitars—to the unfamiliar—a clarinet/flute combination. One gentleman is playing a small hand-held bagpipe, of sorts. Rather than blowing into the familiar standard, tall bagpipe, this one is unique to me. When I ask, someone kindly explains it is a uilleann pipe. This small bagpipe sits on the lap of the musician (minus a kilt) who then uses one arm to inflate the small bag for its sound. This is why it is known as pipes of the elbow. The sound it projects doesn't have the bellowing monotone of the larger bagpipe and this one sounds more like a horned pipe. It's Irish music heaven. I am taking it all in when I once again remember I have my two sisters with me.

For those counting, yes, this is twice now in a short time when I am at a point of distraction that I need to remember these two are with me. They don't know this though. In truth, this must be part of the adjustment of traveling together. Being cognizant of both of my sisters. Of course, this can't be my fault; rather, it's the evil influence of both bars. I figure it's still a good idea to take a quick sis inventory.

Rie is behind me standing at the bar with a drink. She shares that great smile of hers. It speaks volumes to me, starting with the fact she is enjoying herself and it calms me.

Then I spy on Les. She is standing just inside the door. I clearly understand her body language to mean she is not at all happy here and wants to leave. This evaporates my calm.

I start to feel a bit of disappointment well up in me because I want to stay, relax, and enjoy. What this experience is for me is not for her. I get it. Besides, our exhaustion is gaining strength over us. Yet, even so, I make sure to enjoy a few more tunes before polishing off my Jameson. Both sisters know how spending this time in this particular bar with this music is making me happy. To Les, I say, "Thanks, sis. I owe you one. I know you are exhausted, yet I appreciate you hanging around a bit longer for me."

"You bet, sis. I know how much hearing the live music meant to you."

12

LEARNING TO NAVIGATE
THE TERRAIN OF SISTERHOOD

AND IT'S ONCE AGAIN WE HEAD FOR HOME. HOW MANY TIMES IS THIS NOW? THIS time though I expect a bit of momentary tension from Les simply because she is not one to enjoy the inside of a bar, music or no music. I detect a weariness on her face from all the walking, and it is more this than anything else. Then I again gently remind her that listening to traditional Irish music live is one of two things on my list of things I want to experience in Ireland. She understands and this is why she does her very best to let me enjoy as much as her very tired self can bear. She just wants to get home, by the way, albeit without the assistance of a taxi.

Because of the music (and of course the Jameson), my feet feel happy even though there are many more steps ahead for the Moore sisters. And then just like that, here we go again, falling into what now becomes our usual walking pattern, one we manage to create early on in this trip. This is how it goes: It is either me or Rie who lead or the two of us are walking next to each other with Les bringing up the rear. This does not mean at all that she is right behind us because she is not. We typically find her a good fifty paces behind. Rie and I turn to look at her, allowing her to catch up with us. And off we go again. The three of us are chatting away when only too soon Rie and I realize Les is not joining in on the conversation—we are chatting without her once again as she is in the process of sliding backward. Again. Out of earshot. Out of our peripheral view. And this time, it's me telling Les, always in a teasing voice, "Oh. My. Word. Catch up, will you?" And three very tired sisters (who would be home by now if taking a taxi, but we don't. Les wants to save money. Have I yet to mention this?) We can't move from where we each are standing because we are laughing too hard once again. And then there is Les, still too many steps behind.

"Oh, alright. I am coming." And we know what this means. It's a slow process. And now, laughter subsiding, Rie and I wait—again, and then we start walking and talking, again. Three sisters, and then just as quickly we are only two, again. Les keeps trudging and smiling while doing her best to just keep going forward. Again, she is the one who wants to save money and walk, so walk she shall, and if this means Rie and I reach home a half-hour or so ahead of her, so be it.

This whole give-and-take aspect we are trying to navigate? The truth is we are still adjusting to each other as fellow travelers. While in the process, we are making an all-out effort to be better, kinder, and gentler toward each other. It isn't all that hard for us, but even so, after today's long walk, we are ready to have some alone time. The three of us know this; we don't need to speak it. And then finally, we reach our place across from McGowans.

Rie, now as usual, is the one who punches in the code for the front door. She enters. Les follows. I am about ready to step in when the house alarm goes off—it is incredibly loud. (Makes perfect sense. It is an alarm after all.)

We must scream just to hear each other speak. The blaring alarm is in the narrow entryway and the noise hangs in this small space. We can't get away from it, and worse yet Rie can't silence it. We expect someone anytime now to be knocking on the door to help. Any neighbors? No. The alarm company? No. Is a tipsy McGowans customer willing to dislodge oneself even if it is to just yell from across the street how our alarm disturbs drinking? But no; no one is coming. In other words, this very loud alarm serves no purpose. How comforting.

Les and Rie are frantically working together to shut the damn thing up. In the meantime, I rush around the corner into the living room to grab that three-ring binder for guest instructions. My mad pace does not matter one bit because my fingers are struggling to turn the slippery plastic sheets that cover each page. There is information for everything but what we need, to dismantle the alarm. Not even five feet away, I am screaming at Rie and Les. "Nothing in here about the alarm." I am now going between sending a text to calling to a text to calling the management company—no response. So much from the promise of Ms. Young, Skinny, Scrawny: "If you need anything at all, just call the number on the first page in the informational binder. You saw it in the living room, correct? That will be your best resource. And as you can see, we are quick to respond." Well, that sure isn't working because I hear nothing but silence from their end while on our end a screaming alarm continues to terrorize our ears.

Out of sheer desperation and frustration, Les starts to dig through the entry closet in hopes of finding something that might help us. She finds everything in the closet except a magical shut-off switch for an annoying alarm. She comes to notice a small fuse box on the wall opposite the alarm. For some reason, Les has the wherewithal to feel on the underside when she feels a very small object. It's a strange-looking key. Handing it to Rie, Les shouts, "Maybe this will fit somehow? Somewhere?" It doesn't matter at this point. They are willing to try everything and anything. Rie starts inserting the key into any slot on the alarm box.

And then, just like that, sweet silence. Finally.

Another weary climb upstairs. Nonetheless, we are chatting and bringing ourselves to end-of-the-day laughter. We especially laugh about our talent of getting ourselves lost today, and not just today, and probably not the last time either.

Tonight's journal entry covers a lot. When I write about our morning in the CityLink Bus Station, a stunning reality makes me stop: *The three of us were meant to meet Aisling in this Bus Depot, on this particular day, at that specific time. It's only this day we are ready to hear the word "leftovers." I don't believe for one minute that I just happen to be available. Aisling comes to add purpose to our journey and us to hers. And Galway never a part of our plans? It somehow was, even before we knew it was. I'd like to believe today the larger difference was made from the smaller experience at Ultimate Hair. Perhaps we witnessed the Butterfly Effect play out in real-time?*

I include how our sister-tent is taking on a special quality. We seem more determined each day to protect it, preventing it from being blown away from us by even the slightest gust of words.

And all of the walking? Just shy of 16,000 steps today. I fall asleep before I even begin counting the abundance of sheep found in the green fields of Ireland.

13

ALICE IN WONDERLAND'S WILD RIDE, BELFAST STYLE

On my list of Must Experience in Ireland are only two strong desires: listening to live, traditional Irish music (check), and visit Northern Ireland, specifically Belfast. Six days into our trip, the three of us are about to take the train trip north.

Arriving at Connolly Station bright and early, a friendly male employee (he's wearing a uniform; we trust him, naturally, but we don't give our address) kindly points us in the right direction to the train heading to Belfast.

"Sit in that small waiting room there with all of the others waiting to board. Your train stops right here. Listen for the call to board."

No.

Not true.

Not true at all.

We are good tourists. We wait exactly in the place where the station employee tells us to wait. As the three of us sit in the little waiting room happily chatting away, talking about who knows what, we suddenly realize we are all alone.

"Where is everyone?" we seem to ask in unison.

"What about the call for us to board?" Les asks. We turn to see that the locals are settling themselves on the train, our train. In an instant, these three tourists scramble with everything we have in us (Les truly impresses us; herself as well). We board just before it leaves the station.

Note to self: Pay attention to times and schedules on our own from here on out. Do not trust anyone else, including Irish male employees wearing a uniform. This is how one gets left behind.

At the end of our two-hour ride, we arrive at the Transfer Terminal, and from here we must transfer onto a bus for the last twenty or so minutes to the Transportation Centre. Entering the city limits of Belfast, I am not too sure what to expect from today's tour, yet I am excited. "I am looking forward to this. How about you two?" The response I receive is a bit tepid, which surprises me.

From Rie, "I just am not sure what to expect, but, Diz, I know you can't wait." And then from Les, "Hum. We'll see."

I am quick in my response, almost a plea, "Ladies, this is historical Belfast!" Rie reassures quite unconvincingly, "It's going to be fine."

It's at the Transfer Centre where tourists decide which direction they take. We choose the bus to the City Center while others head to the docks. This is where the Titanic museum sits. Over 150 ships have launched their maiden voyage from this port city, including the Titanic. We know how it ends for that ship, yet we know nothing about how The Troubles for Northern Ireland begins.

"By the way, my handsome seatmate on the flight over here? When I told him we planned on a Belfast visit, he recommended taking the Black Cab tour. I'm thinking this is a good option for us because it's a small vehicle, room for three to four only. We can limit the tour to just the three of us."

Rie agrees, "We don't want a repeat of our bus tour to Glendalough, that's for sure!"

Les says, "And this way, we won't have to deal with the quirks of someone else, just our own." We all laugh at this truth because we've got our quirks, no doubt about it.

Arriving at the tour office, I step inside to arrange our tour. And just like that, our driver shows up. His name is Mick. Standing at about 5'5", he is most likely in his late 60s, his hair is silver, his complexion ruddy, and his accent charming while challenging. This will be fun.

Before entering his cab, Mick first directs our attention across the street. It is with rather strange pride (as we hear from him as well as others throughout the day), how "The Europa Hotel is the most bombed hotel in Europe." We are then taken aback when he says "It was bombed at least thirty-six times starting in the mid-seventies to as late as the early nineties. Even so, she still stands, well, thanks in large part to a glorious make-over. Shrapnel," Mick claims, "remains visible in places because it's a part of Belfast's history."

We do not stop for a closer inspection because we are heading instead into neighborhoods once a war zone, as if this spot here isn't. Anyhow, it takes less than ten minutes to pass through the very tall, black, wrought-iron gates and enter the neighborhoods where murals, portraits, and words of protest are as vivid in both message and color as when the rebels first painted them in 1968.

How amazing it is to find ourselves in the middle of such history. On the other hand, I sense in each sister their anxiety rises up a notch. And then the moment is broken by Mick's words. "So, ladies, tell me what you know about The Troubles." (Known anywhere else as a Civil War) Unfortunately, we must confess our embarrassing ignorance. He then launches into a bottom-line explanation for us, which boils down to a thirty-year conflict between two factions identified as Nationalists (Irish/Roman Catholic) and Unionists (British / Protestant). We are now roughly on the same starting page as Mick.

We proceed past more gates; the three of us look at each other. This feels a bit uncomfortable, but we are in for the long haul. Mick points to more walls covered in murals. "They are painted with our heroes. They sacrificed their lives for the greater good." Exiting the cab at this stop, Les, Rie, and I are suddenly standing just a little closer together while Mick instructs us. "Look at the wall over there. Now look at this one, and look here…". And suddenly our tour feels much like Alice in Wonderland; a kiddies ride at Disneyland. I remember the first time how scary that ride felt: dark, twisting, jerky, and objects jumped out in front, unexpectedly. The ride is meant to gently shock while surprising the innocent child. And here we are as adult women in the former war zones of Belfast, our heads twisting and jerking, and stepping back from shocking objects that surprise us. Never have we witnessed anything like this before. It's more than a gentle shock.

On one wall is the year 1968 in very large print. It forces us to pause and consider our own lives on the other side of the world during that time. And then to Mick, I confess, my voice filling with embarrassment, "For us, during 1968, we were just carefree, young American girls living in the bubble of a sheltered life on our cul-de-sac and the small neighborhood beyond." I look over at Les and Rie and whisper. "How are you two doing?" Les makes a confession that takes me by surprise, "I was fine until we went through the gates. You realize anyone who cares about us has no clue where we are, right?" She then quietly adds, "I am feeling a little vulnerable right now. How about you two?" To which Rie adds, "I am feeling a bit anxious to leave. What about you, Diz?"

"I'll admit it is a bit unnerving. But this is understandable since we've never been in a war zone before." Add to the fact that we are spending a great deal of time in the Shankill District, even though it has been forty years since the Shankill Butchers terrorized this neighborhood with mayhem and murder. The song by the Decemberists, "The Shankill Butchers," captures the undercurrent we are sensing. And then I break the spell: "Come on. We are going to be fine," as I try to reassure them both. Turning their focus to more wall murals, I share with them in a quiet voice, "Our lives are so very opposite of this. I mean, how is it that we possibly have any kind of touchstone to the version of 1968 in front of us?" The sisters are not speaking. I get it. It's so much to take in. Yet isn't that a good thing? Fast forward fifty-one years later, 2019, and we are American women aware of the global community, yet still in need of further education. As we observe one wall after another, I comment out loud what I am thinking, "The visual history is stunning though, isn't it?" With each one, our illiteracy on Belfast history is glaring.

All the while, Mick continues. "This was our life. All that mattered to us was to win this war."

Les whispers, "I am feeling boxed in." This is probably because Belfast is only forty-four square miles, yet here inside gates that close off neighborhoods every night, the space has an even smaller feel to it. None of this, neighborhoods gated and controlled by ordinance of curfew, has ever been a part of our lives. But it is for the residents of Belfast, for Mick, and he simply pushes forward with his oral history. "In 1968, there's a peaceful protest with people from Derry, Belfast, and Armagh. It escalates rapidly into years of a bloody civil war." Taking all of this in has all three sisters standing speechless. How are we supposed to wrap our minds around this? Any of this? And with this question, it becomes clear to me: Today I am to be a student in the back of Mick's black cab. And being a student is something I truly enjoy. It's only when I am forty-two that I came to learn this about myself.

After I quit a dead-end job, I enrolled at Ventura Community College. This was my first attempt at college, so I was cautious and chose an exercise class, basic English, and basic math. (Okay, very cautious!) But it was going to be my only semester, nothing more.

I took a basic math class as I finally grew tired of carrying around the voice in my head of my fifth-grade teacher who pronounced me stupid because I couldn't remember my multiplication tables. Fine. I was stupid. A teacher said it, so it had to be true. I only enrolled in math class all these years later to see if her words remained true; I feared she was right.

Before I started my first day of school, my husband Dave, my ever ardent supporter, reassured me: "You've got this, Missy" (his nickname for me). Then I made very clear to him my plan and that I would be sticking to it—no exceptions.

"It's just one semester to conquer my multiplication tables. And that's it. And by the way, I am keeping my head down. I won't be making any friends. Besides, I am old and they are all young."

And then something happened to me. I came to love learning; I came to release my multiplication ghost. Because of all that I had let go of, I embraced a love of being in the classroom with students of all ages. As my self-confidence grew, I became inspired. And from all of the courage I gathered later in life (better late than never), I earned my A.A. My mentor encouraged me toward my B.A.; then she told me I couldn't stop there and that I had to earn my M.A., which I did at California State University, Northridge (CSUN). I finally proved my elementary school teacher wrong, and by doing so I freed my mind. It freed me.

Mick is directing us to stand in front of a short wall that the three of us find rather unnerving. It's about five feet in height and most likely twenty feet in length. This painting is of two gunmen who wear face masks and are aiming their guns at all who stand in front of them. "Stand here next to me, ladies. Look straight ahead. What do you see?"

"They are pointing their guns at us."

"Right. Now slide a few feet to the left. What's going on now?"

"The same guns are pointing at us. The same masked men follow us wherever we move." And then back to the middle and then to the right: The barrel of the guns stay on us. The eyes behind the masks stay on us. We are feeling quite uncomfortable from this lenticular art—where the visual is never stable for the viewer; we are feeling quite unstable at this moment.

We each catch a glimpse of one another, our backs to Mick, when Les whispers to her sisters, "This is so strange, right?" And Rie and I agree. At times, we find Mick's enthusiasm stronger than his accent. And even though this mural is quite nerve-wracking, I am still ready to continue in our classroom on wheels. We do not judge. We adjust. We listen. We take it in.

Mick continues, "At fifteen, I was already in prison with leaders of the IRA. See my photo album back there? Take a look through there and you'll see for yourselves." As our tour moves along, the three of us grow more silent by the minute because there is a lot to take in here. From the moment Mick drives us past the Europa Hotel, to seeing murals of lost heroes on walls of apartment buildings, this is all so difficult to fathom.

Rie now whispers in the back of the cab, "It seems like they are still fighting the same old war." So she puts out to Mick, "Are any of the young men today interested in your same cause?"

"Oh sure, but now they use their methods, through computers and things."

There still is no denying Les' gut feeling. She leans forward for only us in the back of the cab to hear. "It feels as though we can feel the IRA. I don't want to blow up." To be sure, it does project a whole range of emotions, feelings, and fears. Yet in the back of this little black cab, I remain enthusiastic, more so than my two sisters.

The truth is being in this war zone changes us. To paraphrase Ralph Waldo Emerson, all of this history is expanding our mindset to a whole new point of reference, creating an experience of which our minds will never return to their original dimension. This is a good thing. And with that, our Alice in Wonderland ride continues.

Being naive to the experience of living in a war zone, we experience a wide range of both shock and surprise. And as Mick pulls off the road once again and announces the building across the street is a prison, he invites us to get out of the car. It's only now that we see other tours going on as well. It's amazing how Mick's cab had encapsulated us. It's with deep pride in his voice he speaks of this prison. "This is where the rebels, all Brothers-In-Arms, including myself, spent most of our time in solitary confinement, embarking on hunger strikes. Many died here. Have you looked through my photos yet to see what it was like?" I sense he wants to be sure his photos reinforce a personal truth. Mick directs us once again, "Turn around. This is the Hall of Justice." My goodness. The best way to describe this structure is to imagine a weary old woman who has never recovered from shell shock. She still wears countless wounds from the hundreds of rounds of ammunition and bombs that pierced her on all sides and her roof. Imagine the shower of bullets, as if "Belfast Confetti," to borrow from Irish poet Ciarn Carson.

Our tour is winding down when Mick offers us additional time to see more of the area, at a cost, of course; we agree to continue. I volunteer, "Yes. Sure." I believe it's worth the expense and time. I am sure my two sisters see the eagerness and curiosity on my face and are only too happy to go along with me. (Fine. Not at all). What they might be too willing to do is ditch me and leave me to finish the tour alone; they don't.

And then just like that our forty-five-minute tour somehow quickly becomes nearly a three-hour tour. We begin to sense a different vibe. We now become (too late), a tad bit more cautious (again, too trusting), wondering (again, too late), what we might have gotten ourselves into. We feel as though Mick's black cab is the S.S. Minnow (we all know how their tour never ends), heading toward an Irish version of Gilligan's Island.

The configuration for seating in the back of the cab has Les and Rie sitting on the only bench-seat facing forward. I am on a jump seat directly behind Mick, facing my sisters. This allows for the three of us to take in silent communication and/or to talk quietly with each other. And right now, this is exactly what we are doing. "What have we done?" Les mouths.

And me? I am weighing my thoughts. *Why don't we feel brave at this moment? We are together, yet why are we still nervous?*

More whispers from Les, "Are we ever going to get out of here? I am feeling ready to leave."

Rie follows up with her observation, "This isn't what I thought it would be" Then she continues, "In our tidy neighborhoods back home in Southern California, we didn't have to live amongst such violence and destruction such as this."

I reassure them, "It's been twenty-years since this civil war ended. We are fine. This tour has a lot of great reviews. It's just very unfamiliar territory for us. According to the YELP reviews, nobody has been left behind or blown-up, all right?" We chuckle. Perhaps with a tinge of concern? We are immersing ourselves in something that is making us uncomfortable and frankly there is nothing wrong with this kind of discomfort.

What better way to appreciate who we are and where we come from than visiting such areas as these neighborhoods? And truth be told, we are not so ignorant to deny that in America there are neighborhoods with deep poverty, no running water, where gang wars and drugs bring about destruction, just not in our neighborhoods where it remains out of sight, out of mind.

Even though there is a glass panel between Mick and his three passengers, he still hears me whisper to both sisters, "I am getting hungry. Are you, guys?" Both nod their heads in agreement. I say hopefully,

"Maybe Mick will stop at a little market for us so that we might grab some snacks?"

And then from Mick, in the loveliest of gestures, "Here, have my lunch." It's an act of kindness we politely refuse until we realize it's only right to accept his gift. He passes to the back of his cab his crumpled (used more than a few times before) paper sack, and I remove the white bread, white cheese, white turkey mayo sandwich, wrapped in wax paper. We three look at each other. No words need to be spoken, yet we are all thinking it, absolutely we are: white bread! And with this, quickly all fears of location are replaced with a much more disconcerting matter at hand: white bread.

The Moore children always ate a healthy diet because Mom always made sure we had the best quality food possible. This meant never, ever buying white bread for her kids or even brown bread disguised as wheat bread. Only wheat bread filled with solid grains was what she bought. (Oh sure, I beg for her to buy these pink Hostess snowballs. But my ongoing requests always fell on deaf ears. I am forced to wait years before being able to sink my teeth into one of those beauties only to find they were not all that great.) The truth of the matter is, the Moore kids were rarely ill, and Mom always said it was because she made sure we ate a healthy diet full of grains; absent of white bread and Hostess cakes. So even in the back of this cab, her daughters, now in their sixties, can still hear Mom's voice: "How could you even entertain the idea of rolling up a wad of that white dough into a ball and eating it? You know it is not good for your gut."

Okay, let's pause for one moment and deconstruct my absurdity: So it's a no to white bread, ever. But it's a yes to entering an evil bar and drinking alcohol. Correct. And it makes perfect sense, at least to me. I digress.

Two truisms come to mind when weighing Mick's generous offer of his white bread sandwich: "Don't look a gift horse in the mouth," and "Beggars can't be choosers." There is a sense of pride in Mick's voice when he tells us, "My wife made it for me." When I hear this, I immediately picture his wife in her bathrobe, making his lunch all the while never imagining he would be sharing it with his hungry tourists. And now, Mom, here we go. Rie elects to not partake, whereas Les and I do—splitting it between the two of us nibbling ever so little of the white bread, white mayo, white cheese sandwich.

As we ride along, we hear from Mick, "We'll go to the famous line of murals and then off to our last stop, the Peace Wall. It's a must-see!" The murals cover a length of walls for a couple of blocks and are powerful in both images and messages. The Peace Wall? At three miles long, it's impressive. Hopping in the back with us, Mick uses the other jump seat that faces Rie. He starts to explain about this historic wall. "It was erected in 1969. It keeps us away from each other," pointing to the English flags flying on the other side of plenty of very tall wire fences. "See the wires on these houses here?" He points to the house on the Irish side behind the Peace Wall. "They protect the roofs because the English still throw their crap at us."

Seeing this first-hand then hearing this helps Les wrap her head around a lot of what she has heard today. And as she now exits the cab she shares, "I am not feeling so trapped from being inside the neighborhoods and with all of the different tall gates now gone." Makes sense.

As long and as high as this wall is, there are millions of signatures written on every flat space, crack, and crevice. We read words of hope. Of prayers. Of sadness. Of pain. Of love. Of peace. Of forgiveness. I pause to think of all who have come before us, each signing their names and comments. Mick presents each of us with a black permanent pen to join in with all others who record their presence here. It's an honor to add our thoughts, our names, and our date of visit: August 7, 2019.

14

BELFAST, PART II. WE GO IT ALONE

ARRIVING SAFELY BACK AT OUR STARTING POINT, INSIDE THE CITY ZONE, WE thank Mick for the tour, take a few photos and tip him before we walk toward our next destination. Rie wonders aloud, "How do we begin to decipher all the layers of Mick's information? What to believe and what not to? It's so interesting. And by the way," she continues, "I am glad we got out of there safely!"

Les comments, "Now that we are back, I am glad we went." Back in the open city, where there is no fencing topped with barbed wire, we feel ourselves start to relax. We begin talking over each other about the Alice in Wonderland ride we experienced during our Black Cab Tour.

"Deep breaths," I advise. Then, "Without a doubt, it was surreal. How can today not change us? It's a good thing." We turn toward the famous Linen Quarter, home to the highly prized Irish linen. I read aloud from the guidebook, "Ladies, here's the library, and it has a cafe too. I don't know about you two, but I am hungry. And while Mick's sandwich has left me full of gratitude, my stomach feels as though it's running on empty and in need of nourishment. How about you, Les? Feeling the same?"

"I am with you. Let's get some food."

Entering the 200-year old Linen Hall Library, our day learning about "The Troubles" continues to linger with me. I do believe that I am forever a different person because of what I see and learn today. As this ruminates around in my head we encounter some profound and engrossing in-your-face political folk art—either drawn or created—from the feminine perspective of protest. Several pieces are hanging on the wall where we take the stairs to the next floor.

"What? Stop Strip-Searches? Look at this you two." Using black and white construction paper, implementing jagged cuts to create shadows and depth, this piece depicts the upper torso of a female. The foreground includes the diminutive silhouettes of the heads and shoulders of two male police officers, identifiable by their caps. What's so bothersome is that the female, practically nude, must stand in front of these officers who possess complete control of this situation and her outcome. And though this distraught female is in the background, ironically she looms large over them. Still, the cops pay her no mind with their off-putting body language. Furthermore, these officers are comfortable enforcing her invisibility as they nonchalantly disregard her attempts at modesty. The tatters of her shirt fail to cover her even though in an all-out effort she places one arm in a diagonal position in an attempt to cover both bare breasts. Her other arm raises in a manner so that her wrist covers her eyes. The themes of evil, of fear, of silencing the feminine are palpable. To this day, I carry her with me in the front pocket of my memory, readily accessible to me.

Another piece of art is entitled Free Speech in Ireland. This drawing depicts the side profile of a female with her mouth gagged, facing a microphone, its cord knotted. This piece makes visible the deep struggle to voice female frustration and anger in the absence of free speech.

As singular pieces as well as an art installation as a whole, the silencing of Irish women speaks volumes. I try to reconcile why I am drawn to these two pieces when I realize my affinity with them—my voice was silent for a long time, yet my disempowerment was of my own doing. Now I accept that the years I kept quiet my voice was simply lying fallow, enriching it until I finally felt confident enough to share it. Because of this late bloom, my voice resonates from the countless seasons of the give and take in my life. I have sorrow that so many Irish women never lived to experience such freedom of voice.

After we have a small bite to eat in the library café, we head back outside. Because we spent more time on our tour with Mick than expected, we are starting to run short of time. Leaving the library, we head back toward the City Center. I then ask, "Les, do you recognize any of this?"

"No." Her innate GPS fails us once again. What was once so trustworthy is now not to be trusted. Great! Well, this can't be good. "Rie?"

Belfast is in the middle of street repairs and much construction, which only adds to our confusion of city streets and street signs written in 'Irish-language,' further complicating our efforts. Somehow, we find our way back to Victoria Square. Once again, the lost find their way. I ponder out loud, "I am starting to wonder if our frequent experiences of getting lost say something about us?"

But Les disagrees. "Come on. It's just like Daddy always told us when we asked "Where are we?' and he would say 'Right here.' That's where we are, right here, so how can we be lost?" There is no way the three Moore girls can be lost when we are always right here. It's such silly logic to anyone outside of the Moore family, but hearing this from Les reminds us all is fine. Giggling at this memory, we find it so cathartic at the end of such an emotional day. I truly enjoyed the tour in Belfast, but I failed to realize just how tense I was as a result. Les' timing was perfect.

As we continue to meander (our new word for being pleasantly semi-lost), I can't help but reflect on the day. I am also thinking how grateful I am that my seatmate on the flight from LAX to Dublin suggested Belfast is best experienced in the back seat of a Black Cab. He was right. In the middle of our meandering, we make good use of this opportunity and do some window shopping (mostly shopping) then start working backward. I remind them both, "Remember, we need to get back to Dublin! We need to catch a city bus to the Transfer Centre in so we arrive on time at the Transportation Center to catch the last train to Dublin."

We are all in agreement when Rie announces, "I need to find a To Let." We turn to Les and ask if she might find a To Let for Rie. Fortunately, as in Galway, there is a Dunnes Department Store so we head over there. We decide, and for what reason I still can't understand, Les and I will wait outside while Rie goes in, uses the bathroom, and comes right back out. This shouldn't take long. Les and I let her go in, alone.

"Sounds good," are the last words we hear from our little sis. And then I say, "What are we thinking, letting Rie go into a big department store on her own? We know better than this. She will find something that catches her eye, and then another and another." And after I finish the last word of that sentence is when Les and I begin to wait. And we wait. And we wait. I then tell her, "You wait here while I go inside and try to find her."

As I pass through the electronic doors, I hear, "Good luck!" But missing sis is eventually found. It just so happens that while I am going up the escalator I look down and that is when I catch a glimpse of her. She is in a line to make a food purchase. Who else but our little sis discovers Dunnes has a grocery store on the first floor? Nothing slips past her in any store. As I approach her, she explains. "I am buying snacks for the train trip ahead of us." Our thoughtful little sister. Now to make sure we don't miss that train back home. We cannot be late. Missing the train means finding lodging for the night in Belfast.

Back outside again, it starts to drizzle. Wait for it. It is now raining. But only when it starts to rain harder (because it does) do we wait to open our umbrellas; we are becoming more and more like locals. Yet unlike the locals, we have yet to find the right bus. Still looking. We are feeling as though we are participating in the famous Abbott and Costello skit, "Who's on First?" as we continue to struggle to make sense of the road signs and maps and directions and heavy accents explaining which way to go. It all quickly becomes a guessing game and in the middle of their rush hour no less.

In the midst of it all, we keep our cool as we continue to make a few more attempts until we finally get on the right bus. I find myself a seat while Les and Rie grab the two seats in front of me. At the next stop, a little girl sits next to me with her mommy across the aisle. It's a bus full of people yet few are talking, so I start chatting with the little girl. Why not? My sisters shake their heads. I know what they are thinking. *There's Diz again, chatting with a stranger.* They no doubt take pity on this little girl. The conversation goes as follows: "How are you doing?" I ask.

"I am okay." Her accent strong, she's an Irish Lassie.

"How old are you?" Me, trying to break the ice.

"I am ten."

"Oh wow, ten is a fun age. My granddaughter is just a year older than you."

She asks me, "Where does your granddaughter live?" I am getting somewhere.

"In California. It's where we all live," pointing to my sisters. They turn and smile at her.

"I live here," she volunteers.

"Do you? Lucky you! I have been visiting your city today with my two sisters." I then go on to say, "I enjoyed spending the day in your city. I like it."

Without skipping a beat, "Yea, it's alright!"

"What?" I feign horror then she tells me she has been to a city in the US, yet I can't quite understand her. The mom jumps in and tells me, "Chicago. We have family in Chicago."

"Oh, then next time you are going to have to fly much farther to California. Do you know what is in California?"

"Disneyland!" There you have it. Tinker Bell's pixie dust makes it to the far reaches of Northern Ireland as well. Passengers are listening to our exchange, and now we all burst into laughter. From the mouth of babes. As we disembark, I thank her for chatting with me and for letting us visit her amazing city.

We now settle in for the train ride back to Dublin surviving on Rie's snacks.

Back in Dublin, we leave the station and immediately hail a cab. Upon getting ourselves secure in the backseat, we say in unison, "McGowans, please." He gets it. He needs no further explanation. This is good news.

Home, at last, we now begin packing as we leave for England in the morning.

Looking out my tall window, which by the way is open, I notice laundry still covering the clothesline, one end to another. Same clothes, but more added? Perhaps. I smile to myself as I sit for a few minutes on my bed. It feels as though there is some kind of change in the air for the Moore sisters. Interesting, I don't remember packing this, yet it's quite palpable. It feels special. And we still have two more countries left on our journey. I pop over to Rie's room where she is packing her suitcase. It's so organized. "Oh my gosh! You are a proficient packer. I need lessons from you!"

"It's from all my years of traveling. I'll teach ya, Diz. By the way, this will always be a special place for us, you know."

I smile.

"It's been a good place for us to start. I am looking forward to what is waiting for us in England."

"Well one thing for sure, I think my place in Scotland is going to be even better than this." We both start to chide with each other. And there you have it. The subtle, gentle, fun competition we learned so well from Daddy never ceases to flow through us. No doubt he is smiling.

The next morning, patrons of McGowans Pub observed yet another group of tourists departing from the rental across the street. We were glad we had joined them for at least one drink. The truth is, traipsing the country every day, all day, and walking so many miles (we could barely make it up the stairs to our beds), leaves us preferring to be alone in our rooms rather than in a pub full of people.

We take our last sister selfie here then we are gone.

Ireland. Our first place, our first Sister Selfie.
(St. George's/Arran Quay. Dublin, Ireland)

Our lovely neighbor across the street.

This is Les being so very helpful!
(Downtown Dublin)

"If you don't understand

how a woman could both love her sister dearly

and want to wring her neck at the same time,"

then most likely you were not raised with a sister.

—Linda Sunshine

PART TWO * ENGLAND

15

THE MANY UPS AND DOWNS AT THE SHAKESPEARE

EVEN THOUGH IT'S ONLY A SHORT THIRTY MINUTES, LES WAS FEELING A LITTLE nervous about our flight. Landing safely, this time at Heathrow Airport, we grab our luggage and go in search of the taxi queue. We are all feeling how smoothly this is going for us. Les mentions it. "This just keeps getting easier for us, doesn't it?" To that I say, "Us? The flying? Yes, we are and yes it does. And look at you doing better with this flight. It gets easier each time, I promise."

Rie finds the taxi queue, and, as she leads the way, reassures Les. "The more you travel, the easier it will feel for you. You'll be a pro at handling airports once this trip is over." Rie's prediction will come to fruition because months after this trip Les will navigate, all by herself, all airport nuances that come with flying

Is someone yelling at us? We turn our heads to the right where we are suddenly face-to-face with a very no-nonsense woman wearing a uniform. She is talking, more so yelling, at taxi drivers and travelers alike as she juggles both into queues according to the number of passengers and their number of suitcases. She wrangles everyone with her very clear directives that include finger-pointing: "Stand here! Wait there!" We do not question, we do as we are told. Truthfully, she scares us. In the middle of our "stand here" and "wait there," a man and young boy who are not as scared as us are making a mad dash past us in an all-out effort to jump into the next taxi. I am not at all thrilled. "Look at those two sneaking...". And before I can finish my observation the no nonsense voice of Ms. Queue Organizer reverberates throughout the garage: "Sir. Sir, where are you going?" Both man and boy turn around to see the owner of the voice bellowing at them. "You two need to stand here (one stiff finger pointing to the specific spot), and wait your turn." They do as she instructs. Immediately. They suddenly aren't so brave anymore. Watching karma unfold in real-time? It's rare yet oh so lovely when it occurs. I am certain that Les, Rie, and I aren't the only ones who are snickering amongst themselves.

Wait. More yelling. "You three." Yes. Us three. We only listen, we don't speak. "Your cab." She points. We say in unison to Ms. Queue Organizer "Thank you." and we mean it as we scramble to get in the cab as quickly as we can.

"Where to, Ladies?" England is Les's country, so she speaks up, "The Dolphin Hotel, please." And tells him the address of our home for the next seven days.

The Hotel, Part I: The Dolphin. The area is quaint, emphasized by the long line of tall, old buildings. I then notice across a grassy median filled with lovely old shade trees another row of matching old, tall buildings. It's all so very English in appearance. The exterior alone has us looking forward to all that awaits us in country number two.

It is five steps from the street to get inside the lobby. Checking in, we learn that our reservations are all in order. As well, our room is ready, which makes us happy. And then our happiness is gone. It occurs the moment Les is accepting the keys while the clerk is saying, "Your reservation is for one room, one double bed, and a single." Wait. This doesn't sound right. We turn to Les who is quite put off by the news although she reassures us the reservation is specific to each of us having a bed of our own—thinking room as well, we realize later this is not the case at all.

This doesn't matter to the desk clerk. He quickly excuses himself to make a phone call and then returns to us with a suggestion. "There is The Shakespeare, our sister hotel and they can accommodate you. Are you interested?"

We immediately huddle for a sister quorum. England is Les' country making her responsible for reservations and such, yet she asks for our opinion.

"This sounds good, right? What choice do we have?" And with this, Les tells the desk clerk, "Yes. It sounds like it will work, and how far is it from here?"

"As luck has it, it's right next door. Will this work for you?"

"Yes," Les replies, "it sounds good. "A close one. All are happy Les will be getting a room of her own. Rie and I both have lived in dorm rooms, so we are fine with sharing. So now it's just a matter of grabbing our luggage, returning down the 5 steps of The Dolphin, taking five steps to the right, and going up five steps into the lobby of The Shakespeare. And steps? No big deal to us because so far, from August 1st through the 7th, we walk exactly 62,791 steps, or to put it in more realistic numbers: 31.5 miles. So fifteen steps—no worries. It's hardly worth mentioning. I mention it anyway.

The Hotel, Part II: The Shakespeare. They are expecting us. And why yes, the room is ready. This day is once again bending in our favor; back on track. Les is looking forward to enjoying her room. It's her turn after all. Rie must wait until Scotland. While the desk clerk reaches for our room key, I look around the lobby.

It's not that it looks bad, but in comparison to the modern rental home in Ireland, this is much older. Greeting guests in the lobby are lots of potted plants and a few old brown leather couches, not as old as the building itself. Different doorways are leading in different directions. Interesting, but confusing. Pictures and plaques provide the history of this tall and narrow building. It was once the home of an aristocratic family, built in the 1850s. No doubt the owners of The Shakespeare must have modernized the place since then to accommodate their guests. I sure imagine so. I sure hope so.

While Les is tending to last-minute details, I pick up the slick, multi-folded brochure for hotel number two. Good news for us, The Shakespeare touts "we cater to travelers."

All necessary details now completed at the front desk, Les kindly asks, "And where is the lift?" (Just like that, listen to her calling it a "lift" instead of an elevator. She is making an effort in immersing herself in the language of the culture. Impressive.)

Yet, unfortunately this is where things start to go off the tracks. That silly desk clerk is pointing while explaining, "Sorry, no lift. But through those two doors are stairs that will take you up to your room." So stairs it is. So much for modernization.

I tell myself, *Well, it can't be all that bad. After all, we had stairs at our rental in Ireland.* Then we discover that it can be that bad. Our home for the next six days is on the third floor, which by the way is the fourth floor in England. In other words, the American basement? This is England's ground floor. This places the lobby on the second floor although it's street level. Still, there is no need for us to worry because we can handle a few flights of stairs.

Following the desk clerk's directions, we come to the bottom of a twisting staircase of dark red-carpeted stairs. It's at this moment, the three Moore sisters appear to be taking part in a comedic sketch because as if on cue all three of our heads tilt back as far as they will go, and in unison, I might add.

Thinking. Weighing. Laughing, kind of. Sort of. Oh, well! Let the ascent begin, the first of seven days. Left to our own volition (yes, indeed this does mean that there are no employees to help with luggage), we must formulate a logistical way of hauling our luggage as well as ourselves up these steep stairs. With our three heads remaining in the far-back leaning position, I am left to wonder aloud, "What you two are thinking about right now? Any ideas for hauling our luggage upstairs?"

Rie comes up with a plan that sounds as though it might work. "Les, you stay put down here and keep an eye on the luggage while Diz and I start hauling up the suitcases, one at a time. Diz, you carry the front half of the suitcase behind you and I'll hold up the other end in front of me, bringing up the rear."

I agree. "It sounds doable. Let's give it a go." With me assuming the role of Sherpa #1 and Rie Sherpa #2, we begin the ascent. I begin counting stairs, and when we reach stair number forty-nine, we come upon a landing. We stop to catch our breath and then we notice on the wall a delightful painting of an arrow pointing up even higher toward room 301, which again is really room 401. Our trek resumes, which might as well be the two of us ascending the Hillary Step on Everest—that last dangerous stretch. We must navigate climbing up this next flight of even steeper and narrower steps. I count twelve in all, although it feels so much more than twelve; Rie agrees, so it's not just me.

We finally arrive and when we open the door, well, we are taken aback by what we see. Seeing this? It isn't going to go over well at all for Les; I predict for all of us. In fact, in this very small room are three very single beds that gobble up almost all of the square footage. I am wise enough to know that much too quickly we will all feel claustrophobic and the one small window, emphasis on one, won't come to matter.

It's easy to predict this room will set Les back on her heels; understandable. Before heading back down for the next suitcase, Rie and I give the room one more chance to offer up something positive to us. It's a bright little room, and with the window already open for us (no need to struggle here as I did in Ireland), and with a little breeze coming in, the white curtains wave back at us in a welcoming flutter.

"Lovely, right, Rie?" But both Rie and I know better and begin to prepare ourselves in advance for Les' disappointment. "I imagine these two beds closest to each other will be ours," I say as I take a seat on one of them and take it all in. "And there is no denying how the now-defunct fireplace makes for a lovely headboard, right? Sis, this place is old. By the way, should anything fall between our two beds, it is going to be a struggle to find that which is lost. Oh hell, we're just going to leave it there." Rie just keeps shaking her head in disbelief. To the left of 'my' bed is a small nightstand that serves to separate said bed from the other very single bed, that one being next to the window.

"I am pretty sure," Rie expresses with deep apprehension of what's to come, "that Les will want that one, kind of a room of her own. Having a window will help, maybe." Honestly? We are feeling more than a bit nervous right now.

But wait. The management of The Shakespeare reasons there is still enough room for a small desk with an older TV above it, a very small round table-top balancing on a tall, skinny wood spindle, and a tiny refrigerator that barely fits adjacent to the door to our room. Excellent choices. And the bathroom? It's not what one would refer to as en-suite, rather it's more in-suite. With my voice full of trepidation and sarcasm, I say "Les is going to struggle to contain her joy." Then with concern, I add, "Rie, how are we going to make this work?" It's too much like what we had to share as small girls in our small bedroom in our small house on Rutland Avenue in Riverside, California. And what we vowed to never do again.

For many years, the Moore family lived in very close quarters. Our home for eleven years was all of 900 square feet small. The seven of us made do with one bathroom and three bedrooms. For the five kids, the boys shared one room, the girls the other. Les had the twin bed while Rie and I shared bunk beds. Living in such tight quarters was never a choice for us. We had to make do; no complaining was to be heard from the Moore children.

Now herein lies the difference for the three of us: Choice. So when it comes to choosing to share one room amongst us again? Just trust me when I say that sharing a room as adult women is something we should never be doing ever again. We know what we can and can't handle, and an arrangement like this just might be that grain of rice that unbalances our sister scale; what I worried about pre-flight.

"Rie, what are you thinking right now?"

"That these next seven days might end up challenging us."

"Yeah, especially challenging for Les. Disappointment is a tough emotion, at least it is for me, and we both know Les is going to be disappointed."

"Without a doubt."

"The good news here," I determine, "is we are all mature enough to handle it. And at least we each have our bed versus at The Dolphin where two of us were going to have to share a double bed."

"Well, Diz, it is what it is. We'll make it work. I mean, we will be spending every day out exploring, so what's the worst that can happen?"

"Yes, what's the worst that can happen?" As soon as I speak those words, I regret it. But I'm going to take in a deep breath and decide to let this moment unfold organically. (I am getting so good at this whole no-worrying mindset.)

Before heading down for the next suitcase, Rie and I start laughing, a very nervous laugh mind you. And then I wonder aloud, "Which one of us is going to gently explain to Les our one-room living arrangement for the next seven days? Sherpa #1 or Sherpa #2?" Neither Sherpa is quick to volunteer in relaying this particular bit of news. "Let's decide to not say anything to Les but let her see our lodgings for herself. I mean, why not? Let her form her own opinion without being influenced by us." To which Rie agrees.

Down the stairs we go.

We say nothing to Les.

Up the stairs with another suitcase.

Down the stairs, again.

And again we say nothing to Les.

Up the stairs with another suitcase, and this time Les follows. Here again, don't let the word follow mislead you. Again, she is not close behind us. As her two Sherpa Sisters sit on the beds waiting (waiting, still waiting) we are getting more than a bit anxious for Les to enter the room. We do feel sad for her, truly.

Just as quickly as she enters is just how quickly her face drops. Her surprise slash disappointment at first glance matches ours at first entry as well.

"What? This isn't what I expected, not at all!" And there it is. The disappointment in her voice.

"So I don't get a room for myself? Just great." Not a great start.

"Les, let's talk about maybe getting a different hotel, better amenities. More room for you."

"But if we move I'll lose my deposit. We don't have much of a choice. I don't want to lose the money and then pay more for another place because it will be a late booking."

Rie steps in by trying to find the positive. "Look at it this way Les. We are only in the room in the mornings and at night. Otherwise, we will be outside all day."

I try to fix things. "Les, we are so sorry this is what we have. Pick whichever bed best suits you." As much as I want this to be a grand gesture, right now it falls short of cheering up our sis.

Earlier, Rie and I guessed Les will most likely pick the bed by the window; it's as we figure.

"I'll take this one." And she points to the bed by the window. While facing the white curtain maybe she can at least create her own private space by turning her back on us. By the way, she will incorporate this leave me alone method more than a few times. Have I yet to mention that Rie and I are experts in interpreting the non-verbal language of our older sister? Why yes, yes we are.

With this tense moment over, we begin to relax. By reasoning this out, talking about it upfront, we have avoided any future problems. Look at us working so well together. We've grown closer while in Ireland and here in England we will continue doing so as well.

Everything now put away (thank goodness there is a small closet where we can store our suitcases), it's time to go out and get the lay of the land, starting with finding a place for lunch.

On our way out I have the front desk reserve a portable fan because the three of us are going to require a lot more air movement than one small window can provide.

After lunch, we head over to Hyde Park/Kensington Gardens to explore what we can with what is left of the afternoon. This park happens to be within reasonable walking distance from our home-away-from-home; about ten minutes for the three of us.

If I must choose the best word for me to describe this park, I believe enchanting does it justice. Everywhere we turn stands magnificent old trees with their gnarled trunks and branches. My imagination goes into overdrive. I convince myself once dark settles in these trees come to life. Such a concept is embedded in the thinking process thanks to fairy tales and animated movies.

As we follow along 'The Diana, Princess of Wales Memorial Walk,' her loss weighs on our hearts. Many Americans, including the three of us, think of her as our Princess too. This walk soon has us wandering about. Truth be told it appears to me we are doing more backtracking than finding new areas to explore. I say to my walking companions, "No, we have already gone this way." Going in circles is another way to look at it. It's quite easy to get turned around. Well, it is for us. And now that the sun is getting ready to set, we start to make our way out of the park. (I am not in favor of encountering a craggy branch reaching out at me with its outstretched limbs after dark.)

Looking around, we quickly realize many paths are leading to entrances/exits. Where did we enter? Which way to The Shakespeare? Thank goodness for cell phones. Now, if we can only agree on which is the best direction to take.

Well, we are off to a familiar start in England, the whole getting lost. But this feels a bit different from our getting lost in Ireland. There we were still learning to navigate directions, ourselves, and our sister-hood. Now, after eight days together, we are a bit more relaxed about all of this—each other and directions. We eventually come upon a road leading us back to our hotel. It's all good. The truth is if we were desper-ately lost, we—no, I—would ask a stranger for directions. Heaven only knows I have no qualms in doing so. Besides, I have Les and Rie as my backup. Why, I feel better just knowing that.

As we ascend the stairs to our three-bed suite (not magically con-verting into a three-bedroom suite during our absence), the three of us are chatty and laughing, even after walking five miles this afternoon. And then just like that, the day hits us and we are ready to sleep. But sleep doesn't come because it immediately becomes painfully clear to us just how single the beds in room 301 are; exceptionally narrow. And lumpy. The "Oh My Aching Back" next morning kind of lumpy bed. And the pillows? To make it through this first night requires the addition of small towels in the pillowcase to add a bit more cushion on to which to rest our heads. This sort of works. Barely.

From our mother, we three inherit a highly sensitive head. If our head spends the night out of whack, it's a horrendous headache that will be greeting us in the morning. Come morning, each of us will be buying a pillow of our own rather than trying to survive with the ones The Shakespeare provides.

We'll make do, because, after all, we were tent campers for years. We became used to sleeping on the hard ground. This has me starting to think we all might be more comfortable removing the sheets and blankets off the beds and sleeping on the hard floor, most likely softer than these beds.

16

WE WERE DOING SO GREAT

FOR HER LIST OF WISHES, WHILE VISITING HER COUNTRY, LES WANTS TO SEE
The Changing of the Guards at Buckingham Palace and go to Wimbledon
Stadium. Most of all, Wimbledon. Even though this sister is not a player
herself, she is a huge tennis fan. It's time to put the plans in place but
first, breakfast.

Our hotel provides breakfast for their guests, a bonus, well at this
point we believe it to be. We'll find out for ourselves. We head for the dining hall, which again is the American basement although England's first
floor. To get there we must first descend the sixty-one stairs to the lobby
and then forty-one more steps down even narrower and even steeper
stairs. (Think of going to a lower deck on a small boat.) Navigating this
set of stairs can get a bit tricky because guests must (at least should)
first look either up or down to see if anyone is coming back up or going
down. Yet for those guests not courteous enough to check first if anyone
is coming or going this is where it gets awkward. Someone is going to
have to shove their body flat against the wall as a method of letting others
pass—be it up or down. This silly dance occurs for us more than once,
the whole thing of planting our bodies against the wall while clueless

guests just mosey along. *Right, you bet, it's all good. Just as long as you're happy. Please, take your time.*

This being our first breakfast in England, we are not quite sure what kinds of food await us. Having had the kitchen in Ireland, we ate whatever we wanted to prepare for ourselves, which often came down to what was familiar. But here we are embarking on something new to us: English food and whatever that encompasses. Food brings out a whole different aspect of our personalities. Starting with Les who, again, is not at all adventurous when it comes to food. The more familiar, the better for her. Me? The most adventurous. Then again. Perhaps not. I base this on a recent experience in Iceland; eating horse proved a bit of a stretch for my taste buds.

Dave and I traveled with another couple to Iceland. One place in particular where we stayed, the host announced the various food choices for breakfast.

"We have horse on the menu this morning," just as I am ready to get myself a tiny slice of roast beef, or so I thought. Then I asked the host,

"Excuse me, is this roast beef?"

"Oh that there?"

"Yes."

"No. That's horse." I immediately think, *Gee, I sure hope it wasn't one we saw a few days ago trotting about so carefree in a lovely pasture.*

"Horse you say?" And with that, I was pretty much done with my breakfast before I even took my first bite. One of our traveling companions was braver. He declared horse "Not bad" as he went about eating some horse with scrambled eggs and sliced fruit.

I am happy to report that with my first glimpse of food choices in this English dining hall the food looks comfortably familiar: toast, eggs, and some fruit. I see no evidence of horse, and if it is on the menu I won't be eating it. This is of course one strike against me. (I sure hope this isn't a competition.) Rie is perhaps more adventurous as long as it is in the sphere of her dietary needs/restrictions. Our little sister now eats pork, which Les and I do not. (A religious belief but no longer the issue for us; rather, we are just fine not including pork in our diets.)

The trip isn't even halfway over, so here's hoping this isn't in any way a contest of adventurous eating. Maybe it will be. Let's see how our eating choices unfold. It's Rie's willingness to eat pork that might upend my opportunity to win. I might have to re-think cloven hooves. Dang it, Rie. But then wait. She didn't participate in the nibbling of Mick's white bread sandwich. Okay, I've got this.

Back to breakfast at The Shakespeare. The staff in the kitchen and dining hall represent The United Nations. We enjoy it, and though we do not speak any of the variety of languages we are hearing we clearly understand their rules as they direct the guests: follow the pointing finger to your assigned table. Confused guests who fail to understand this delicate dining hall dance get to experience at least once the correction from staff. And yes, even the attentive Moore sisters get to experience this shade-of-blush embarrassment.

Table assignment established, we now take a plate because guests get to serve themselves, although it is all orchestrated under very watchful eyes and communicative nods.

Our typical breakfast fare at The Shakespeare? It ranges accordingly: Every day, there is a choice of fruit from bananas to watermelon and sometimes canned apricots. Oh, and toast. This is where it gets a bit tricky as guests do not toast their toast. No, such a delicate task is left to a trustworthy member of the kitchen staff. It works as such: The Toast Professional toasts slices of bread, naturally, yet does not proceed as one would expect. Instead, the Toast Pro grabs about a dozen or so slices of bread then begins the process of toasting, which, by the way, is only two slices at a time. Ever meticulous, the Toast Pro keeps an eye on the ever-growing pile of toast that is soon towering on a small plate while at the same time grows ever colder. Yet it's still not time to serve it. We all must wait for the Toast Pro to move the toast tower onto a larger platter before it is available to guests. With the cold temperature now perfect, it's ready to be served. These three guests are thrilled. The trick is to slather the slice, or slices, with a choice of jams or other spreads, including Nutella, especially Nutella, thus aiding in the eating of this cold yet professionally toasted toast. (I must admit that I am most curious about the application process to become a Toast Professional.) The Moore sisters eventually break the code for getting warm toast: Arrive a bit late, but not too late. One does not want to seem ungrateful. It's a delicate balance, to be sure.

Besides toast, the kitchen also provides sweet rolls, an assortment of crackers, and a variety of cheese. And always some breakfast meats which Les and I ignore and Rie eats. Suddenly she takes a lead in the Who's the Better Eater contest. There is still time for me to gain on her. I am weighing if I should even reveal to her that she is a participant in my undisclosed contest. Better not as she might eat something gross just for spite, just to win. It's settled. I'm not going to tell her, for now. And no, I am not too sure when. Perhaps when I am winning? Not that winning is everything to me. It's just my enjoyment of winning. That being said, I am not so competitive that I want to win at all costs. I think. Still, Rie remains unaware of it. We'll see how this plays out. For me.

London awaits us, but first, we make sure to stop and take our morning sister selfie in the entryway of The Shakespeare. The moment now recorded, our first destination is only a block away, Paddington Underground Station. We head below ground to catch The Tube (or train; it's all interchangeable) only to come up and meet head-on the mighty Trafalgar Square.

Here in this enormous public square is a 170-foot tall statue honoring Admiral Horatio Nelson and the 1805 Battle of Trafalgar. This was the battle when the British established their naval prowess by destroying several Spanish ships. It's also during this battle they lost their revered Admiral.

In one upper corner of this monstrosity of a square is Charing Cross, the gateway to the Theatre District. We head off in this direction because our goal is to purchase theater tickets for the one play we all want to see: "The Lion King." While in the planning stages of this trip, we agree this is a must-see. Walking up to the Theater Box Office, we ask for three tickets, please. When we learn the cheap seats are $250.00 each, suddenly "The Lion King" is not so much of a must-see. We agree to look at other plays that might be just as enchanting. In other words, cheaper.

As we are still working on deciding, Rie remains in line to purchase tickets for a play we have yet to choose but need to do so quickly as she is inching ever closer to the ticket counter. Because there is only room for one of us on the stairs leading to the basement (I mean, the first floor) to buy tickets, Les and I leave her to the line as we step into a luggage store next door to check out things.

Yes, okay, to be more specific, finding me a teensy bit larger piece for my carry-on. After looking around, we check up on Rie who is in a rather deep conversation with others discussing various plays and seeking recommendations. Ahead of her is a gentleman who encourages all in line to see the Canadian musical "Come from Away." No one has heard of it, yet this gentleman goes on to explain how it's the true 9/11 story when all flights coming into NYC face immediate diversion to the tiny town of Gander, Newfoundland.

Yet I can't resist responding to him. "But a musical? It's just difficult for the three of us Americans to picture the events of 9/11 as a musical." It seems almost sacrilege, considering, after all, it was a terrorist attack on our country.

Rie was at the gym when the images began to stream across the televisions. One man leaned over to her and made a frightening prediction to her, "We are at war." Of course, these words frightened her. Who wants to hear these words?

As the attacks were taking place, Les was on her way to work and heard it on the radio. So many morning talk shows have prank calls, so this is what she believed she was tuning in to hear until she realized it was real. She shared how "I instantly thought what a horrible thing to happen." Her mind does not travel down the same rabbit hole of worry as Rie's. As mine.

I was getting ready for work when Dave called to tell me to turn on the news, which I did. I called Dave back, and he rushed home to be with me. I was terrified. "This is so frightening. How is this even happening in our country? Oh no, the second tower is going!" As we stood frozen in our living room in California, unable to grasp what was occurring in real-time, we, along with so many others watched the tower collapsing to the ground. Years later, we learned that at this same time our future daughter-in-law, Erin, was standing amongst so many others on the streets of New York City witnessing the fall of the second tower.

September 11, 2001, and Erin was on her way to work—her first day on a new job. She was on time, and then she wasn't. When the subway train halted, Erin quickly concluded, "Great! I am going to be late on my first day." Of course, this made her nervous but thank goodness after only a fifteen-minute delay she reached the street level and headed to her new office building as fast as she could. Her new office was nearby. "My only focus was that I am starting a new job, and I'll be showing up late. It's not a good way to start. I then shift my thinking and am now focused on what is going on. I've yet to realize that the first tower has already fallen. I saw taxi cabs were pulled over, their windows down with radios blaring the news. And then as we all witnessed the fall of the second tower, it was as if in some strange unison we all turned toward the Empire State Building because we believed we were under siege and it was going next. We watched The National Guard, who had machine guns at the ready," Erin told us.

Erin further explained that because the cell towers were jammed, she was unable to call any family to let them know she was alright. "I was definitely in a bit of shock; it all felt so surreal," she'd said. Understandably, Erin experienced a broad spectrum of emotions, from her first-hand experience and the loss of an old friend who perished in one of the towers.

"It's not about the tragedy in the city itself" the gentleman goes on to explain, "but rather about one community helping another community in the middle of 9/11. It's when thirty-eight wide-body aircraft are flying toward NYC and all pilots must immediately redirect their landing to Gander, Newfoundland." In essence, this play unpacks how this tiny town of fewer than ten thousand people instantly swells to almost seventeen thousand and the townspeople don't blink an eye. In the midst of it all as they host all passengers and flight crews. This same airport, by the way, was once the stop-over for American flights to refuel before they could continue the flight to Europe. But with the dawn of the age of jumbo jets and the capacity for long-distance flight, planes no longer had to stop off at Gander before making the long flight over the Atlantic.

"If this helps at all, I am a TV producer from Canada. I've seen this play more than once, and I have no doubt you will enjoy it and yes, it somehow works as a musical." And because the ticket price ($65) works just fine for us as well as the first curtain call, we buy tickets to watch "Come from Away."

Theater tickets now in our possession, we head next door to spend time in "The National Portrait Gallery." To best understand the power amongst the kings, the queens, the famous, and the infamous in the British lineage (birth order), this is the place to visit. We just simply follow alongside the countless portraits for a greater understanding of who's who and why. Finishing up at the gallery, we venture off to Piccadilly Circus, Leicester Square, where we come upon the largest LEGO store in the world. With a young grandson still a fan, Les wants to buy him something from this particular famous and behemoth LEGO store.

When we arrive, there is a very long line winding around the outside, yet Les is not put off by this. She is going in. Rie just wants to see inside, of course. I want nothing to do with it, so I find a place on the grass to wait. I wait with all of the others who wait outside for the same reason I wait. (We quickly reason we are the intelligent ones.) The good news for shoppers is most of the waiting is done on the outside. The better news is Les finds what she wants right away. The best news is that checking out is even faster.

The rest of our day is spent in and around the Theater District. Because part of our theater ticket price includes dinner reservations, we head over to the restaurant with enough time to be in our seats before the curtains rise.

Oh, and by the way? The Canadian TV Producer is correct. It is a play worth seeing. And a musical? Yes. It works because it is not about tragedy, rather the goodness of humans when tragedy arises.

Upon exiting, we discuss the play while strolling along the sidewalk with all of the other people in the Theatre District. There is an electric vibe in this part of town that we three rather enjoy, although it's time to point ourselves back toward our place. But first, we must (yes, must) find a store still open where we each buy ourselves a pillow. At least our heads will be comfy for the rest of our stay at The Shakespeare.

It's late, yet we reach our hotel happily chatting away with each other. We determine it to be another successful day on the books for the Moore sisters. Look at us. We continue to agree, get along, be happy, laugh, and joke with each other. This can't be a good sign.

17

SISTERS SLIDING SIDEWAYS

OUR NEW PILLOWS WORK FOR US. AFTER A GOOD NIGHT'S SLEEP FOR OUR HEADS at least, we can have a fun day; no headaches from crooked necks.

Breakfast in the basement over, we head back up all of those stairs. All three of us have come to feign protest with each step up while we merrily laugh taking each step down. Ready to exit the hotel, I have my cell phone out so I can take our morning sister selfie. This morning though is different. A group is standing outside of the hotel waiting for a taxi when one gentleman offers, "I am happy to take your photo for you." Handing over my cell phone, I say, "Nice. Sure. Thanks." After taking a couple of shots, he hands me back my phone. I take a moment to scroll through his handiwork. I notice immediately we are not in our birth order. I am on the left, Les is in the middle, and Rie is on the right. It's so glaring how out of place we are.

It's not that we haven't taken other photos out of our birth order before. It's not a must; rather, it's more of a developed habit for us—plain and simple. For instance, every time we are with our brothers, we automatically line up as if we are once again little kids sitting on the piano bench for a family photo: oldest to youngest. One of Mom's favorite photos is of her five adult children on her back porch steps in a line that mirrors our birth order. It's what we do.

It's just different today. An odd feeling quickly passes through me. I can't explain it. I never can. I often pick up on these weird vibes crossing in my brain; I've learned to pay attention. I usually act on them as well. For example, on December 8, 2019, I was listening to Christmas Carols when Tchaikovsky's "Nutcracker Suite" came on the radio. This was a favorite piece Mom performed when she played the stand-up Bass Violin with the Riverside Orchestra, so I decided to wait until I heard the conclusion of Act II, Pas de deux (my favorite part) before I called her. Because I waited, when the phone rang on her end I heard in her voice she was having a stroke. If I were to have called any sooner, I would not have heard this. I would have not called 911. It might have been too late for her.

So here on the steps of The Shakespeare, I can't help but comment, "This doesn't feel right, does it?" Les and Rie squeeze in to see what I am seeing. One of them says, "We aren't even in the right order. We need a Do-Over."

"I agree. And no more guest photographers." Do-Over done. Everything is once again right in the world and we are ready to head out to explore more of London, starting at St. Paul's Cathedral. Pre-photo, we checked the bus routes and schedules closest to our hotel. Now as we are about to leave, Rie points out the most direct route to reach the bus stop. "We turn right from the front steps of our place, at the end of the street we turn right and then turn right again; all right turns and a few blocks straight up."

Les does not agree. "No, we should turn left from the steps; then go right after two blocks."

I stop her mid-sentence. "You guys, it's a short distance, either way, so Les, how about you go your way and because I agree with Rie, I'll go with her. And by the way, we will beat you to the bus stop." In truth, it's all good ribbing, as usual. Besides, the two of us are quick to recall when in Ireland how Les' internal GPS went haywire. We decide to leave her to her own devices for this short amount of time. I guess we are feeling a bit reckless this morning. I mean after we remedy the photo fiasco it's going to be a good day. And truthfully, she could be right this time so why not a plan that works for us all?

Not that it's a contest. But then again....Rie and I might (okay, we do) walk a bit faster than usual; Rie, my willing accomplice. It's always a friendly competition with us, thanks to our dad.

I recall one time when our old family camper broke down during a summer camping/road trip. This was nothing new, but this time we were somewhere in Missoula, Montana. To keep us busy, Daddy promised a shiny silver dollar to the first boy and the first girl who reached the top of this nearby hill. (By the way, Doug won/I won that day.) But today, there will be no silver dollars for the first to arrive at the bus stop, only personal glory. Bring on the contest. Les will realize soon enough who won.

"You two are taking a long way." Les insists as she takes off in the wrong, okay, our opposite direction. It takes Rie and me just a few minutes to arrive at the designated bus stop. Here is where these two winners (because we are) keep watching for Les. No sign of her. According to my cell phone photos, we split up at 9:35 a.m. I elect to start walking in her given direction, but still no Les.

I scan the street Rie and I take to get here, to win. Because we do. "Wait, Rie, is that Les coming up the same street as us?" I ask hopefully. Rie looks, "It sure looks like her. Why is she coming this way?" Sure enough, it's Les. We know by the way she is walking, her gait has *I am weary* all over it. When she reaches us we are curious why she ends up coming our way? Her remark is classic Les: "Don't ask."

Our older sis has long believed ignoring problems means they magically disappear. You bet, this is exactly how it works. Ask Les what's wrong, and all one will ever hear is "I am fine," her classic response. And no, it's not always as she protests. Rie and I have come to better understand our older sister and know when she is putting up her protection shields. She is doing this right now with her "I'm fine." This is how Les silences questions and cuts off conversations. Rie and I know to give Les some space because the silence of our older sister will pass—she will move on with no further discussion.

If we were paying closer attention to Les, we would see that she is tiring out from the strong walking pace we've set. Not on purpose, it just happens. Up to this point, Les most certainly puts in a noteworthy effort, yet because she keeps most all things to herself she begins breaking apart before we become cognizant of this fact.

As we continue to wait for the bus, a very chilly wind moves in on us. Perfect. This should make us feel better. Even better, a delightful level of irritability for each Moore sister rides in on the same wind. With Plexiglas on three sides, it's still not strong enough to hold our emotional weather at bay; suddenly, a real chill is bearing down on us, and it's one we create all by ourselves.

Joining us this morning is a tall young man who must stand due to the short bus bench. There is only room enough to accommodate three sisters who are not speaking with each other. The mood on the bench shows no signs of improvement; tough crowd. I'll fix that. In a rather short amount of time, I have this young man sharing that he is eighteen, has a twin (male), and is on his way to work with the bus company we are hoping to ride with soon. He asks about us. I am the only one willing to respond. "Are you three friends traveling together?" Right. Friends.

"We are sisters," is all I can muster (or, mutter?) at this point. He likes it that we are sisters. Us? At this moment? Maybe not so much. I am thinking to myself how "like" is a pretty strong word to describe us right now. I am quite sure we are all struggling just to remain on the bench as the undesirable weather squeezes us uncomfortably close together.

In the middle of our sisters' silence, I ask the young man, "Would you be so kind as to take a photo of the three of us?" I figure it might break the ice. He is happy to oblige. I just need these two to cooperate, but our young bus stop companion doesn't wait and instead starts snapping away. The results are true classics: three photos of grumpy Moore sisters. It's only later I discover my camera in the live setting, so movement is included, which only makes these photos better.

The first attempt: We can witness ourselves fixing our hair before the shot freezes. The three of us are squishing together the best way possible. I do believe quite uncomfortable best describes our body language at this point. Rie is sitting back, fiddling with her hair. No smile. I am sitting forward. My head tilts away from Les. I am not going to acknowledge her, and by the way, I am not smiling either. And Les? She is sitting as far back as she possibly can. She even refuses to look in the right direction for this photo. In other words, intently looking away. The friction in this photo jumps out at the viewer.

The second attempt: Sure, what else have we got to distract us while waiting for the bus? Our clueless young man takes more photos of three off-putting mature (I use the term loosely) women in their mid-sixties, who at present, are acting more like petulant thirteen-year-olds. This time, Rie has an ever-so-slight smile. Me? I have a very, very slight smile. And Les? Well, look at her. She turns her head just ever so slightly for the photo, but still no smile.

The third attempt: I have our young photographer wait for a second while I tell these two knucklehead sisters of mine we are going to do the three wise monkeys for the next photo. (This might help the two of them see how silly they are behaving right now. Oh sure, the three of us.) Rie covers her eyes. I cover my ears. Les covers her mouth. And just like that, it's as if a warm breeze knows to pass over this particular bus stop at this particular time to thaw the blades of ice separating these three stubborn, silly sisters sitting on this very chilly bus bench.

Forever capturing that moment, we always laugh at this photo. In fact, once home, Les has 5x8 photos of us as three wise monkeys made for each of us. All sit in prominent places in our homes and serve as a funny reminder for us. But before we are home and laughing at ourselves, at this moment we need to realize being stubborn does not serve us well, and in fact, it's the snag that possesses the power to unravel our sister tent. We all need to be much more vigilant in this regard.

Thinking back on our planning. To hear us then? "Three countries? Oh, that sounds like fun." Surprise. Still on the bench one of us comments, "Ladies, a three-sister journey? It's not for the faint of heart! We can do this though." We all just shake our heads and chuckle. And in the midst of it all, we hit the sisterhood restart button.

Today, we plan on hopping off at St. Paul's Cathedral. And just like that, it's my fault we hop off much too soon and end up walking more than we want to. My screw-up aside, walking around a corner and coming upon St. Paul's, well, it ends up being (at least for me) well worth all of our extra steps. Sitting at the highest point in this city (or even if it were at the lowest), this cathedral is impossible to miss.

It's been almost 350 years since the construction began in 1673, and upon entering this magnificent cathedral, the breadth and scope brings me to a halt. I take it all in, which is a lot. Inside, its highest point is 365 feet. To grasp its enormity is to appreciate its 3,500 seating capacity, though there is so much more inside these hallowed walls.

Saint Paul's is not meant for just wandering in, looking around, and leaving. Here is where one pauses in awe of the stunning capabilities of men so many years ago. It is here where believers can experience the majestic presence of their Lord. It is here where I sense a sacred quietness, a remarkable reverence. The enormous stained glass here does not disappoint. Although it is what visitors expect in a cathedral, few admirers realize these artistic renderings are what the illiterate medieval masses 'read' to learn the stories of Jesus, his disciples, his miracles, and more. These picture stories become a means of proselytizing, the stained-glass method if you will.

Perhaps many might know this church from sitting in their living room while watching the 1981 wedding of Prince Charles and Lady Diana Spencer. I can still see the beautiful Diana gliding down the aisle in her wedding dress, her twenty-five foot veil following behind her.

Running along parts of the walls are numerous sarcophagi, yet we are on the hunt for one in particular, that of Lieutenant-General Sir John Moore. Our daddy always expressed hope that this military hero might be a relative, and so today we plan on introducing ourselves to this young officer and gentleman, two hundred and ten years later.

While standing in the midst of so much to see and so much going on, I realize there is a small wedding taking place in one of the many alcoves, near where I am standing. Each alcove is about the same size as a small wedding chapel. Not wishing to invade their privacy, I look elsewhere to step only to find myself standing next to the larger-than-life marble sarcophagus of Lt. General Moore. "I have been looking for you," I whisper. A fat little cherub is accompanying a male and a female angel. All three are forever frozen in perpetual motion as they lower the uniformed hero, forever suspended in the youth of his forty-eight years, into his final resting place. Moving over for a closer look, I search for any family likeness in the marble carving of his face. Then I read the engraved inscription:

Sacred to the memory of Lieutenant-General Sir John Moore, K.B.
Who was born at Glasgow in the year 1761.
He fought for his country In America, in Corsica, In the West-Indies,
In Holland, Egypt, and Spain: And on the 16th of January, 1809,
Was slain by a cannon-ball, At Corunna.

This hero and his last days of life spent in battle are the subjects of a poem written by Charles Wolfe, "The Burial of Sir John Moore after Corunna." With eight stanzas in total, the first two stanzas tell of the battle still waging on, the setting in which Moore's men must quickly bury their beloved leader. The last stanza captures the haunting sadness as they have no choice but to leave Moore without a proper farewell.

If Lt. General Moore might not be a distant relation, so be it. Of course, today it is much easier to find out if this is the case, yet we prefer to let this all rest in peace along with our daddy. Either way, it's still an honor nonetheless sharing the last name of Moore with this brave war hero.

After spending time inside, many visitors choose to go outside and climb up to the top of the highest dome, all 1,100 steps; one thing is for certain, these people must not be dealing with the lack of a lift like us at The Shakespeare. Because we already have too many stairs in our life right now, we choose to catch the next Hop-On/Hop-Off bus coming our way.

Crossing over the London Bridge, we drop in on the 900-year old Tower of London for a visit. Though small in size and land (12 acres), the Tower is seeping in both royal jewels and spectacular history, including where King Henry VIII's Queen, Anne Boleyn, faced her executioners. It's surreal to stand in this place. One that is so old on this side of the River Thames, while on the other side of the river is modern glass architecture. It creates a remarkable juxtaposition of then and now.

"You ladies ready to head home?" I ask. They are, so we seek out the closest Underground stop and head back to Paddington. Lucky us, we end up sitting next to a young man and three young women. Thomas introduces himself, his girlfriend Betty, and the other two; they are returning from an afternoon of pub hopping. I start the conversation with Les and Rie joining in as well and it continues through several stops until we reach ours. During the ride, we share what we are doing and where we are going when I decide to throw out a question to them, "Oh, by the way, any advice for places to visit in Scotland?" They all start laughing while looking at us and each other, still laughing. "I guess I asked a funny question?"

Thomas turns to me. "We've never been to Scotland, ever, and have no plans to do so."

"What? Why?" I ask. "When you are living so very close? I don't understand?"

Betty then fills us in on how "Brits travel to Spain or Italy. We want to see and enjoy the sun, the warmth. It's much too cold for us, so why go from cold England to colder Scotland?"

"This makes sense to us but is it really cold there?" I am now thinking about the early planning stages of this trip with Rie and Les and deciding to avoid Italy because of all of the European tourists—here is proof we picked the right direction for us to travel. Before our train comes to a stop, we exchange phone numbers. I invite them to use my home in California as a jump-off point if they ever visit—feels comfortable doing this. They appreciate the invite.

Back at Paddington, it's time for some dinner so we make our way to a small restaurant we have been wanting to try. We relax as we wait for our food. Although a bit weary at best, we still feel upbeat. As a matter of fact, we are rather happy.

Chatting over dinner, Rie's unexpectedly enormous meal has me taking a silly photo of her showing shock over the abundance of food. It has us laughing. It's what we do best, laugh.

Dinner over, we walk the short block back to our hotel where we have too many stairs waiting for us after walking too many steps today.

Beginning our ascent, we all join in commenting on the stairs, the too many stairs. Entering our room, we each plop down on our beds and start to get comfortable for the evening.

Dusk settles in at the end of this enjoyable day. The fading London sky has just enough light to push through our small window to expose a slight tear in the canvas of our sister tent. Just. Like. That.

And then the small rip starts to grow with words directed at me, spoken by Les, "Must you complain about the stairs? I get it. You don't like my choice of hotel."

I am completely knocked off balance. As I struggle to regain my equilibrium, my mind is scrambling with an overview of today.

If everything is fine, as Les mentioned earlier in the day, then how does this tear get here? When did it start? This glaring failure takes me by surprise. By the expression on her face, I can tell Rie is taken by surprise as well. If it takes Les by surprise she keeps this very close to her chest; we are only left to wonder. And then we are no longer left to wonder. "You just don't get it, do you?" Because her voice is above a whisper and because no, I don't understand what she is saying, I lean in toward her. "It will help if you explain to me, to us. Get what?"

She replies in words that form two- to three-word sentences, halting as she speaks each of them. "I thought. We were having. A room of my own. It's not. All my fault. This room. I asked you both. You both said. It looked fine. Online." To be fair, she is right. We agreed The Dolphin looked fine online. And now? The Shakespeare is fine. Rather, we are making it work. At least I thought we were.

"Les, it's okay. It's been okay. Why isn't it okay now?" While I am quickly responding with reassurance, she remains busy struggling to form all of her internal frustrations into words.

And then once again Les huffs out some words toward me less audible than before and yet they push me back on my heels with such a very hard shove. "It doesn't help you keep complaining."

I am at a complete loss as I try to make sense of what she is conveying, and then I hear myself voicing my confusion. "Les, why are you thinking this now? I'm confused. Again, what makes you think we are complaining, that I am complaining? When we climb up all of the stairs, we all laugh about not having a lift."

But now, on this night, our usual laughter is no more and in its place an unharnessing of feelings and emotions, yet few, very few words. Even so it has such a force to it that it rips the small tear into an even larger, more painful gap. In the direct line of whatever Les plans to unleash, I attempt to diffuse her and our situation by asking as calmly as possible, "Les, what's wrong?"

She has only two words to give me: "I'm fine!" Right. So much for any clue. But we know better. And without any more words from her, we are unable to help ourselves through this. And to drive home the fact that she will not be sharing any further, Les is bolting for the door. This isn't going to turn out well.

Following my August 1st pre-dawn flight wake-up call at 3:30 a.m., I made a mental note to discuss stomping off with Les and Rie. And though these two reassured me several times how I worry (because again, I carry 'The Worry Mantle' in our family), we still needed to have this cconversation about how none of us are not happy. not getting our way, just over it, or wish to avoid, we take to stomping off. So one evening in Ireland, we talked about this and agreed that for this trip we will not partake in this specialized behavior of stomping off.

"Diz, we'll be having too much fun rather than too many problems." My response? "Fine, Rie, but let's all agree, no stomping off on our trip." To which we do, "Yes. No being stomper-offers." And with this, the three Moore sisters who are stomper-offer prone seal the deal with a good laugh.

Yet now in the process of running from the room, Les grabs her phone as well as taking with her the words of promise to not do exactly what she is doing: stomping off. We are at the beginning of a storm. One that we are brewing, and it's not good. As Les is in mid-flight, I am quite certain I detect some tears in her eyes. Lord, I hope not because if Les is crying we are in big trouble.

Preferring to be lost in a book, Les is anything but an open book. Despite all of the millions of words she has read over the years, she still prefers to keep the majority of her own words buried deep inside for safe-keeping. The same with tears. They are stored deep inside her. It's just how our older sis functions; it doesn't mean it's wrong. Up to this moment, I believe I have witnessed our older sis crying four times, total, throughout our lives. It might be an exaggeration. Too high of a number. And now this cry is brought on by yours truly. I cannot bear being the reason Les is so sad. Here I go again, believing I must fix this, somehow. I am not always successful, by the way.

At forty-five years of age, Les suffered immeasurable pain. Stephen, her twenty-five-year-old son, had walking pneumonia but it was diagnosed too late. Sepsis started to claim his body and then Death showed up to steal the last breath from her beloved son. And though Death arrived quickly, before departing he made sure to leave our sis in a broken heap of fragments and splinters; she continues to pull slivers out of her heart. I wanted nothing more than to fix this for her. But of course, I couldn't breathe life back into Stephen, yet perhaps I could help Les breathe because she found taking her next breath near impossible. The truth was, she had to do it on her own, and though she sought some therapy, it was much easier to shove her pain deep inside her. Her heart will never be whole again, because when Stephen died he took pieces of it with him.

Now, many years later, in our rapidly shrinking room at The Shakespeare, I don't know how to fix her, to fix us. I seek wisdom from Rie. "Give her time, Diz, She's never walked like this before. No doubt she is physically beat from all our walking. It's a lot." True, we are averaging seven miles a day. "And even though we have all been laughing at our living arrangement, right now it doesn't seem to matter if we all poke fun at our lodging because Les has lost sight of this." Rie is right. It's just that what Les has not lost sight of is me being her problem. This leaves me gasping for air.

We can't ignore the fact of how this small room robs us of alone time, of privacy. Here we are again, three little girls living together in our small bedroom, yet we had no choice then. These many years later, we are used to having choices, of making our own choices. And our first choice needs to be doing better than this. Yet, we need Les here to be a part of who we are: sisters giving our best effort at being good traveling companions.

Les has been gone for almost an hour and it doesn't feel comfortable. Yet her two sisters resolve to give her a little bit more time. In our effort (more of a struggle) to respect her space, we fluctuate between being nervous and being angry because Les is the least savvy of us when it comes to traveling.

During her absence, I begin writing what I am thinking at a furious pace in my journal:

I regret coming. I'm doubting my decision to be here. I continue to quickly scribble down my feelings and fears, of course not even stopping to consider how Les might be feeling at this moment, in the middle of her first big trip. My fingers are feeling the clench around the pen as I write down everything as it pops into my head:

We aren't as close as I believed. Are we going to lose us, our friendship, to forever struggle with each other at the end of our lives as we did at the beginning? We are very strong. Very stubborn. Very everything RIGHT NOW. How do I bite my tongue? This isn't good. Rie thinks we'll be okay. I'm lousy at hiding my feelings. I'm too easy to 'read.' I can never read Les. I never know how she is feeling. I don't know what she wants. She simply tolerates me. I see this now. Why do I frustrate her—because I do. I've got to write this frustration out of my head, or we are in trouble. Big, big trouble. Forget the whole 'sister tent.' Let it blow away, damn it! It seems our tent stakes were never that strong. Do I even care if we stay grounded during this mighty headwind we are facing? Being so far from home does not help.

I continue, page after page:

I took this trip on the premise we will be okay. Now we are not. Have we just always ignored these dynamics? I'm feeling so empty. So very, very sad. And now, to think we are already reaching for some 'justifiable self-defense' and 'heart-piercing verbal ammunition.' Why so early in our trip, or even at all?

Rie is reading as we wait for Les to return. My hand is tired of writing. I don't like this feeling. It's as if some family poltergeists smuggled themselves into our suitcases, magically conjuring up old feelings and dissolving us into an ugly pile of unhappy sisters. We feel the presence of these entities as they continue to unpack all of our old crap with the greatest of gusto. Working at a furious pace, they recklessly toss our feelings, our hurt, and our fears right into our faces, around our small room, and every which way. Our room, now a bitter-'suite,' was already small but it's feeling quite minuscule now. I'm mad. I'm unsettled. I'm fearful that three hearts could be broken tonight.

Still no Les, so I return to writing in my journal.

I now wonder if sisters can travel together. Perhaps not these three sisters. I am ready to go home right now—leave before it is too late. Before Les returns. I can be as good of a 'stomper-offer' as my older sis.

Greg, Les' husband, says he knows when Les is on the phone with me because she is always laughing. She is great fun to tease and joke with, and I enjoy making her laugh. Yet, right now? Suddenly, we are no longer laughing about the stairs? About anything? Why not? Thanks to her insight and wisdom, Rie walks me back off the ledge. "Diz, just give her the time she needs."

"I know you're right. But it's hard to do."

"I'm thinking she is not too far. She is too tired." This reality brings a "huh" out of me because Rie is right. It helps.

"You are right, again. I get it. She is exhausted. We missed it." Our older sister reached her limit; she didn't voice it but displayed it. Piling on to her reality, the lack of privacy must be overwhelming (she never experienced life in a dorm full of girls like her two sisters), add in sheer exhaustion, and never having been away from her home this long. Even so, we have a lot more "long" ahead of us.

"I'm going to try to get some sleep, Diz. Les is going to be fine. This will all work out for us, don't worry too much."

"Rie, aren't you worried?"

"Not too much. I think once Les feels rested, she will be back to her usual self. We'll figure it out. We always have." She is right. Yet I do worry. Worry about us and the rest of our trip. What are we going to do? Because this is about we. This is our trip. About an hour and a half later, Les returns.

I apologize.

Silence.

She prepares for bed.

Silence.

She crawls into her bed making sure her back is facing her sisters. We 'hear' her body language loud and clear: She wants no conversation.

Silence.

Then sniffles, yet no words, dang it! Still some left-over tears in her yet no offer of communication. Fine. She screams her silence at me, so I mirror it right back at her. And she can just sniffle herself to sleep for all I care.

I notice that our one small window is wide open and our little portable fan is chugging its rotation back and forth as best as it can to move about the thick air in our room, yet it remains quite stuffy. It is not at all comfortable as the three Moore girls struggle to settle into some kind of slumber.

18

THREE DANCERS, SIX LEFT FEET

No jumping out of bed for me this morning. Instead, I begin the slow process of opening my eyes under great caution and trepidation. I decide it's best to leave my lids in a narrow squint as I take a cautious survey of my surroundings: Who is awake and who is still sleeping? Being careful to not draw any attention to myself, I suspect my two roommates are opening their eyes with the same wariness.

Wimbledon day is here. I can't begin to imagine the internal chaos Les has to be waking up to. On one hand, she no doubt remains unhappy with me while on the other hand, she has to be thrilled about seeing this famous tennis court and surrounding area.

Les does not play tennis. She never played. Yet Les is completely enthralled with everything about the sport of tennis, including knowing the professional players and their stats. For her to be stepping foot on the holy ground of the High Church of Wimbledon? It's an answered prayer for our older sis.

Leading up to this morning, Rie and I hear of Les' excitement about this particular patch of grass. And now that today is finally here? What can I say but no doubt today is going to be such a delight as we head there together because we go everywhere together. Even today. Such joy. But first, to wake up and face each other. This should be comfortable. I wonder how we will be negotiating our tiny patch of real estate? And then my question is answered; let the negotiating begin. Imagine a piece of music stuck on a non-ending loop to which the three of us are performers in the most intricate of ballets. Is it possible this room has become even smaller in square footage during the night? I do believe this to be the case. And our overwhelming politeness? It's reigning supreme this lovely awkward morning. And the words we carefully select to speak to one another? Few, polite (naturally), and in an uncomfortable staccato:

"Excuse me."

"Done in the bathroom?"

"May I use this outlet?"

"May I get by you," and so on as our ridiculous dance around each other continues. With each passing minute, an invading tension is strengthening its grip around each of us. And all of our unspoken words? The ones we are too stubborn to speak? They jam themselves into every inch of any open space within our cramped quarters. This hurts. For all of us.

"Do either of you want to go to breakfast?" I break the stiffness in the room by removing the blunt words and replacing them with more words in the form of a question? (Someone has to model civility, right?) Rie merrily answers with "Yes, I'll go" and then turns to Les, "Do you want breakfast?" To which Les shakes her head in a slow back and forth. And then a "not hungry" is ever so quietly spoken.

I think to myself *progress*, then I say out loud, "All right then. Rie, ready?" And with that, we head down those damn stairs.

Breakfast over, we return to the room and take care of what we need to do while remaining ever so polite in words and movement. We are ready to head downstairs for the day. Together. At this juncture, I am set on walking straight out through the front door as a silent signal that I'll be skipping our daily sister selfie, thank you very much. I plan to pretend it escapes my mind. The sisters won't notice. Besides, I can't imagine either of them wanting to take our now traditional morning photo. Hey, all good by me. I am now telling myself, *Just keep walking, Liz.* And I do just that. I am in the middle of one last long stride to clear the door frame when I hear Rie call after me.

"Diz, let's not forget to take our morning sister selfie!" Dang her anyway, this close. And because I am the picture-taker, we always use my cell phone. Rie plays it cool as she wisely wedges halfway in between me and Les. This is the most miserable morning selfie to date, and I hope it's the last. And birth order? Who cares?

Let's just get through this day, better yet, how about the morning? I am wondering if it's possible. Everything about today is what I am not looking forward to. My emotional scale right now? Somewhere between sad and frustrated. Wimbledon, oh yeah.

Making our way to Paddington, we all deliberately avoid walking too close together. I take a glance at the selfie. Rie's smile is especially big. She lifts herself above the sister fray, unlike her two sisters.

The photo gives away just how much Les is straining against a smile, doing her best to show just how damn happy she is about all of this. I've got a slight smile myself. I match Les smile-for sort-of-smile. At least the two of us agree on this—we are uncomfortable with each other and not thrilled about the day ahead of us. Good. She is hurting too. And with that, I feel a twinge of justification.

Reaching an intersection, we just miss the green light. Great. We are forced to stand in place, together. I am over this whole sister togeth- erness. And then I do believe I hear Les make a snippy comment, just not quite under her breath so that I might hear. Why yes, in fact, I do hear it. "This is my country, not yours."

"Did I just hear you mumble something at me?" Being who I am, I just can't let this go. And then I am not at all quiet as I snip back at her in a worthy outdoor voice that allows those in the crowd near us to hear as well; they'll never see us again. Who cares because I sure don't. By responding to her, I am now fully engaged and it makes me just as responsible for my part in this mess. At my boiling point, I wonder, will this light ever change?

Yet, Les tries to deny me a reply, "It wasn't directed at you. Never mind."

Bullshit, I instantly think. "No, tell me what it is you said."

"Forget it."

"No!" And as we are standing at the street corner my thoughts begin racing in all different directions:

Les has been great all of this time, why is she now being a brat? Mom always told Les she was like the little girl with a little curl in the middle of her forehead. When she was good, she was very good and then when she was bad? Horrid. Sounds about right, except for the horrid part. Oh my gosh. Our suitcases. Of course. We all pack our suitcases with some self-defense and heart-piercing words for ammunition. Why, under God's heaven, do we even think to pre-pack such verbal hurt and harm when we are planning such fun together? Are we this way at home with each other? I sure don't think so. Or it's just easier to ignore? Are we just so insecure with ourselves? And with each other? Is this why we all arrive pre-armed? I didn't even think we would need any of this. How sad we are taking this journey subconsciously prepared, so it now seems, to defend ourselves in an instant. And here we are in the middle of.... Wait, incoming!

"I'm done with this," from Les. (I'm hearing a sound I don't like. Has the small rip from last night just ripped into a larger one?) I observe Rie as she places herself farther ahead of us (smart girl) while still standing on the corner. Les and I do all we can to avoid any kind of eye contact. The light changes, although we sure aren't ready to. Now finally crossing the street, Les and I still hold firm to our sullenness and unhappiness toward each other. As we are making our very individual way on the sidewalk that leads to the underground entrance of Paddington, I spy a little alcove. I make a quick decision to pull both sisters aside and then I look directly at Les as I let her know how I feel in a loud, hissing voice, "I can't do this!" And whatever else I am expressing in both voice and manner absent of any calm. Les quickly shoots back at me. "Fine!" And instantly I am thinking to myself, *Oh my gosh, what a surprise. I never expected to hear this singular word from her. So clever!* But then I demand from her, "Tell me what it is you said to me earlier and why?"

"This is my country, not yours. Your time is over. It's my turn now."

"And what does that mean? That I already have Ireland and England is your country? We all know this!"

"We did everything you wanted to in Ireland and now it's my turn."

"Who says it isn't?" My patience is over. "What the hell, Les?"

"You keep suggesting places to visit. It's my country."

"Les! You want to see the guards at Buckingham and visit Wimbledon. But when we ask what else, what do you say? 'I don't care.' So why do you say this then when it's a lie because you do care?" Silence. I am trying hard to read her, her frustration toward me, and why she just doesn't speak up. She finds it so hard. I find it so easy.

Her first husband robbed his young bride of her self-confidence and her opinions. None of those mattered to him; he convinced Les they would not matter to anyone else as well. All of his horrific, rotten lies she took as truth so of course this is who Les brings on our trip: to speak up with suggestions is to create problems. All the while, I believe I am helping Les by interpreting her silence as wanting suggestions from me. Do I ASK her if this is what she wants from me? Are you kidding? Of course not. Instead, the rhythm for our dance is provided by assumptions: I ask, "Where to next?" And from her, "I don't care" is her not knowing how to voice to me, to us, what it is she wants to do, to go see. I then take the lead by assuming once again that she is either not interested beyond her two choices, or she is unsure because she failed to complete her pre-travel homework. This is how we arrive here at being none too pleased with each other. But in all honesty, who wants to be wandering around all day and miss out on opportunities, is what I am thinking, so I take the silence of Les and fill it with my voice of suggestions. All of those reasons are why we are standing here right now on the sidewalk leading down into Paddington Station yelling at each other with the thinnest line of discretion; sort of. Barely. Who cares? Rie does.

In a quiet and calm manner, Rie steps in. Thank goodness. Except, she is neither quiet nor calm. Instead, Rie is speaking in a voice several pitches above her typical quiet pitch. And with that she lets us know in no uncertain terms, "You two are being so very stubborn!" Hearing this immediately confuses my thoughts. *Rie is taking charge of her two older sisters? What? Wait, both of us? It's Les you need to go after, not me.* And when my brain registers her words being stubborn, My brain quickly relays *No. No, I'm not. Les is. She is the most stubborn of us all. Oops. Isn't this something a stubborn person says? Never mind.* My comments stop just short of coming out of my mouth although I so much want to speak them all.

And then Rie, shouting in our faces, takes on a parental tone, "You both want the same thing!" Once again I stand there biting my tongue, *ah, I don't think so.* And here again, I don't vomit these smart-ass words tumbling around in my brain. Rie then asks Les what she wants from me: "An apology." Now my brain is going into full laughing mode. *Oh, that's rich.* I am this close to screaming this, yet once again I keep my clever retorts to myself (why I don't know), and then I do say out loud and firmly, "I did say I am sorry. Last night. You refused to accept my apology. And you sure haven't apologized to me." She vehemently disagrees, her outside voice now matching mine. "I did say I'm sorry."

Then, it's Rie again who is speaking, but this time a few pitches lower as she directs her words specifically at Les, "You never said this to Diz." There it is. (And by the way, I am certainly loving Rie right now.) And then silence. It's such a palpable silence that we three seem afraid to move. It's as though any movement might make this worse. We all sense it, afraid that all of the words we speak and do not speak will create a tear in our tent so big that it will be beyond our ability to repair. A gaping hole as large as this no longer offers enough shelter for the three of us; one sister will be left out. I am so afraid that the damage we have caused might be too large to stitch back together. Yet neither Les nor I are backing down, starting with me. "What is it, Les? What is it that I do that seems to always have you coming after me? Not just this time either."

"Why should you care, you've never liked me."

"Never? Not true. You always keep me at arm's length. It's you who never likes me." And here is where we both lose sight of our many wonderful times together, of when we were so close when pregnant at the same time. Of her as my trusted confidante.

"You don't like me. You haven't since we were young. Mom even told me you left for Thunderbird because of me."

"Les, what?" I must take a moment to balance myself, catch my breath. I struggle to speak the words. "What. Are you. Even talking about?"

"You went to Thunderbird because you didn't like me. This is what Mom told me."

"Wait. What? Explain."

"You left because of me. I guess I was the reason you were always so sad. Didn't you ever wonder why I was never around when you came home for a weekend visit? Because you hated me so much, you scared me away."

Whoa. What a big heap of emotions and words. And they are coming at a fast and furious pace. Up until now, Les withheld this conversation from me. Fifty years later, standing on some random sidewalk in London, England, is when I hear these historically sad words. And even if Mom didn't speak those exact words, this is how Les took them in, and in turn here is yet another false truth she claims for herself. And it has kept me at arm's length from her all of these years. I am deeply saddened.

"Les. Les. Sure, I was jealous of you. So strong, popular, beautiful you. And in true sibling fashion, especially since we are so close in age, I was always comparing myself to you, my beautiful older sister. A much less frustrating option for me was leaving. We were just young teenage girls, for heaven's sake!"

And then Les speaks words that shock, "Well, you should know I was jealous of you. No responsibilities, so carefree and funny."

We are in our late sixties and I am just now hearing this? And yet, it's only now I understand why she never felt comfortable around me. "Les, this is such a punch to the gut hearing this. And now that I know, I'm so very sorry."

"I'm sorry too. What a mess this is!" Rie steps back a bit. She knows to leave the difficult patchwork to the two of us. Somewhere in the depths of our souls, Les and I are willing to save us as well as our sister tent.

"Les, you do realize had we not taken this journey together we would have most likely continued to keep each other at arm's length, taking all of the sad and false beliefs with us to our graves? How horrible would this have been? It sickens me, yet gives me hope going forward together."

To which Les replies, "Yup, sis, who knew." And with this, we start walking down into Paddington Station, together, closer together.

Once inside, we find the one free bench for the line to Wimbledon. Our tent stakes have held us with an incredible strength the three of us never realized we had. When we sit down, I feel arms reach for me. To my sheer astonishment, it's Les who encircles her arms around me with such care and sincerity. Though speaking in a voice with lingering caution, Les says, "I love you, Liz. Very much." She is full of acceptance and grace toward me. It's all rather lovely. I didn't expect it. Les continues, "You are making this trip such fun. You do what I wish I could do, talk

to everyone. It's just not easy for me. I wish it was. But it's who you are."
And because I love her so, it's easy to say,

"Thanks, Les. I love you too. I'm so sorry about all of this, then
and now. I truly am."

"Me too." And then all frustrations and worries instantly evapo-
rate out of my body. Les and I reach out to Rie so that the three of us
can embrace one another. And as we await our train for Wimbledon,
three bodies begin exhaling in unison. Once again, we hit the reset
button. This shoos our pesky poltergeists back to our room where they
hide once again in the tight, dark corners of our suitcases. Gone. For
now. Hopefully for good. Then again, we are only halfway through this
three-week journey.

Even so, some damage is done. But this is okay. I'm remember-
ing how uncomfortable we were in Belfast, wanting to escape, even
though we were all together. Well here we are again, uncomfortable
in yet another unfamiliar emotional place, in spite of being together.
(Why doesn't "together" afford us some sense of security?) One thing is
certain, we remain a work in progress. Our sister tent, made of hope and
faith, is held in place with stakes of laughter. We find incredible strength
the three of us never realized we had.

It's true, Les and I created quite a large rip on our sister tent, yet
we don't wish to deny it. To stitch the torn sides completely shut after
what just occurred between us is to make it appear as though it never
happened. It would be like putting a small Band-Aid over a gaping wound
and calling it healed. Today, we gained incredible knowledge about each
other, so why ignore this when it will help us as we continue our journey?
We need to figure this out for the better of our sisterhood.

When we planned this trip, we exchanged excitement about seeing this part of the world. We talked about the weather during this time
of year and how to best pack. We agreed on layers as the best choice.
We also discussed how we would be experiencing something unique to

us: the three of us traveling without husbands. Living with them every day, we are not always cognizant of how we forget to flex our muscles of independence, as daily living is often a comfortable routine, which in turn can lead to atrophy of self-reliance.

Hindsight reveals we were like brides caught up in the planning of this journey while we failed to look at what life would look like after that whole ridiculous fairy tale ending of living happily ever after. Right. We all know the Prince will soon be ever after throwing his dirty laundry on the floor, something the Princess never imagined. What was her plan to deal with this? No plan. The same for the Moore sisters. No plan.

Later, as I reflected on this day, it was frightening to think just how close our sister tent came to flying beyond our grasp. Rie is why it stayed grounded. And yet despite her nature of not wanting to make waves, she didn't elect to step back and silently observe her two sisters in their process of falling apart. By stepping in, Rie saved us. She saved her sisters, our sister tent, and our journey. We will become better as a result.

The Moore sisters share the same mindset when it comes to what we want to accomplish today: Always start furthest out and then work backward toward 'home.' First stop, Wimbledon Stadium. A fifty-minute ride on the Blue Line, literally at the end of the line. When we get off the train we see the sign WIMBLEDON. We ask a uniformed worker, "The best path to Wimbledon is?"

"Get back on the train and disembark off three stops back at Southfields." Well, of course! Don't get off the train at the Wimbledon stop. We foolishly let logic and reason lead us and look where it got us: Getting off at the wrong stop for Wimbledon at Wimbledon. Backward we go; Southfields exit it is.

Now in Southfields, we decide to make the walk to the High Church of Wimbledon. Entering the area where we purchase tickets for tours, Les is careful to choose from the menu of tour options as she is hyper-aware being here is her special once-in-a-lifetime opportunity. One tennis enthusiast and her two non-tennis enthusiast companions will be touring a museum and of course seeing the holy ground (Center Court). In the stands for about twenty-five minutes, the guide provides history and gossip about the courts, the players, and the famous. We also take advantage of her offer to take our photo with the grass court serving as a backdrop. It's a wonderful moment for Les; Rie and I are very happy for her.

"I'm finally here." Les proclaims in amazement. "I don't see myself ever coming back any time soon though it would be fun to watch a tournament. For now though, this one time is fine by me! Thanks, you two." We cap off the moment with a visit to the museum and then the gift shop. Les struggles to contain her excitement. All-in-all she spends about 75.00 pounds, which for her is a lot of money to part with. It's not that she cannot afford it. It's not that she doesn't have it in her wallet. Oh no! Rather, she simply hates to part with it. Rie and I just shake our heads at our big sis.

Neither Rie nor I were born with the same frugal gene as Les. A better description is extremely frugal. Even as a young girl, she was thrifty with her money. There were no ATMs when we were young, and banks closed at 3:00 p.m., sharp. But the family had 'The Bank of Leslie.' She was the go-to source to tide over family members, including Mom and Dad in emergencies. Noteworthy, all borrowed money was expected to be returned, naturally. (I wonder if she charged interest?)

We choose to grab our lunch from a little market on our way back to the Tube. As Rie wanders off (no surprise) to find what she wants, Les and I decide on the same ready-made fresh pesto pasta salad along with some slices of mixed fruit. Upon exiting the store, we decide to carry it with us on the Tube then eat it once we arrive back in London at Parliament Square, adjacent to Westminster Abbey. But first, we must get to the platform.

Rie and I carry our large, thick orange plastic grocery bag with handles while Les is working hard at carrying two bags—her treasures in one, and food in the other, and, oh, her purse is hanging over her shoulder. Rie wisely determines that to make it easier for Les is to combine her two bags; placing the smaller bag of Wimbledon treasures inside the much larger orange grocery bag. One less bag for our sis to guard and/or worry about.

As mentioned earlier, Les, having very little travel experience, is extra cautious. She is especially wary about possible pickpockets—she has every right to be as there are copious amounts of posters filled with travel warnings, especially concerning theft. So Les is on high alert and keeps a strong grip on her purse as well as her bag of treasures and food. Rie and I notice Les is beaming from her Wimbledon experience. Truthfully, she would be happy going home right now.

We eat our lunch in the shadow of the grandeur of Westminster Abbey. Les and Rie find a place to eat while I decide to sit on a set of stairs, a bit away from them. Here I begin to engage with a young mother with her infant and the grandmother. Finishing up with my lunch, Rie approaches me with one of those orange grocery bags now containing their garbage; she offers to dump mine along with theirs. Then asks, "Are you ready to go inside the Abbey, Diz?" I am certain my smile says it all. "Yes. I'm thrilled I finally get to experience it." Les joins us, orange bag in hand. She decides to keep it because the large size makes it much easier to carry her Wimbledon treasures.

Because I was born the same year and the same day the young Queen Elizabeth was crowned in Westminster Abbey, Mom and Dad named me Elizabeth. Daddy's parents immigrated to the states from England, so they were pleased their newest granddaughter shared their Queen's name. We came to share our nickname as well, both of us called Lilibet by our dads. So going inside the Abbey will only strengthen my affinity with the Queen.

Once inside the Abbey bookstore to purchase our tickets, I read: The Abbey is CLOSED for the day. I try not to show my disappointment at 3:30 in the afternoon, never imagining such an early closure. Even so, both sisters get it and are very empathetic toward me. Les offers up the suggestion, "How about tomorrow after we watch the changing of the guards we come back to visit the Abbey then?" It's kind of her to offer, but I must remind her, "No. That won't work. We are planning to visit Stonehenge and Windsor Castle tomorrow."

"Okay, we will do it the day after next. That works, right?" It sounds like a plan. Okay, no Westminster today, so we head over to Shakespeare's Globe Theatre, which is also exciting for me. We elect to hail a taxi this time because we are done putting in steps today.

Lucky us. There is no line of people waiting to get in. Finally, timing is in our favor. We step up to purchase our tickets.

"We apologize. We are closed today for a private showing." I beg, "I can't just step in and take a peek?" The docent is on the verge of being rather rude in her response. "Not by any means!" I give her a sort of smile while I match my internal voice to hers. *Well, Alright then.* My only option is the gift shop/bookstore. A poor substitute for not getting to see inside this historical theater, yet it's out of my hands. Making a couple of purchases, I make a sneaky dash out to a side patio to grab a peek inside the theatre from this location. No view or entry from there either. I end up doing the last best thing: Les takes a photo of me standing on the outside of the theater. I am standing there with a smile but I am thinking, *Yeah, look where I've been! The outside of The Globe Theatre.* This had better be funny later because it isn't too funny right now. Oh well. So it goes. The three of us head toward home using the Southwark Bridge. With the London Bridge serving as our backdrop, we stop for a windswept selfie, more windblown. As we proceed across the bridge, I say, "Well, you two, where to next?" Give us credit. The three of us keep trying even as the day is starting to wane.

On the south side of the bridge, we come to a tourist office. Here we find a bench under a very large tree where Les and Rie sit while I go in to get some tourist brochures and suggestions. I bring them a treasure trove of pamphlets and as we decide what looks best Les asks, "Do you two smell that?"

"Smell what?" Rie and I ask, in near unison.

"It smells like pesto." I chime in, "It's just a leftover smell on your breath from your lunch."

"Yes, but I don't smell it on your breath, only mine. That was some strong pesto, at least mine was to smell like this." And then with the orange bag still in her steely grip, Les lifts it off her lap to smell and make sure the pesto scent isn't permeating her treasures. Well now, this is odd. There are two rather large stains—say the size of two tennis balls—on her jeans, both legs, mid-thigh. The texture appears green and oily. She doesn't understand. Rie and I don't understand either.

Les opens the precious bag that holds her valuable Wimbledon treasures. Her expression is one of instant dismay. And then we all come to understand why the smell of pesto remains as strong as it is. Since leaving Westminster she has been carrying the empty food cartons—hers and Rie's—from lunch meant for the garbage. The pesto pasta Les didn't finish has leaked. Onto her pants. This confuses us all when one of us wonders aloud. "The trash? So if this is the trash, then?" We all immediately know the answer to this question: The trash can at Parliament Park holds Les' treasures. Les or Rie. Rie or Les. One of them hands it off/ takes the wrong bag and dumps it in the trash. A deep disappointment for each of them, to say the least. My disappointment comes later when I realize I am so caught up in all of this that I don't have the wherewithal to take a photo of her pesto-spotted jeans. It's the photo that got away. Talk about regret.

But right now? To be brutally honest it's good news for me. Hold on. Don't judge. I only say this because I know for sure I have nothing to do with the orange bag mishap. I am in the clear. Les cannot turn her frustration toward me (I feel quite certain she has used it all up anyway. At least toward me.) But okay, it doesn't matter much right now because Les is quite sad, especially when she realizes she has been guarding trash for the last couple of hours. And of course, it is not an option to return and try to retrieve it because we will not be Dumpster Divers for her. It's not happening. Yes, without a doubt we feel so very sorry for her, yet very sorry has its limits.

And then I feel it rising in me. I know it's not the time, but I just can't help myself. I start to laugh. Though not funny in one way, it is quite hilarious in another. And then I look over at Rie who is making an all-out effort to not join me in my poor attempt to stifle my laughter. If we don't look directly at each other we should be good, and if we do? It's not good as we always feed off each other's laughter.

Rie's husband, Tim, drove us to the airport to catch our flight to Ireland. Rie and I were riding in the backseat of the car, which we shared with all our carry-on luggage. From the front passenger seat, Les (who gets carsick) turned slightly to ask me, "So what do you have in your carry-on?" She barely finished her question when I quickly shot back to her, "My Wayward Son." I couldn't finish the sentence because I found what I said funny (and yes, quite clever), and I burst into laughter. As soon as I spoke those words, I turned to Rie because I knew in an instant that she got my joke; good girl, she was already laughing. From this, we both launched even harder into laughter. In the middle of our hysterics, Les looked at us, confused, then wondered aloud, "Okay you two, why are you laughing? My question wasn't that funny."

"Les, you know. The song?" No. No clue

"Carry On My Wayward Son?" Still no. Nothing from Les. And then I had to tell her, "The song by Kansas?" Each time I explained further, Rie and I only laughed harder. And then as if on an invisible cue,

Rie and I both started singing in perfect unison: "Carry on my wayward son, there'll be peace when you are done, dah-dah-dah-dah-dah-dah-dah (filler when lyrics are forgotten; often by me), don't you cry no more."

Les, now in on the joke, could only shake her head at her two silly sisters who can start laughing quite easily with each other. All it takes is looking at each other.

While our laughter worked on our way to LAX, it's not so much now as we've got pesto stains, garbage, and the like. So, with Les sitting on the bench, Rie and I, naturally being hyper-sensitive to the situation at hand, must turn our backs on Les as we fail miserably at stifling our laughter and calming our shaking bodies. We don't want Les to have to watch us. In fact, we try to spare her. Honestly. But we are unable to contain our giggles.

And then we hear Les. Turning back to face her, she is joining in the laughter but hers is a bit more of a laughing/crying. What else is there to do?

It seems that Rie knows what to do. Ever the caretaker, she steps in and takes care of Les. Her laughter is now under control (not mine), she offers up to our sis, "How about tomorrow I go back with you to Wimbledon so you can buy your gifts once again?" I now turn around and face them both. Then Rie continues, "I will skip Stonehenge and Windsor Castle to go back there with you. And here is 20.00 pounds to put toward the repurchase of your souvenirs." Les immediately agrees to the idea while also taking Rie's gift of money. I turn my back to the two of them. I mouth something kind of like these words but not exactly, "Ugh! Just grrrreat!" Taking a deep breath, I turn back to them. "Okay, I will go too, and here is 10 pounds toward your purchase." Les takes my money even though I am not even a part of this orange bag caper and she is not asking for the money, so why do I feel I need to chip in for her re-purchases? She has plenty of money. Here I am hopping on Rie's feeling guilty train.

And then I make myself pause—take a moment to deconstruct the course of events this afternoon. Rie's choice to return to Wimbledon makes sense. First, these two are not sure who is responsible for the mix-up although one believes it is the other yet by now it no longer matters. What does matter is Rie is being gracious in her offer to return with Les to Wimbledon the next day. She understands what this means to Les. The one who typically always goes along with the program, Les would not ask for us to make such a sacrifice. Rie knows this, so our little sis speaks the words for Les.

Rie then turns to me, "Why don't you go on ahead to Stonehenge and Windsor Castle while Les and I return to Wimbledon?" Les supports this idea as well. Even though I am not to thrilled about canceling plans (although I'm getting used to it, thanks to the Abbey and Globe), visiting Stonehenge and Windsor, they do allow me the opportunity to go off by myself and visit what we were all going to do together. Then again, I believe it's important to stick to our agreement of sticking together. So I tell both, "Stonehenge and Windsor Castle have been standing for centuries, they will be standing just as long in the future. We will save it for another time." Back in Ireland at The Cobblestone, I told Les: "I owe you one." It's time I pay up my verbal debt to her. I am happy to do so. One of them then suggests we visit Stonehenge and Windsor our last day in England, yet Rie has been hoping Bath would be one of the cities we visit as well. It's something we need to consider, together.

The Orange Bag Caper put to rest, we start walking toward the tube when we happen upon a beautiful art installation. We come to learn artist Ottmar Hörlwatch is responsible for this delightful aerial exhibit, "Lunch Break." There are forty little gold angels on swings, all the same size and same contemplative pose (one hand on the chin). High above an intersection is some sort of netting, and this is where the angels hang from, at varying heights. The angels swing yet not in unison because their push comes from cars or buses passing below. Like others, we stand in admiration and awe. And just like that, the cacophony of the city seems to slip away and in the midst of it all I'm smiling. I look over at Les and Rie, and they too are smiling. I'm feeling grateful for who we are: Three Moore sisters on a journey exploring new places and things, including us; we're getting it. Or to borrow Les' words, we'll be "fine, just fine."

That evening we come to broker an agreement: tomorrow we catch the changing of the guards at Buckingham Palace first. Les suggests we then go to Westminster Abbey, and then on to Wimbledon. Nice. Even so, I think we best get back to Wimbledon to be sure no hiccups prevent us from returning to the gift shop before it closes for the day. Then back to Westminster.

Again, she offers Westminster first. Again, I decline. I hope I don't come to regret this decision.

19

AN EPIPHANY, OF THE SECULAR SORT

LISTENING TO THE ADVICE OF OTHERS, WE ARE SURE TO ARRIVE EARLY FOR THE pageantry at Buckingham Palace in order to secure a good location for viewing. Our wait allows for some fascinating people watching; our wait is longer than the length of time it takes the guards to complete their maneuvers. Next, to the Tube and back to Southfields. (We catch on rather quickly with most things and in this case, we know not to exit Wimbledon for Wimbledon.)

The irony does not escape us: Les wanting to visit Wimbledon on this trip. The joke the three of us make is she can now say she's had the once-in-a-lifetime experience twice, two days in a row, sans tournament.

From the Tube, we catch a bus back to the courts (not walking there today.) Les duplicates yesterday's trash treasures, yet this time instead of the $75.00 she spent yesterday of her own money, today she only spends $45.00, thanks to the $20.00 donation by her willing young-est sister and the $10.00 donation from her 'Why Did I Donate?' middle sister. One of the three Moore sisters is quite happy.

Leaving the gift shop, we are on the lookout for the bus to take us back to the Tube to return to London. With no bus is in sight, we start doing exactly what we don't want to be doing right now: walking. The top of our feet feel as though they are melting through to the bottom of our shoes while our shoes feel as though they're laden with cement, making every step a grind. The fact that we are averaging six and a half miles a day in England might explain this. Still no bus as we inch ever-so-slowly toward the tube. And then we pass a restaurant—Sourdough Pizza.

In a quick instant, we decide today will be a down day and make an immediate right turn into the restaurant. As we go over the menu we start discussing our howling feet. In the meantime, I step outside to answer a phone call from my husband, Dave. While talking, I find myself standing in front of a sign advertising the Mani/Pedi Salon next to Sourdough Pizza. It's a sign. Okay, two signs. The sign to advertise and then a sign telling me it's time for the Moore sisters to get pedicures. I return to the restaurant and make a proposition to my sisters. "How does a pedicure sound?" I hear the response I'm expecting. With a resounding "Yes!" from both, I immediately pop over and make three appointments for three sisters with six very tired feet.

Because right at this moment pedicures win over any hunger we are feeling, we finish our pizza in record time and move on to the nail shop. It's in the middle of the foot washing when I have an epiphany. It's almost like a religious experience. Today? It's not just about repurchasing gifts. It's about us being together. It's about faith in ourselves that we can work through difficulties as they come our way.

Post pedicure, our feet feel calm and happy—for the time being—and in truth all three of us are feeling the same calm and happiness. When we walk past the grocery store with the big orange bags, I offer up to Les. "How about a lovely, oversized orange bag to once again carry your Wimbledon treasures? You know, for safekeeping?" They both give their sassy middle sis a "ha-ha!" We agree nothing will interfere with our good mood. Wimbledon gift repurchase? Check. Pedicures? Check. On to Westminster Abbey? Check. I try to imagine the Pomp and

Circumstance that has taken place in the Abbey over the many years. Once again, I can't contain my excitement. And once again it is not open for visitors today. The sisters are upset and apologize profusely. "It's not your fault the Abbey has closed again, but darn it I do feel some strong disappointment starting to creep in on me." Disappointment is one emotion that is tough for me, and right now I stand very close to jumping in with both feet and wallowing in it for a good long while. Instead I take a deep breath then silently reason with myself: There is nothing you can do about this. The Abbey is staying put, so you can visit another time, on another trip. I also recall what the mother of a long-time girlfriend would always tell her daughters:

"You can get glad in the same shoes you got mad in." Okay, well, I can do the same. I mean, here I am on the vacation of a lifetime with my sisters so why not be glad? I shift my mood, my body relaxes, and I am feeling good once again and ready to keep exploring. So I ask them, "Where to next?" With this question, Rie suggests, "How about the Chelsea District?" This will work as we have been talking about visiting this area. Heading there, we talk about how we remain fans of the movie "Notting Hill." We find Portobello Road and the store run by Will Thacker (the character played by Hugh Grant) then we take to wandering about the long rows of wares vendors have set up outside. We come. We browse. We buy. We are ready to go 'home.'

It's 5:30 p.m. when we exit Paddington Station. Once back in our dorm room, I mean hotel room, we do the usual: connect with the husbands, share the day, and get ready for bed. Then before going to sleep, we solidify our plans for the next day, our last in England. The three of us agree that an excursion to the ancient Roman city of Bath sounds much more relaxing (just the name "bath" influences us at this point seeing as we have a very tiny shower to match our tiny room) rather than heading off to see Stonehenge and Windsor castle. We reason that we can't see everything and every place. I had been trying to get us to Wales, yet it just isn't possible this trip.

During our early planning stages, Rie's siren call included trying to draw us in for a quick visit to Paris by way of the Chunnel. She loves Paris and wants to share it with us, so this night she mentions it again. "Why not go? It will be fun to ride the Chunnel and pop in for a quick visit to Paris!" When we consider the expense as well as the time spent in Paris, we conclude we will be in the Chunnel more than in Paris. We three cast our vote for Bath.

With this evening ending on a much calmer note than last night, I finally catch up on my journal writing, as it pertains to the day and the ranges of emotions. I am sure to include my fun surprise today: The three Alvarez sisters, Danielle, Nia, and Courtney, are in London. Years prior, at one time or another, each sister was a student of mine, and it just so happens we have remained in touch. It turns out they are staying in a hotel only a few blocks from us. The girls and their parents jumped across the pond to celebrate Courtney's graduation from a university in England. We make attempts to meet up, yet the travel gods have other plans that leave me to journal about them instead:

I naturally juxtapose the three Moore sisters with the three Alvarez sisters, Danielle (27), Nia (25), and Courtney, (23). Although these sisters are on the opposite end of the age spectrum from us, even with our forty-year age gap the six of us eerily align in birth order, behavior, and nature. For instance, Danielle considers everyone's interest and oftentimes remains silent about what makes her happy while wanting the group as a whole to have a good time; Les all the way. Nia, the middle, is the most vocal. Like myself, she too can struggle being sandwiched between two sisters who seem more alike to each other than to her. The difference in their personalities can often have Nia feeling like an outsider; a feeling I have been familiar with. And then there is Courtney. She is very aware of everyone else's feelings, and she comes equipped with a desire to please. Much too much like Rie.

Unlike the Moore sisters with many years of living now behind them, the Alvarez sisters have a riot of life running ahead of them, so naturally, we look at life through a different lens. I, along with my sisters, have come to understand age mellows us, well, somewhat. As far as the Alvarez sisters being in their twenties, it's wonderful that they are as close as they are and lucky for them that they get to enjoy many years sharing their sisterhood. Les, Rie, and I didn't have these early years as sisters because we were getting married, having children, living our own lives. But we get it now. Let me rephrase that. We continue to get it now as we practice at our sisterhood. I know the Alvarez sisters, and they are no different than the Moore sisters—they too must practice getting along.

Honestly, no matter the age of the sisters, the number of sisters, it's just not going to be entirely easy. It does help though if sisters fall under the Why not? category when it comes to taking a journey together. Here's to us, to the Alvarez sisters, and all other sisters who ask Why not? as they embark on a journey together.

20

SOAKING UP BATH

Traveling to Bath today, we take the sleek, modern, and comfortable Great Western Railway (GWR). We grab a table to share for the smooth ninety-minute ride, a direct line from Paddington.

The village of Bath is quaint, beautiful, and inviting. At the City Center stands the stunning Abbey of Bath, officially known as the "Abbey Church of Saint Peter and Saint Paul." The many spires of this church first pierced the heavens in 1611 and 400 years later, still do so. The elaborate carvings and intricacies on the outside alone are beautiful.

Before we go exploring, we first find a place to eat. During lunch, I thank Les for our blow-up. We all talk about how it helps to relieve pressure from our constant togetherness, and it allows us to enjoy this trip even more. I write in my journal, "*Odd, isn't it?*" Then again, perhaps it's not.

Finished with eating, we take the Hop-On/Hop-Off so we can decide where we want to visit first. It's Rie who speaks up. "Since we didn't go to Paris, I would like to visit the Fashion Museum here, if that's okay with you two?" As one who has sewn costumes from every period, Les and I don't hesitate, "You bet. It's perfect for you. Lead the way."

Within the two floors are beautiful fashions presented in various collections. This museum houses over 100,000 items and objects from a very early era to modern times. We find a few unique and clever installments that manipulate women's gloves now aged to a burnished golden yellow. There is a wreath made from hundreds of gloves. A glove crucifix. Without a closer inspection, the viewer is none the wiser that gloves are the artistic element.

"Rie, Les, look at this." Under very heavy protective glass, I get to admire one of the ceremonial gloves the young Queen Elizabeth wore during her 1953 coronation. "Take a picture of me next to the glove. It's like me standing outside of The Globe; this close to Westminster Abbey." I can only shake my head. But, in all honesty it's fine.

We hear from Rie, "There's an interactive space I want to try. They have gowns from the Jane Austin period, and I've always wanted to wear something like that." We follow her as she finds various outfits to try on, specially designed for guests to put on over their clothing.

"Rie," I tell her, "don't forget to try on the hats." It's our turn to witness Rie being happy in a setting special to her. Here, she is me in Belfast. Here, she is Les at Wimbledon. It pleases me that we can experience joy for and with each other. It's time to get back to the Hop-On.

We Hop-Off at the Roman Baths, construction built for water causeways and baths for people, all around 60 A.D. no less. It took about 300 years to gradually build up the rest of this area. Understanding the antiquity that remains standing before us, I take a few minutes to gently touch these very old walls. I am always curious about the workmen, most likely slaves, whose hands were placed, centuries ago, where I now place mine. This never ceases to stun my senses and stir my imagination.

While immersing ourselves in ancient culture, we realize too late we forgot to bring with us our modern technology, more specifically charging cords. All three of us end up with dead phones. Oh well.

Because tomorrow we leave for Scotland, we linger in Bath until the last train leaves for London. The ride back signals our time exploring England is ending. We purchase dinner (Les declines anything pesto) from the high-end food market inside Paddington Station and take it back to the room.

When we return to The Shakespeare, it is a good three hours past our usual return time. I only make note of this because our husbands have come to appreciate hearing from us at day's end. Isn't it nice being the traveler rather than the one staying home? The travelers know exactly where they are (okay, at times the three of us are an exception), and how they are doing. Those who remain at home can only wonder. And for our last day in England, it's been an all-around good day, ending on such a good note. At least for us, the three travelers.

Entering our room first, I see a piece of paper on the floor. Reading it I see I need to call Dave right away. With my phone charging, I call. "What is wrong? What is happening? Is it Mom? The kids? Is it Sully? What?" The response I get? He seems quite upset. (A rather mild interpretation, by the way.)

After not one husband hearing not one word from not one wife? Our three husbands decided their three wives to be victims of kidnapping. (Who in their right mind is going to kidnap three *Golden Girl*-ish broads?)

Oh wait, it gets better. The husbands concluded we went to Paris today (we never confirmed this with them), so they put their heads together and came up with the notion we are trapped in The Chunnel. No, we are dead in the Chunnel. But wait. No, we reach Paris but it's where we die; being dead makes it difficult to call. Okay, no we are alive (again/still?), and someone robs us of our money and cell phones. From what I am hearing, all scenarios of worry playing out in their (wild) imaginations fail to include the possibility of three dashing men pursuing the three Moore sisters. This could have happened. We should have gone to Paris, because we ended up missing so much fun. Well, not the dead part.

Oh, by the way, did I make any mention at all of how the three sisters also failed to share our relocation to The Shakespeare from The Dolphin? Right. Important information nonetheless. Back to this evening. When the guys don't hear from us, Dave takes the lead and calls The Dolphin. Funny, right? Yes, on our end. Not so much on his end. His conversation unfolded as such, and yes, I do recall this conversation rather vividly because he repeats it to me word-for-word:

Dave: "This is Dave Kraus. Please connect me to the room for Liz Kraus."

Front Desk Clerk (FDC): "We don't have phones in the rooms. I can take a message."

Dave: "What room is she in?"

FDC: "Let me check. Sorry, we don't have anyone checked in with us under this name."

Dave: "Yes you do."

FDC: "No, sir, sorry, we do not."

Dave: "What about Leslie Patch or Rie Dekker? One of them has the booking."

FDC: "No, sir, we don't have anyone checked in under either of those names."

Dave: "Yes. Yes, you do."

FDC: "No, sir. We do not."

Dave yells, I mean, Dave explains to me later just how incredibly nerve-wracking it is to be hearing such words; how there is no reaching me from the other side of the world. He feels so helpless. What does one do? Then again, I know exactly how it feels....

October 22, 2008. Dave was about to begin a trek to Everest Base Camp. He called me from the remote mountain village of Namche Bazaar nestled in at 11, 286 feet elevation, basically on the opposite side of the world. The signal was spotty at best. We struggled to hear each other. Dave's voice, at times, garbled at best. So, he figured shouting was the best option, and of course the only part of the conversation I heard loud and clear: "And I won't be talking with you again." Then the phone went dead. There was no calling him back. Instead, I must wait for two weeks before learning why he became so upset with me. Is this him telling me our marriage is over? On a phone and so far away? If so, oh, he'll regret this decision. This is me being pre-emptive. Not that it always works in my favor. This is really my fear taking over me.

That first night I was unable to sleep at all because I was so upset and confused, trying to make sense out of the last words he yelled at me. The next morning, when I reached my classroom, I went into my first ever, full-blown panic attack. There was no way I would be able to teach, so I called my dear friend and colleague who taught down the hall from me. She rushed to my room and found me sitting on the floor, sobbing. I could barely catch my breath as I told her I had lost Dave, and there was nothing I could do about it. With the expansive distance between my classroom in California and Dave trekking in Nepal, the only thing I felt was out of control. Completely out of control.

As my girlfriend held me, she tried to calm me. She knew Dave well, which made it believable when she assured me there was no doubt a misunderstanding. She arranged for someone to cover my classes so I could go home and bury myself under my covers for the rest of the day. What a kind gift. And weeks later when I am in a calm-enough state, I'm even willing to accept his collect call, he explains he was unable to hear me so yelling in the phone should help. We both agreed it didn't.

Water under the bridge, right? Where he waited only a few hours, I waited two weeks to hear from him. I guess I shouldn't compare. No. I compare. I digress.

Right. Now back to the matter at hand; husbands in panic mode. Not one sister answered as usual due to dead phones. No one called the guys. One of us always calls one of the guys. And now silence. Nothing but terrible silence on their end. So Dave makes the difficult call. Yet now? Dave is hearing nothing regarding the location of his wife and sisters-in-law, only dead air from The Dolphin's Front Desk Clerk (FDC).

Now, many might jump to the conclusion our current husbands are being too overprotective, perhaps even controlling. Yet, Les, Rie, and I know what it was like to live with husbands who did not care about us but decided to take control over us, which worked for a brief while.

But this time around Les, Rie, and I managed to choose better for ourselves. We are partners with men who adore us (why of course they do) and their masculinity is not threatened by a strong Moore sister as a wife. So this call is not meant for us to answer to them, and they are not controlling us; rather, they place this overseas call out of deep concern.

And then, for Dave, finally:

FDC: "Oh wait, I believe they are now at The Shakespeare. It's just right next door. Would you like for me to connect you?"

Dave: (Uhm, I think it best not to add content here at this time.)

Dave and I manage to walk ourselves back from the ledge. Mostly, I am sorry he has to experience the horrible fear that unknowing-ness brings.

It's time to change our conversation to our Golden Retriever puppy. Sullivan "Sully" James came home with us three days before I left on this trip, and now I fear he won't remember me after being gone for twenty-one days. Just to clarify, "he" being Sully, not Dave, although I do mention something about me being hard to forget. We laugh. He agrees. We are all feeling better and ready for a good night's sleep. But first, I make another entry in my journal:

The ancient city of Bath reminded us of how far we have come from our past while learning so much about each other in the present. How is it that we are now halfway through this twenty-day trip together? Honestly, I'm grateful for all that has happened to us here. With our sister tent remaining intact, we are Scotland-bound.

21

OUR CLOWN CAR AWAITS

I scheduled an 8:30 a.m. pick-up to transport us to Kings Cross Train Station. I was also very specific: "We require a large sedan or mini-van as we are three passengers, three suitcases, and three carry-ons."

"Yes. Got that. Right away, ma'am. No worries." So efficient and helpful. Yup, "no worries" at all.

Facing us next is the momentous task of getting our luggage back down the sixty-two steps. The three of us and our luggage make quite a sight, enough for a young teenage girl and her dad to take pity on us and help carry a couple of suitcases down. While very grateful, I can't help but think, where were these two when we were hauling the luggage upstairs? Oh well, grateful, nonetheless.

Settled in the lobby, I check my watch: It's 8:30 a.m. I suggest Les and Rie wait with the luggage while I go outside to wait on the front steps for our car. Okay, some concern. We have a train to catch. And trains are all on time, so if passengers are just one minute late they are left behind. So it's imperative we arrive at the station on time.

Overlooking a very small car pulling up to the curb, I continue to search down the road for a car that fits our needs, as per my request. The effervescent driver jumps out, greets me with a big smile and a happy, "Good morning to you."

"Well good morning to you too." I think to myself, *what a pleasant man. And he even goes inside to help his customers. Nice.* And then I think I hear my name although I'm not quite sure due to the very strong accent of this gentleman.

"Elsbeth?"

"Elizabeth? Yes. I'm Elizabeth."

"Do you need a ride to King's Cross Train Station?"

"Yes."

"Well, let's get your suitcases in the car."

"Sir, thanks," I say in a joyful voice. "I guess it wasn't made clear that we need a bigger car. Not only me but also my two sisters need to go to the train station, not just our luggage." He laughs at my comment, which makes me happy that he understands I am not being rude, rather curious how in the blue blazes he is going to make this work. Better yet, he will see we need a bigger car and get one for us. I turn around to signal to Les and Rie to come outside. When they see our transportation, I can see the surprises on their faces as well. "He says he can make it work." And just like that, he makes everything fit, with one caveat. Putting Rie's suitcase on the front seat requires being covered up with a sweater or a jacket. This only makes sense once we learn it is illegal in London to have a suitcase in the front seat. We need to catch a train, so sure, happy to be in cahoots with him. I also reassure him if he gets a ticket, we will pay for it. More specifically, "The Bank of Leslie" can pay for it, because, after all, England is her country. Rie and I both agree with this idea with laughter in our voices.

Though the three of us must squeeze in an extreme sardine-like position in the back seat, we start a conversation with our driver. He shares how several years prior he fled his war-torn country and escaped to England. And even though he brought with him a high level of education and skills, he drives a cab in this new land as a means to survive. The three Moore sisters shake their heads in disbelief because once again, as with our experience in Belfast, such visible suffering from war has never been on our radar. What's important is that it's there now.

We arrive at the station on time and citation-free. The real trick becomes extracting our bodies and luggage. It comes to us that we must look very much like clowns exiting our small car. Once we passengers and luggage are out, our driver sends off to Scotland, with prayers and blessings of "peace, health, and safety." We truly appreciate his verbal gifts.

Tickets purchased, we make our way to the gate for our next destination: SCOTLAND. Taking turns getting something to eat and use the facilities, I jot a few thoughts in my journal:

England is a country steeped in centuries of royal lineage according to birth order, their struggles in bitter battles, and the waging of wars. It's also in this country where we as sisters came to struggle, disagree, argue, yell, and cry only to then put down our armor to hug, forgive, and experience grace for each other. For all three of us, losing our sisterly bond is a hill not worth dying on. We move toward Scotland as an even stronger unit than when we first start this journey together.

Cheers, England!

Photo 1: A very cold bus bench; not just the weather.
(Paddington; London, England)

Photo 2: It's getting a wee bit warmer.

Photo 3: And we're back!

We finally 'meet' this respected and beloved military leader.
(St. Paul's Cathedral; London, England)

Center Court, Wimbledon.
(Merton, England)

"Lunch Break." Art Installation by Ottmar Hörlwatch.
(Next to St. Paul's Cathedral)

The Abbey in the City of Bath.
(Somerset, England)

The 'Moore' we get together, together, together,

The 'Moore' we get together, the happier we'll be.

(Children's song; lyrics modified)

PART THREE * SCOTLAND

22

EDINBURGH AND THE PROMISE OF AN ELEVATOR

THE THREE OF US RIGHT NOW? FROM HEAD TO TOE? WE ARE TIRED AND MORE than a bit weary. Feeling the last forty miles we demanded of our feet, we are looking forward to the five-hour journey. We're seeing this time as a bit of a respite, especially for our feet.

Our destination, Edinburgh (ED'n-burah. All who choose to pronounce it Ed-in-burg receive a gentle correction from locals.) As a reminder, this is Rie's country, which means she gets to choose her room and her special place to explore. Here I go, getting ahead of myself again. We need to arrive first.

As our train speeds along the tracks, the lovely countryside races hard to keep up with my field of vision. The slowing for each stop allows me to take in a longer view of the Scottish landscape. It does not disappoint.

Upon arriving at our destination, Waverley Station, we disembark the train only to end up in a very long and very slow queue. It's not all dire news when we meet our queue mates—a dozen or so elderly gentlemen wearing beautiful long, vibrant red coats, many with various ribbons and shiny medals splayed across the left breast. We learn (because I ask) they are of the retired division of the Royal Guards, as in Queen Elizabeth's Royal Guards. I am guessing that the youngest one in this lot of jolly-looking fellas has not seen fifty for about twenty years. Even so, they are so darn cute and hard to resist. I make mention of the crowded train to some of these charming gents, "Is it always so crowded on the train to Edinburgh?"

"Oh no, Love, it's Fringe time." Ah, yes. I recall Rie sharing about this month-long event while in the middle of planning for Scotland. "There is The Edinburgh Festival Fringe Society, we can check it out."

The Fringe is known as one of the largest celebrations of arts and culture worldwide. During this time, Edinburgh's population swells from 482,000 to over a million–for the entire month of August. And yes, we will be there in the thick of it. "It goes on during the day, most of the night, and for the entire month of August. We can check that out if we want."

On this particular weekend of the celebration, these gentle and once gallant warriors arrive to participate. They proudly share that they will be taking a lead role at the opening of the festivities each day this weekend. "We will be playing our instruments as we lead the charge." I am thinking *Uhm, "charge" seems a bit aggressive for these older lads.* And then just as quickly, "Is that an American accent I am hearing?" Starting the last third of our trip, all three of us now roll with the whole accent question and say what they want to hear but what we still do not. "Yes, yes it is." And then? It's as if they are now finally free to confess a soldier's long-held secrets, their stories come tumbling out all at once, in particular the joys of meeting American girls during war time. One talks about a girl from Texas. Another about a sweet nurse he met from Virginia—he thinks, that is if his memory serves him correctly. The memories of these girls still light up dim eyes, and I find it all rather sweet.

Then they bring themselves back into real-time and start asking us questions, which are both charming and funny, to which we reply, "No, you can't have our phone numbers." "Yes, we are all married." Put the uniform back on these aging soldiers and their mind convinces them that they are young once again and ready to pursue (middle-aged) American 'girls.' Sly old dogs. Well good for them: the mind is willing, but the legs? They need to save their strength and energy for leading the charge into the stadium.

We take a few photos together before we say our goodbyes. It's our turn for a taxi, and we find one that is more appropriate in size for our needs than in England. We are ready for our last home away from home.

As our driver eases his way into the right lane, he then makes a slow turn. I am not sure if it's on purpose, yet I appreciate that he does because that's when we see her and are instantly smitten with her beauty and can't quit staring. She is majestic as she stands in such grandeur high above her city. All heads must lift toward the heavens to acknowledge her. She is simply breathtaking in her unadorned presence. She is "The Castle of the Maidens" and this grand dame remains stunning even at 900 years of age. Created out of large stone, her builders embedded her foundation into an extinct volcanic "plug" (volcanic landform when lava hardens), making her impenetrable to all enemies. We are definitely going to make time to visit this beautiful lady.

While taking in all the city sights, we realize our driver is leading us farther and farther from Edinburgh's City Center. We aren't too sure about this, being so far on the outskirts, yet the driver assures us we will be happier residing in the town of Cramond, staying at Fair-A-Far. The name evokes an image of a thatched cottage in the woods. Our driver reassures us. "By residing farther out, the constant festival crowd and their noise will not be a nuisance. Trust me, it never stops."

Good to know. Besides, we love that our third home has a fairytale name. But when our driver announces our arrival, there is no magical cottage but instead a cluster of multi-story residential buildings. On the outside wall of our building is the sign Fair-A-Far Cottages. Home. Rie double-checks the paperwork to confirm our address; our imagination got the best of us. "Well, at least it has a lift! See here in the paperwork?" We will much appreciate a lift. But the affirmation of having a lift isn't the point, not at all. What is the point is that we reassure Rie she has this correct because we know the last thing our little sister wants to do is make a mistake. To better understand what drives our sister is to better understand our mom.

When our oldest brother was born, Mom was nineteen. When our baby sis was born, Mom was twenty-seven. Mom delivered five healthy babies in eight years (put another way, forty-five months being pregnant.) And by the way, each baby was larger than the last, which brought Rie in at over 10.15 pounds. Needless to say, by this time mom was fatigued, as was her body. Fast forward a few years, and at some point in her young life Rie heard Mom say, "I cried when I learned I was pregnant with you." These words were grouped as such because they best represented Mom's exhausted physical and mental state. And while spoken aloud in a moment of absolute weariness, Rie's young ears took them to mean Mom didn't want her, which was not the case at all. And even though the true intent was reconciled many years later, until that time Rie's young mind took Mom's words to heart and conjured up for her young self the will to quiet her voice, which evolved into being an outside observer within her own family. To avoid detection, Rie also practiced the art of invisibility. She didn't play with her siblings but instead her baby dolls; they wouldn't cause waves and in turn, not draw attention to her. But most of all, Rie decided to be as perfect as possible; now there's an easy life decision, to be sure. Our little sister was driven to prove that even though Mom didn't want child number five, she would come to change her mind and even appreciate Rie because this little one worked especially hard at pleasing by staying out of sight, out of the way, and out of trouble.

When Rie repeated this to her sisters in our later years, it broke our hearts. It has broken and shaped Rie's heart and mind for much too long. Even so, here it all is, packed in her suitcase, just waiting to make an appearance at just the right time, which is now. So when it comes to getting the elevator right, Les reassures Rie, "We believe you, sis. It's fine." The particular truth at this moment though has nothing to do with Rie but rather how we are a bit gun shy after The Shakespeare. Yet once again, the paperwork Rie is holding in her tight grip does in fact list a lift is one of the amenities. We again give our little sis kudos.

Getting inside the building proves a bit tricky due to the first set of heavy glass doors meant to keep out the winter weather (storm doors; not found in Southern California), and then another set of heavy glass doors that prove a bit unwieldy. We finally juggle ourselves as well as our luggage through door number two where we find ourselves ensconced in the small lobby. We see the flight of stairs. Then again, who cares? We sure don't. We turn our focus to the elevator.

And just like that, all the magic drains from the building that houses our magical cottage. There is yellow caution tape everywhere. It goes across. It goes diagonal. It goes vertical. And I go "**" when reading the elevator ceased to operate the day before our arrival. (Ah yes, the lucky Moore sisters. We know this by the lovely typed note taped over the middle where the two doors meet (this will most certainly stop anyone pushing through the caution tape to use the elevator). The typed note reads as such, sort of, as it seems the person responsible forgot to include sarcastic commentary, so I must do it for them.

OUT OF ORDER!! (Huh, we were struggling to discern this.)

We will have it repaired in eight to ten days. (Really? So soon? Please, take your time.)

We apologize for any inconvenience. (Please, don't give it another thought.)

Thank you, The Management (It's fine. And no, thank you!)

For the curious? Yes, this is the only lift in this multi-storied building of cottages (a/k/a apartments.) And how about I just go ahead and spoil the ending? It is still not working when we leave. It appears lifts will not be a part of our holiday experience.

Back to the present. There is nothing left to do but stand on the pedestrian side of the yellow tape and laugh. And laugh we do. Then we laugh even more once we tilt our heads as far back as we can to take in the stairs. Hmmm, now this pose has a familiar Shakespearean Hotelish feel to it. Our floor? The directory in the lobby places our "cottage" on floor 3½. Yes. That is correct. I verbalize my concern to Les and Rie. "Perhaps it's good news after all that the elevator is not working. How does an elevator stop on a half-floor? Well of course it's broken!" As we are trying to wrap our brains around this, the ascent begins.

These stairs.

They go this way.

They go that way.

And once again, they go this way. It's now we better understand the Scottish children's song, "Did you ever see a Lassie?" Picture if you will: these mature Lassies trying to haul luggage, heavier now with travel treasures, up floating steps made of cement. Each time a suitcase wheel hits against the next step up, a "we're here" clunking noise echoes loudly throughout the tall, narrow atrium because of the great acoustics.

Of course, the neighbors must be most pleased with our noisy arrival. Even so, I am here to confirm that it is not so easy going this way and that. But we finally reach the landing that leads us to the front door of our last temporary home.

"Great news, there are only forty-one steps. Hey, look at it this way; it's fewer stairs than at our favorite place in London." This information doesn't seem to help that much right now.

Upon entering, we see it's much like our first rental in Ireland: clean, tidy, modern, and blonde hardwood floors. This place differs in that it is only one floor. The one bathroom is on our immediate left. It has a bathtub and plenty of counter space for three women to spread out their products. We give each bedroom a quick peek then move on to the living room. (I imagine Les and Rie are doing exactly what I am doing; thinking about the sleeping arrangements.) But on to the living room. It has a couch, two stuffed chairs, a long oblong bench for a couple of people, a TV, and two large windows. The kitchen is large enough to include a dinette set, the right size (minus the stern warning to not move the table and chairs). Like the living room, the kitchen has a large window. We can see Rie is relieved. "This is a very nice and clean space. And plenty of room for us to spread out." Said another way, we now have space to distance ourselves from each other. And yes, we are ready to do so.

It's time to focus on the rooms. It's Rie's turn to pick the room she wants. And by the way, there are only two rooms. Needless to say, she chooses the master with one lovely big bed, a lovelier big closet, and the loveliest big window. (Closet and window are interchangeable, according to taste and personal opinion.)

Oh, and for those who are keeping track? Yes, Les, for this trip, is indeed the winner of 'Who Does Not Get A Room of Her Own?' Rie and I look at each other and burst out laughing, and there is no stopping us. (We will continue to laugh about this every time the subject comes up.)

"Ha, ha, yeah, real funny you two." And Les starts laughing as well; she is usually the first one to laugh at herself.

"Sis, it's funny to us. Hey, what isn't funny at this stage of the trip? And lucky you getting to share a bedroom with me. Who's the winner now, huh?"

Les responds in a voice full of laughter, "Oh, that's me, alright. I'm the winner! No doubt about it!" I'm now laughing so hard I have tears in my eyes. "See, you turned your frown upside down and look who is smiling."

The three Moore sisters continue to stand in the space between the two bedrooms and belly laugh. We know we are tired, road-weary, and about ready to be done with this journey, but first, Scotland.

After all of the crap Les and I had heaved out of our sister tent and left behind in England, sharing a room here shouldn't be too difficult. I am going to go with the flow; not fixing anyone or anything. (I've got this.)

The room Les and I share has two single beds, a single closet, and an even smaller single window, but the sill is deep. Let the room-sharing negotiations begin:

"Les, since you don't get a room of your own, just saying, in case you forgot I thought to mention it, the least I can do for you is to let you choose: window sill or little table? This is me being thoughtful of you, and I am even going to let you choose between the two beds. See how I am? I just want you to be happy because you don't get a room of your own. You know this, right?" I can barely finish my sentence because I am laughing so hard. We hear Rie cracking up from the other bedroom. Les throws a couple of pillows at me. She plops herself down on the bed of her choice.

"I prefer the table, thanks."

"Perfect."

I remember the oblong sitting bench in the living room and decide to employ it for the week keeping our suitcases off the floor. It's perfect for holding both suitcases. And the window in our room is easy to open, no fighting with an uncooperative screw like the one in Ireland; this one has a hand-crank instead.

The room works well for us. With our suitcases shoved next to each other to fit on the bench, they soon become one long suitcase. It doesn't take long before we are not sure where her things end and mine begins; both eventually regurgitating whatever we keep tossing into them. At this point in the trip, who cares? We sure no longer seem to.

Now that we are unpacked, we take a moment to just relax and for the first time on this trip we watch some TV. To be honest? We are each starting to fray a bit more around our edges. I have a sinking feeling we might soon be employing some of our unused jabs and comments shoved into those small zipper sections of our suitcases. We each still have plenty to aim at a sister or two even while we continue to make an all-out effort be better than that. At this moment I am sure to remind myself: *Don't invite trouble, Liz*

It's time to find a grocery store. Rie looks on her phone, not a Cost Cutter in sight, thank goodness, then she announces, and I kid you not, "It doesn't seem that far. Let's walk it." I go into instant face palm mode as I shoot back at her, "I cannot believe what you are saying to us. Really? It's not that far? Ireland? Ring any bells? Walking for miles and hours, maybe an hour, out of our way?" And yet we begin to walk. (Yes, we amaze even ourselves.)

We walk along the sidewalk (fingers crossed it's in the right direction), lined with old gray mossy rock walls with a multitude of flowers peeking their heads out between the cracks to see who is passing by, as well as flowery vines so curious that they twist and turn to see up over their walls. I whisper to them all, "Carry on. It's just us travel-weary Moore sisters."

The background to this chorus of color are the green hedges. Lots of hedges. A plethora of hedges: Round hedges, square hedges, low hedges, high hedges, and clever topiary hedges. And then in a category all of its own, the magnificently tall hedges. The most noticeable, according to some neighbors, are those encircling author J.K. Rowling's home (only the roofline is visible), which we will end up passing quite frequently to get to the market. At one point during a walk, Rie stands for a photo next to this hedge. It dwarfs her by at least thirty feet. Why so many hedges? Naturally, I am curious. And then, as it so often does, travel and life eventually intersect.

About a year and a half post-trip, my issue of Smithsonian magazine arrives and on the cover? "In Scotland, Living Life on the Hedge." Taking a photo of the cover, I immediately text it to Les and Rie so that they too might enjoy the immediate rush of memories flooding back from Scotland. Then I quickly flip to this piece: "Scotland Yards," by Peter Ross. Delving into the fascinating history and phenomena of hedges in this part of the world, Ross posits "what the white picket fence is to America, the hedge is to Britain" (54). As an American, I get the whole "white picket fence" mindset, and now I get the hedges in Scotland too. It's because Scotland and this first-hand experience hedges are now forever a part of my memories. No matter how much time passes, even words on the cover of a magazine have the power to evoke memories. This is what traveling does to a person: It opens up both the mind to new experiences and holds them there as a touchstone to enjoy any time later.

It's because of the beautiful hedges, walls, and landscapes (so much green) that we don't seem to be minding this walk. So far. For right now. Well at this moment. We shall see how long we convince ourselves with such foolish thinking. Les reassures Rie again that even if the lift is not working she has done a fine job with her reservation. Seeing our beautiful surroundings, she has every right to be proud of herself. I take a deep breath of the beauty around us. I exhale the joy of the surroundings in our new environment. It's a peaceful place tucked away in this corner of Scotland.

I add to the praise because it is lovely here. "Good job choosing an abode outside the City Center. I do believe you've selected the most peaceful of all three places."

And then, "Hey you two, what's that disturbance? It sounds familiar, yet I can't seem to put my finger on it." As it continues to get louder I turn to my two sisters who are not paying me one bit of attention but instead to their conversation, so I call back to them, in a louder voice, trying to interrupt them as they busily chat away, "What's that noise?" As it gets louder, so does my call to them. "Les. Rie. What's that sound?" Steadily it continues getting louder and louder, and it appears to be coming from—and then in unison all three of our heads bend skyward.

To our astonishment, and for one very quick minute, we find ourselves standing directly under an enormous passenger jet as it rapidly skims over us and the rooftops of the lovely village of Cramond on its final approach to a runway. And then everything fully registers. "What the heck? That is one big jetliner. And where is it going to land because one that size requires a lot of space for a runway." I immediately went to Google Airport near me. "Ladies, here's some news. We are just a ten-minute drive from Edinburgh Airport." Yes, our magical cottage just keeps getting more magical all of the time. Good luck strikes once again. I'd like to say out loud, *It can't get any worse*, yet even I know this would be just plain foolhardy on my part; I choose silence. While some things are out of our control, others are, such as how our relationship continues to get better between the three of us. So here's hoping all of our suitcase poltergeists are now nothing more than thin air, and we will come to enjoy the last stretch of our journey together. We can do this. I let them know "Our cottage is in the flight pattern for Where Scotland Meets the World," as I cite Edinburgh Airport's motto from their website. "Rie, perhaps go back to your paperwork and see if the owner also happens to include this in the list of things to enjoy while staying at his property. Hmmm, I think not." And then the three of us do what we do best: laugh. To be in the flight path of passenger jets to Scotland's major airport? It doesn't get much better than this for the Moore girls.

As time passes, we find ourselves assuming the behavior of the locals by learning to shut out the sound, most of the time. With each approach to the runway, it feels as though one need only reach up an arms-length to touch the underbelly of these silver birds, of which I take a lot of photos and videos. Even though each approaching jet begins to become familiar, they never cease to amaze me. But more than anything else, watching these jets has us thinking of our daddy. We each long for him. Les, Rie, and I have often shared how we were happy that in later years daddy became a source of support and understanding. As grown women, we each came to enjoy our own special, unique relationship with this Renaissance man. After his passing, we have refused to let him fade from us no matter how many years pass, and aircraft experiences bring him back into our presence.

All aspects of flight—from gliders to jets—forever fascinated our dad. If he were here with us, he would be on his back on the lush green Scottish grass waiting for the next jetliner to pass over him, smiling, happy, and thrilled. He pulled off the road countless times just to take in the thrill of a low flying aircraft, especially military jets. Perhaps his ultimate thrill was to witness the landing of space shuttles at Edwards Air Force base. So yes, he'd get a kick out of our location in Scotland.

As little girls, we struggled with Daddy's absence. It was Mom whom we counted on. It was Mom who did the heavy lifting raising five kids; such a parent doesn't often get the praise and accolades deserved. She read to us every night, and we would fall asleep to the hum of her sewing machine. All the while, Daddy was somewhere else singing or rehearsing his singing, often with his new chorale of which he was the leader and lead singer. He was where he preferred to be because our parents' marriage was coming apart, and nothing was able to stitch them back together ever again. Attempting to raise five little ones when they themselves were still growing up, they began to break apart before our very eyes and very sad hearts.

Once we became adults, Daddy's three daughters got the chance to know this ever-evolving man better. We found this busy music man to be warm, funny, intelligent, competitive, kind, and comforting, with a hard-to-miss twinkle in his blue eyes. We saw snippets of those traits while growing up. Too many times it was as if he was Mom's sixth child, the fun prankster. He modeled for his kids how to pull off one great prank after another, and from our family's large repertoire of pranks, there is an all-time favorite. It's when our parents took us for a hike one Sabbath afternoon. Rie, only four at this time, stayed close to Mom and Dad (avoiding trouble) while the rest of us kids advanced to put our plan into motion. At twelve years of age, Doug, the eldest, was the mastermind behind this plan. Oh, and a grand plan it was: "Let's move the car off the hill down into the valley and let Mom and Dad think the car has been stolen." That sounded like something our daddy would appreciate, even admire. Our plan worked as such: Doug would get behind the wheel, shifting the car into neutral. It would be up to ten-year-old Les, eight-year-old Liz, and six-year-old Brad to give the car a heave-ho but not until we heard Doug's command out the window from the driver's seat.

"Okay, push!" And so we did. And just like that Doug and the family car, a white Valiant station wagon, coasted down the hill (probably the height of a thirty-foot story building). When it finally settled to a stop, his three partners-in-crime rushed down and cheered Doug for his great idea. Then the four of us raced back up the hill and carried out the last bit of our plan, which was to act casual. It was hard because we could hardly contain ourselves as we waited for the moment of discovery.

And then it came. In a voice that reverberated throughout the hills. Our confused Dad turned to Mom, "Where is our car? "He rushed to where he parked it. Mom then screamed, "Someone stole it!!" And it was about this time Daddy crested the hill only to see the car at the bottom. "I must not have put on the emergency brakes!" We might have been wise to let them believe this to be the case, but we were too young and too full of excitement. "Fooled you. No one stole it. We pushed it down the hill. We hid it from you." We all were then puzzled by the absence of laughter.

Our parents decided early on that Kangaroo Court worked best for their crowd of kids, the four oldest in particular. What this came down to was 'All for One and One for All' and the beauty for our parents was no evidence was required for punishment. In this method, they dished out punishment equally for all; saved time. It was always Dad's job to deal with us.

For quite a while, we had a lovely, elderly woman as a babysitter. She knew our parents well because our families attended the same church. Because the five Moore children were so well-behaved she never hesitated to babysit. One Saturday evening with Mrs. Folks, she happily accepted our offer for some chocolates. To clarify, "our" being the four oldest. Later that evening Mrs. Folks gushed to Mom and Dad about us. "The kids were so sweet. They even offered me some chocolate from the prettiest box." Both parents were hyper-aware of what was in the "prettiest box." Most likely our trusting babysitter ate a chocolate-covered cricket, one of the many exotic choices bestowed upon us by an older cousin. I can't remember where he got them, yet how kind was he to share with his fellow jokesters? And yes, we found ourselves in Kangaroo Court the following morning. So there was that time.

And here we were again. The four of us are gathered over the whole 'hide the car' prank. We are in one of the bedrooms lined up in front of daddy and he started in on his questions, the same was applicable no matter what mischief we had concocted: "Whose idea was this?" He met only silence (I am thinking, *Don't you think it's at least one of us?*) "Tell me or you are all going to get a whipping." Daddy still hears only silence. (I answer the question in my mind, *Yes! A whipping sounds lovely.* Whenever faced with that age-old question so many of us have heard, "Do you want me to pull this car over and spank you?" My mind would race to *Sure, you bet. How did you know? Is now a good time?* I never figured out why we were asked when we didn't have a choice in the matter. But this is just how my brain works because it's always on overtime.)

Back to daddy and his questions: "So you are all willing to get a whipping even if you aren't to blame?" Silence. (Nothing new here.) Not one of us tattled on the other. We were pretty proud of ourselves. But this time, from Doug, "We just thought you would like our funny prank." And then there seemed to be a real struggle on Daddy's part not to crack a smile, but he remained stern in his position. Sort of. It didn't last long, and while he lectured us, no spankings were given. Instead, behind closed doors, away from Mom, his blue eyes took on a twinkle of recognizable mischief. He knew he had taught us well, just not quite this well.

The Moore children have a treasure-trove of memories. Right now I especially appreciate how these many years later they continues to come along to create deeper memories and add greater joy to this journey.

Now after some walking, we locate a small store that seems to stock everything we need. Laden with groceries, we begin the trek home. On foot, of course. As we continue to add to our current count of 7,700 walking steps, busses are passing us. We want to be on one, but how? Where?

As we reach home, we notice a bus stop across the street. "Do you guys feel up to figuring out the comings and goings of the various bus schedules and their routes? No time like the present, right?" And as I begin to look over the schedule I call Les and Rie over for some assistance. "What do you two make of this?" And as they attempt to make sense of it too, I volunteer, "Hey, I have no shame in admitting this is a challenge for three travel-weary brains. Maybe we tackle it in the morning after some sleep?"

But then an opportunity comes knocking. An elderly gentleman is slowly approaching. Guess which sister will be asking for assistance? And he looks like a local. (Clearly, our pattern of trusting any man whom we determine to be a local is now well entrenched in us. So much for working on this, yet then again this trip is almost over so who cares at this point.) "Hello. Yes. Excuse me. Would you please be so kind as to help us figure out the bus schedule?" He looks at me. He speaks to me. What on earth is he saying? I am only able to nod then add, "Sure, Yes. Thanks. Most helpful." He then follows up with some other words of which I can only guess what it is he is saying, so I give back to him, "Oh no, you have been such a help. Thanks." I turn to my sisters, who are of no help whatsoever. I whisper to them, "Do you think he understood me?" And as we watch this gentleman disappear around the corner, it's as if on cue the three of us can no longer stand but collapse onto the bus bench into nonsensical laughter. We can't seem to stop. Tears are flowing. We can't move. Oh but wait. Here comes another opportunity for assistance. A woman, about thirty, is coming down the sidewalk toward us. Failing miserably with the first effort, I am game to give it another try. What the heck. I warn with a giggle in my voice, "Okay you two. Straighten up. Quit laughing. Let me handle this." As though they would disagree in protest, but stifling their laughter is another thing.

My second attempt is a success. For this effort, I am happy to report that amongst the three tired brains of ours we collectively make sense of not only the bus schedules but also a majority of what this Scot is speaking to us. "Yes. We've got it. Thanks!" And this time, I mean it. We are almost giddy now as we make our way back to our faux cottage: No more walking for these six feet. No sir, from here on out we will be taking the bus. We unpack the groceries, eat, and then without much ado all head to bed earlier than usual. It's fair to say that we are beginning to run out of energy before each day is even near being done.

23

THE "I LOVE YOUR CALIFORNIA ACCENT" TOUR NEARS THE END

After a fairly restful sleep, Les and I wake to Rie offering to make us breakfast. The sis who nurtures others with her cooking is back in her comfort zone. We are most happy to oblige.

While eating, we make our plans for the day and decide to explore downtown Edinburgh. This means we will be catching the city bus, of which our confidence level is extremely high. Breakfast over, we take our first sister selfie in Scotland and then cross the street with confidence ready to board the bus that will take us to get downtown, Number 41. And just as quickly as we board the bus, we exit it. Yes, it's bus 41 alright but not going in the direction we need. So close.

On our second try, and from here on out, we catch Number 41 with such ease that we even assist other tourists at our stop, offering to all (who clearly need assistance) the correct direction, and the routes. "Oh sure, happy to help. No big deal. It's quite simple." Look at us. Experienced travelers, well, at least when it comes to bus route 41, and in one direction only.

For the first bus ride into the city, a Scottish woman introduces herself. "Hi, I'm Linda, good morning. I have been listening to you talk. Is that a California accent I hear?" Les is the one to respond to Linda. What? Fourteen days in, and look at Les being social with a stranger. Her confidence is blooming; it's lovely to witness. "Yes, yes it is."

Linda responds with a big smile, "I have a dear friend who lives in Southern California, and I always look forward to talking with her as I enjoy her accent so very much."

Then we learn she also frequents a town called Camarillo, just a few freeway exits south of where I live. Again. This world!

Linda is very helpful in advice as how to best negotiate downtown and the best stop for the Waverley Train Station. It's there we secure tickets for a variety of sights including the Castle on high (she keeps an eye on all as they move about her town), the Royal Yacht, and Holyrood Palace. We will take in the castle today and save the others for tomorrow.

Off the bus, we start with a direct path to Waverly when in true Moore sister fashion one of us—okay Rie—makes a sudden sharp left turn. Something bright and shiny has caught her eye. "Oh wait, I want to pop into this shop!" This will become our norm in Edinburgh. And we are completely fine with it. We soon find ourselves enjoying being in town, wandering around, and exploring. Right now though we grab something to eat and then purchase tickets for self-guided tours.

We then get on the bus at 3:00 p.m. with the promise that it goes directly up the steep hill to "The Castle of the Maidens." However, once on the bus, there is nothing direct about it as it travels every street, back alley, roundabout, and any other detour. We doubt our driver is lost, yet we have somehow landed ourselves on a version of Hotel California-on-wheels. We get on, yet we can't seem to get off. We must devise an escape plan because the castle doors close at 5:30 p.m. We conclude we have no choice but to pick a random stop for what appears to be a reasonable walking distance to the castle. The more appropriate word here is hiking distance. Lucky for us, it's a beautiful day for a hike we did not expect to take.

When we finally storm the castle doors, it's 4:00 p.m. With only an hour and a half to explore and admire, we start in the Kirk (church) of Fallen Soldiers. Here we pause to take in the names of thousands of Scotland's brave who gave their life for their country. Upon exiting, we tour inside the castle before heading off to the Red Room. Here is where the king sat with his knights. On display are full knight armor and their weapons of war. This great room leads us to the Regimental Museum for The Royal Scots Dragoon Guards. Time is running short, but we stop to take in the stunning panoramic view of Edinburgh spread out below. And much too soon we must pass through the castle gate before it closes, and yes the original spikes remain in place.

We leave the castle in time to catch the early evening bus ride. It is nice to be so relaxed in our temporary Scottish town and 'home' even though it feels so very far away from our California.

24

FAIR-A-FAR, A BIT TOO FAR FOR ONE OF US

THE NEXT DAY, WE HEAD TO THE COAST TO TAKE A TOUR OF THE QUEEN'S LITTLE boat, the 133-foot long Her Majesty's Yacht (HMY) Britannia. We find it at the docks of Port of Leith, and when we see what is at the dock, we are very surprised: an equally large shopping mall. I know, it sounds weird, yet it works. Once on the Britannia, we spend a few hours exploring all five of the decks from stem to stern and port to starboard.

We are enthralled as we tour this ship. We have access to the living quarters, and although partitioned off with Plexiglas, we see where the Queen had her room, her prince another. The informal living room. The honeymoon suite for Charles and Diana. The formal dining room is rented out for events, and because there is one occurring later that day the tables and room are beautifully decorated. On a lower deck, there is a full surgical suite, dental area, laundry room. It was a floating city and able to handle emergencies of all kinds.

We find the only exit is via a souvenir shop. We look around, make a few purchases, and head outdoors to catch a bus back into the city.

Back in Edinburgh, we walk over to The Royal Mile, named as such because it's the distance between "The Castle of the Maiden" at the top of the road to "The Palace of Holyrood," at the bottom of the road. In between are churches, statues of famous Scotsmen, a variety of shops, restaurants, and street entertainers, including men in full Scottish regalia playing bagpipes on various corners. The area is a fun place to stroll.

As we make our way toward the bottom of the hill, we enjoy the eclectic Fringe groups of entertainers. Les, Rie, and I are in complete agreement that the men in kilts playing bagpipes are by far our most favorite. The whole kilt thing is so romantic, thanks to the books and series, "Outlander."

Pausing along the way, we come to find ourselves stopped alongside the ever-growing crowd of spectators also appreciating the street entertainment. I notice the couple standing next to us enjoying all that is going on around us. I start talking with them; they seem nice enough. "Quite the fun place, isn't it?"

"It's a lot to take in but we are enjoying it. We had planned for some time to be here specifically for The Fringe, so this is exciting for us. Are you here for the same reason?"

"As it happens, I'm on a vacation with my two sisters," who have now joined in the conversation, "and we happened to book our trip during the same month as this wild party."

"We booked a cruise that stopped here specifically for the festivities."

"Wow. What a fun idea. By the way, I don't hear an accent. American?"

"Yes, you too?"

"California. Southern California. (Because our state is so large, it's a quick identifier.) How about you?"

"Yes, the same. We are from San Bernardino." I turn to Les, "Well are you going to tell them or do you want me to?" With that lovely smile of hers, Les shares, "I live in Riverside." The couple could not believe it.

"How random that we meet here yet our cities where we live are pretty much next to each other?" I say, "I guess it's true, the big world becomes quite small rather quickly at The Fringe."

We all enjoy our shared disbelief, say our farewells, and continue walking downhill toward the front of the gates of the "Palace of Holyrood" (rood, a very old word for cross). The petite palace is where Mary, Queen of Scots, once reigned and it remains an official residence of Queen Elizabeth and her family when they happen to be in town.

It's only after we complete our self-guided tour of the interior that we discover the best part, at least for us. On one side of the exterior is the Abbey, a stunning structure built by King David I of Scotland in 1128.

Many sources recount the same story behind this Abbey:

The King is out hunting when he is thrown from his horse. A stag appears—not at all pleased to be disturbed. Looking up at the stag, the King notices a crucifix between its antlers. For some miraculous reason, the stag leaves instead of mauling the King. It's a grateful King who takes this as a miracle, so he builds the Abbey in response to this sacred moment.

And because countries do what they do, it's around the sixteenth century when the English set about doing their best to destroy this palace and its Abbey. The aftermath of their destructive intentions is still visible as the ancient Abbey, now so very frail, is without a roof. Her stained-glass long-gone leaving the window casings vacant, their only purpose left to them is to provide unobstructed views of the royal gardens and land beyond.

We visit when the sun slants beams through her broken openness, delicate carvings, and odd-shaped holes that in turn produce beautiful mosaic patterns scattered all about the uneven Abbey floor. Standing about her beautiful ruins, she mesmerizes us. I find upon quiet reflection her brokenness leaves me somehow feeling whole. Perhaps the sacredness of this Abbey has never diminished.

Upon leaving the grounds, we make our way to a bus that will take us back into the heart of the city. Along the way, we notice some new banners heralding a craft fair. It's taking place at the foot of the castle, so we make our way there because it sounds like a place to find unique gifts. And although over a hundred artisans sell their handcrafted wares here, their product must first be approved by a jury of local design experts. This ensures all work being sold is of the highest quality, as well as offering up a diverse choice of items. Sounds good to us. Let the hunt begin.

I turn to Les and Rie, "Is this magical or what? I feel as though we've stepped back in time." Perhaps it's because instead of open space between the booths, here sellers use a decorative cloth that demarks their space. The fluttering cloth adds to the romance of an earlier time. "Don't you love it?" Les is making a statement of joy. I agree. "The castle adds to the magic too." It fills the entire skyscape. Rie describes it best, "It feels as though we are about to have an old-world experience." I nod my head in agreement then add, "It truly does. I can't put my finger on one specific thing but combined they all permeate the senses and make me feel as though we are about to travel into the past. Are you two ready to enjoy it?" We take this time to wander off on our own (I know. What?). And then feel delighted when bumping into one or the other or both. We share what catches our interest, split up again, resume the hunt.

There is a feeling of lightheartedness as we go about searching for treasures. I have fun bantering back and forth with the merchants and when I hesitate on an item due to its price, they encourage me to barter, which I always enjoy. "Give me an offer, Love." Let the delightful back-and-forth begin.

After more than a couple of enjoyable hours spent wandering about in the past (or maybe the delight is from alone time?), we find each other back at the entry and are eager to share our favorite finds from the fair.

First Les. "I bought this glass-blown fairy for Lacy (her daughter) because she loves fairies." Great choice! Now Rie's turn. "I bought these dryer balls made of wool, but I also saw these beautiful salad serving utensils made from the burl of a tree, and I couldn't resist them." She holds up her treasure for us to admire. I can't resist praising her choice of purchases. "You have such exquisite taste." Now it's my turn. As I begin reaching into my bag I tell them, "I have this pair of the most beautiful wooden salad serving utensils made from the swirled burl of the Scottish Elm." Yes, exactly like Rie's. And no, both unaware of the other. And she can't resist. "Why Diz, you have such elegant taste." It's true, I do. Oh, so does Rie.

It's time once again to rejoin the bustle of modern Edinburgh. We head to the bus stop, truly content about our day. I shoo away that passing thought once again. *Never mind. No need to invite mischief. Besides, our sister tent is feeling rather secure and comfortable.*

Getting off at the stop by our favorite little market means we have a mile to walk back to Fair-A-Far. At this point in our lives, our journey, what's a mile, right? I don't believe I have yet to mention this walk is not entirely level. To walk it is to feel a bit of incline. So the mile to the market? Quick and enjoyable. The mile back to the cottage? A bit more tiring.

Just as we did in Ireland, we always carry our small umbrellas. Well, two of us are carrying umbrellas on this particular day although each of us carries our treasures from the fair along with a bag of groceries. As is our usual, Rie and I are several paces ahead of Les, so I am only talking with Rie about noticing a change in weather. "The sky is getting darker. We'd better make a fast sprint home before it starts raining on us."

"We've got this, Diz." And then again, not all of "we've." Rie and I turn around to look at Les. Our non-sprinter sis is walking, then again, more of a trudge I'd say. While we wait for her to join us, some fat raindrops reach us first. "Wait. No, we don't 'got this.' A quick sprint home won't work for one of us. We'd best turn around." Rie is right. So we make a U-turn back to Les and the bus stop that has a lovely shelter, and we wait. At least taking the bus means we have a much better chance of reaching our "cottage" nice and dry.

The merciful and thoughtful Rain God waits until we step into our building before opening the skies and letting the rain come with a force. And it comes. And it comes. Rain and more rain. More rain than Galway. More rain than these Southern California natives have seen in ages. It is delightful. With no sign of the downpour subsiding, we get comfy in our sweats and our cozy socks. Relaxing in front of the TV, feet up, Rie volunteers to make toasted cheese sandwiches for dinner, and we accept without hesitation.

Hearth and Home. This is where Rie is most comfortable. She enjoys sharing her home, including when our nephew Stephen came to live for a long while. Rie makes room for one and all.

It was because of Les' son Stephen, we came to call our little sis Rie. When Stephen was quite young, he struggled to say Laurie as he seemed to hear only the last syllable of her name. He pronounced her Rie and from then on we all joined in (except Mom, who still calls her Laurie).

As mentioned earlier, Stephen lived a spell with Rie and Tim along with their son Jacob. During this time frame, Stephen was twenty years old and Jacob (who had by now assigned me the nickname Diz) was just two. This age gap didn't stop these cousins from what they each enjoyed doing every morning together, watching cartoons. Their routine went as such: As soon as Stephen sat down on the couch, Jacob climbed up right next to Stephen who in turn put his arm around his younger cousin. Settling in, Stephen would ask Jacob the same question, each time, every morning, without fail, "Are you comfy?" Saying nothing, Jacob would simply look up at his older cousin and smile. This continued for several weeks when one morning Jacob reported his confusion, "Mommy, Stephen thinks my name is Comfy." Sweet logic from the mind of a two-year-old. It's also a sweet memory that forever tugs at my heart. Tears bubble up each time I think of it.

Dave, Brent-Stig, and I were living on the property when Stephen was there and he reaped the benefit of both aunties; we doted on him. It was Aunt Rie who provided home and hearty meals while it was Aunt Liz who provided the humor. Stephen had a quick wit, which was the source of much laughter. He also spent a lot of time with his cousin, my son Brent-Stig. From the time they were little guys, they called themselves brothers. And then it was time for Stephen to return to his home in Riverside. It was only a couple of years later when he became fatally ill. His passing left broken hearts strewn all about his friends and family. And then there is Jordyn, his daughter. Now in her mid-twenties, she was only a two-year-old at that time, and now she must depend upon stories to learn about her daddy.

And now, this evening, as the three of us Moore sisters sit around the table enjoying both food and conversation, we realize we are feeling quite grateful for what we have and had.

With only three more days before we return home, we all agree we are feeling less human and more like zombies, which leads Rie to come up with a brilliant idea, "Let's soak our feet in the tub!" Les asks, "Why is this just now dawning on us?" No matter, one of us starts to fill the tub with very hot water. Rie adds some table salt and lots of coconut bath liquid; it works at this moment because it's what we have, and no one volunteers to walk the mile to the market in the rain to get anything else, so we are happy to make do.

And then of course, true to form, we turn silly. I capture on video the three of us on the tub's edge. Us silly, us lucky, us fortunate Moore sisters.

Perhaps it is Rie's cooking.

Perhaps it is the foot soaking.

Perhaps it is the steady rain.

Whatever it is, sleep comes easy to us all.

25

THIS IS GOING TO GET EASIER, RIGHT?

WE HAVE NO EARLY BUS TO CATCH THIS MORNING, SO WE ARE SLEEPING IN. IT'S a lovely way to start our day. While still in bed, Les shares how she is already feeling about this day. "Let's keep it low-key. Maybe Rie wants the same." I just listen as I begin getting out of bed. Les is right behind me, and soon we join up with Rie in the small hallway between our two rooms. She greets us only to follow with, "I need to tell you something." She then proceeds to tell us of her plans: "I want to sketch today. To be by myself."

I reflect on last night. *Hum, too much closeness soaking our feet?* And then I switch to becoming more realistic. We know this about Rie. It's who she is. She needs time to herself, so it's not her words that surprise, yet Les and I are caught completely off guard. Interesting, she didn't mention this last night. So now I must ask our youngest sis in my calmest of voices, "Rie, how many times did I ask you about three sisters for three weeks? And remember what you said to me?" She looks at me and says, "Probably how we needed three weeks. And it will be fine? Something along those lines?" I give her a nod and say, "Yes. Yes, you did." And then comes a reality Rie is only now sharing at this very late juncture in our journey, when she educates us on the fact that no matter who she travels with she starts to wear thin of everyone around 2.75 weeks. "Even with Tim. It always seems to be around two and three-fourths weeks when I'm ready to get back home. But once we are home, I forget about it. I love the whole planning part, the packing, all the while thinking this time it will be different." This isn't great news for her sisters to be hearing during weeks two and three-fourths. We are almost ready to head back home. Yet in the meantime, Rie requires time alone to ponder, to meditate, to sketch. Whatever. But after these many days of travel, we now find ourselves with a different Rie from the one who we started with. Again, part of her mind's hard drive has her not wanting to make a mistake. She reasons aloud to us. "I know what's best and it's to be separate from others when I feel this way because I will make a mistake somehow by saying the wrong thing." So this is where we are. My mind is trying to reconcile her decision while my heart understands. She continues. "I know it probably doesn't make sense to you both, but I'm hoping you understand."

"Les and I want to understand, yet what about our agreement? This is confusing. You must see this, right? We need to know how to reconcile this. To understand this for you, for us."

Although we've each had our turns when we had no other choice but to be strong women, I have never suffered the difficult losses my sisters have experienced. Les, the horrific pain and unbearable loss of Stephen. How my sister puts one foot in front of the other, I will never truly understand. And for Rie, along with the heart-wrenching losses of her unborn children, she later also suffered the total loss of her home.

In early December of 2017 in Ventura County, the infamous Thomas Fire erupted. It almost instantly transformed into a monster snake that made its way up the steep and hilly terrain to reach Rie's family home. It was with spite that it slithered in through her new windows. It squeezed tightly all things with its searing red grip then left only heaps of ash before it moved on to destroy so much more in its wake.

Les and I did our best to alleviate Rie's sadness from this remarkable loss. It didn't seem like much in the grand scheme of things, but we surprised her by gathering up all of the photos we had of her and her family; she was thrilled. But even though the fire has long been out, it continues to singe our little sis.

I understand what Rie has been through. I just don't understand the decision to take a day for herself. Les doesn't either. Perhaps we were too nonchalant with Rie's proclaiming: "I will be just fine, I've traveled this long and even longer. I'll just go to my room." Yet now she wants to leave? Her sisters, especially Les, are struggling with Rie's emotional shift, and then Les clears the thick air, "You need to think about what you are asking!" Well now, look who learned from London how we all benefit when we share our words rather than stomping off, or trying to. This trip just keeps generating more and more surprises. Then I try my hand at not fixing but reassuring Rie. "Trust me when I say how Les and I understand the feeling of wanting to break away from the whole feeling of being joined at the hip." Then, Les interjects, with the ever-so-slightest hint of older sis sternness. "You are not going to do this because Liz and I didn't do it in our countries." (Cue the suitcase poltergeists.) She continues, "I think it's selfish! Why do you suddenly think it's okay for you to break our agreement, because this is what it's about."

Say what? I think to myself as I take in Les's determination. And me? Trying not to be the fixer. What is going on here? I know for one thing, we are no longer road warriors but rather weary of being on the road, together. Then Les continues with what's frustrating her. "Tell me how is it that we stick to the plan and now, come to Scotland, we scrap the plan? We are just as weary as you are but why are you going to change up things now?" And there you have it. Les. Yes. This sister is the one to speak such risky words at this most vulnerable of moments; Rie could become our second "stomper-offer." What also makes this difficult for Les is how she operates: Go along with the program, and fairness. She is not seeing this in Rie who is set on going rogue. At least it feels like that right now.

We seem to have a squall brewing. And at this delicate moment, it's for certain our sister tent will not withstand another storm of words, emotions, and now weariness as well. With my mind racing about for ideas, solutions, anything, it settles on uncomfortable words from Homer's epic poem, 'The Odyssey': "Let him lose all companions and return under strange sail to bitter days at home." *Why, oh why does my mind torture me so? Is this what we are in the midst of right now? Losing us? No. No, we are better than Homer and his men, by far.* And then my mind is distracted once again, this time by something so very difficult: Silence. It might as well be a pair of cymbals clanging around our heads as we stand so very still waiting for Rie's decision. More silence. More waiting.

Rie continues to weigh, to consider. It is so sad that she struggles not to make a mistake. It's a tough wait, I must confess. All that repair-work to the side of our sister tent in London? This time we might be creating a gaping hole so large our tent will be sent flying away from our grasp. And if it does? I am not chasing after it. I am too damn tired. And by the looks on their faces, Les and Rie have to be sharing the same sentiment.

So at this very moment, even with so many steps, laughter, and growth behind us, who cares? We sure don't seem to. And what about our strongest tent stake that secures our sister tent above all else, laughter? It's sure not working for us now. We all know it. No one is laughing.

And then from Rie, whose honesty can poke: "I don't think you guys should challenge me or deny me a day to myself. You two will be together after all. Besides, we are all adults, so why the pushback?"

Rie's questions are valid. Fair. Yes, we are all adults, so why indeed are Les and I not happy with her decision? It's as though we all are frozen in our thoughts. It's as if we are unable to move—in any direction. Rie seems to repeatedly hammer our feet to the floor with each word she speaks. I give reassurance another try. "The fact that we are all adults, and how the two of us will be fine together--is this the point? Isn't the point facing us right now how we always struggle when it comes to the three of us spending too much time together? And now, this is our gauge? Eighteen days is too damn long for the three of us? How does one of us going away from the other two help us solve the three of us? Because we need solving if we are going to make it to the finish line of this journey. Better yet, to keep our sisterhood intact once home again." Okay, my old habit of fixing is difficult to break, yet this is me hoping for us to get a conversation going, which shows no signs of happening. We have a real struggle on our hands. It's not just Rie, it's really all of us.

Les and I are standing side-by-side facing Rie, who happens to be standing in the doorway of her bedroom; metaphorically visible how this can go either way. Still silence. Rie finally speaks again. "I get it. What I also understand is when I separate myself from my words, this is just me being very tired. I am tired of traveling. This is me pushing you two away because I made the mistake of saying three weeks will work. Now my mistake is obvious, and I feel I have let you two down. Even so, when I stop and weigh all of this, and how I'm feeling right now? If we don't stay together, if I don't go with you two today this very much might break us and might very well separate us for a very long time, if not always. And I'm not ready for this to happen to us."

What to do with all of these words, all of these feelings, all of these truths, all of these hurts, all of how far we've come. Come to think of it, it's pretty remarkable how the three of us are even still talking at this point. So how do we begin a conversation about why being three for a length of time challenges us? We agree we need to do better for each other. But how? Rie asks, "For us, what does doing better for each other look like? I mean if we close our eyes and envision what it looks like for us to be better for each other, what do we see for ourselves?"

My first response is, "Being three sisters who embrace the gifts of being individuals, allowing us to be who we are and enjoy each other without a feeling of exclusion. Grace and acceptance."

From Les, "It looks like being there for each other no matter what is going on. We love each other. We need to build on that."

And from Rie, "Mine is tolerance (for our differences), patience, kindness, and love."

And from me, "We need to put into practice our list of words."

All of the jealousies, the self-consciousness, the insecurities, the wanting to belong, these all pound our sister tent with such a force. And as for our poltergeists, skulking nearby in the dark waiting for the next dog whistle calling them in haste, we have pushed them back, once again, together.

The decision to stay together is more work for us, but we hold our sisterhood dear. It's what traveling this length of time with sisters, at least these three sisters, looks like. We are willing to face together what we need to do to keep us tethered to one another rather than drifting too far apart, forever just out of reach from each other.

Settling back in with one another, Rie comes into my bedroom a little bit later. We start talking about packing and the possibility of shipping things home, deciding to make a plan later in the evening. But for now, we elect to stay local today and explore the Cramond Old Mill Trail. It's a wooded path directly behind our apartment complex. (Cottage sounds so much better.) Though this trail is a little less than six miles away from the City Center, it's a lovely place that tourists seem to miss; fine by us.

The direction we take ends up being a lovely stroll, not too much over a mile, which is easy for us considering we leave behind almost 88,000 of our steps in England. As well, the dirt pathway has gentle climbs and is easy to navigate. A river happily meanders alongside the trail while taking in shade from the ancient trees leaning over from the river bank.

Because walking in nature is so familiar to us, we take in all that this path has to offer, including any fauna and the abundance of flora.

When we were little kids, our parents modeled how to notice as well as appreciate all that Mother Nature was showing off to us. From Dad, we learned to identify birds and from Mom, plants and flowers. We all enjoyed being outdoors. And on the weekends we weren't camping, we were still hiking on Sabbath afternoons because Mom and Dad challenged their children with different elevations of hikes. With five kids underfoot, what better way to keep them from squabbling than the beautiful distraction of a very long trail?

For instance, once we hiked up to Half Dome in Yosemite. It's an elevation gain of 4,800 feet to reach the stunning dome—about seventeen miles round trip and almost ten hours to complete. I was twelve, which meant Les was thirteen. At fifteen, Doug was away at summer camp. Brad was ten and Rie nine. I have always struggled with dizzying heights, so when we reached the base of the dome I chose to remain behind with mom and Rie. Les and Brad successfully climbed the rope ladder (as it was then) to the top with Daddy.

Mom and Dad shared their deep love and enjoyment of nature with us. Camping and hiking was probably the strongest bond our parents shared and it helped in raising their kids. Outside of this bond they struggled financially. Daddy worked manufacturing tools during the day and attended college at night. Mom drove a school bus. Their combined income was much too little. For so long, we were a family with so very little money. I believe the words of essayist and poet Charles Lamb perhaps described our family best: "Content with little, yet wishing for more."

At that time, all those years, the five of us kids were never cognizant of how the camping, the hiking, the singing, the joking, and the laughter—all of it was an investment our parents put into their family. As a result, they left our family with such vast wealthfrom which even today all five children continue to benefit, even three stubborn, road-weary, yet strong sisters.

Now as we come upon Cramond Village, we see a massive ocean inlet and causeway, a raised road across low, wet ground. We do our best to venture out a short distance when a powerful wind (oh joy) makes even walking upright a real challenge. Les even makes a few attempts to take a photo of me but all that she captures is my hair blowing in all directions; only one earring is visible. No matter which direction we turn, the wind blows and pushes quite determinedly even the most reluctant of pedestrians. I will not mention her by name.

Coming to the end of the path, we find the tidewater of the inlet out at least a mile. Turning toward the causeway to Cramond Island, we are deciding if we can make it there and back before the tide comes rushing back in. Why are we even thinking this when there are multiple warnings about the tide stranding visitors out on the island? One sign, in particular, makes up our minds for us.

"Call 999/112 in an Emergency, ask for Coastguard.... DON'T GET MAROONED ON CRAMOND ISLAND. Safe crossing times are as follows." From all of the capitalization, we conclude too many people don't heed this warning and must be rescued. Comparing the "safe crossing times" and the time it is right now? It's a gamble we are not willing to take. So we do the next best logical thing, we look for a place to eat.

Backtracking a bit on the path, we return to a little cottage we had spied earlier tucked back in the dense woods. It's a bakery/café. Hansel and Gretel come to mind. Perhaps we should rethink this? We don't and instead take the last vacant table out of three inside a charming little gazebo with glass encasing. And then the Scottish heavens open. A big soaking was avoided once again. It's rather magical watching it rain all around us while drinking our hot drinks and eating something freshly baked from the oven. Right now? Heaven on earth is Scotland.

Although the rain subsides, we still decide to skip the return trip home on the wooded path and take the street instead. Here we quickly fall into a very familiar pattern modeled to us by our Mom: critiquing houses and yards. All the while, we are commenting if what we see pleases or displeases us.

Growing up in Riverside during the sixties and seventies, we witnessed the beginning of an era when too many orange groves were destroyed, replaced with new housing tracts seemingly overnight. But these came with model homes and instant landscaping, which mom always enjoyed. Whichever of her brood wanted to tag along with her, we knew it was there mom came to dream. To wish. To imagine. to whisper her quiet sigh of "someday."

Now all of these years later, Jan's three daughters are in Scotland, considering, commenting, and judging each house and landscape. It's automatic. We need not discuss or explain what we are doing. It makes for a fun walk back to our cottage, okay, apartment.

This night I write the following in my journal:

A rough start this morning. Rie wants to spend time alone. Didn't happen. We are starting to buff up against each other. Later Rie and I talk. She leaves the room. I call her back. We know this trip forces us to work things through vs. just leaving. (Hard. So hard.) We find ourselves becoming braver with each other as time passes. We are trusting our voices, silences. We all work at not being a stomper-offer. We are stronger together. If Rie had not gone with us today? But she did. We enjoyed critiquing houses on our walk home. A nice bonding. Our love, sisterhood, and friendships are stronger because of these challenges. Our sister-tent holds steady even now into day eighteen. And like our rough day in London, this day in Scotland ends up being one of our better days together as well.

Just like sailors too long at sea, we start to imagine ourselves turning for home, feeling a restlessness that comes from such a distance, both in space and time. We are finding ourselves ready for the miles between us and home to be gone.

The next evening, I write in my journal:

We are beginning to see the end of our trip. First, Rie is struggling. She is ready to go home. Weary. I get it. That said, here we are again. Before booking this trip, I fear it is just too long. Is it four days longer than it needs to be? Rie has many stamps on her passport. "Oh yes!" she said, sure about the amount of time. Les agrees with this as well. The good thing is we continue to improve at being travel buddies, practicing the art of us, which means thoughtfully encouraging one another.

In truth, we each have our turn at an all-encompassing weariness. What better way to lift all of our spirits at the same time than to get out of town and change up our scenery? The three of us only add to the ever-growing crowd in the City Center, so we sign up for a bus tour. We will be heading out of town in the morning with a tour of the West Highlands. In planning the night before, I share some not-so-good news. "Ladies, we need to be up early enough to catch bus 41 at 6:24 a.m."

26

MAYBE A SMALL TOUR WORKS?

WE MUST FORCE OURSELVES TO GET READY THIS MORNING. IN THE PROCESS, Rie comes up with a great idea. "Let's eat breakfast in town. It will be much easier." Les agrees, "I like it." I echo her. Why look at how we are so agreeable with each other. I determine it to be a good sign, dagnabbit, and somehow it will be an amazing day. I am willing this to happen as we make bus 41 right on time.

Arriving at the City Center, our bus comes to our stop and we line up ready to step off, yet when the doors open we all step back into each other in a rapid retreat. (I do believe I hear the driver chuckle.) This morning, there is a force from a fierce cold wind (lovely) that greets us. In this instant, we now understand the appeal of Spain over Scotland, as our London Underground acquaintances explained, "Why go to Scotland? It's too cold." Yes, yes it is very cold, even in late August. Well, it's too late for Spain, but staying on bus 41 for the rest of the morning? We are considering this as a realistic option.

Paying the weather no mind, the driver keeps the folded bus door open all the while giving us a sly Welcome to Scotland smile, although we understand what his smile is conveying: *Ok ladies, off you go.*

Fine, but this morning will have me walking behind both sisters. Unfortunately, we come to realize too late that we are too early for restaurants to be open, not that there are a lot. We are fortunate to find a place, only because it's the one with an employee sweeping the sidewalk entrance and the doors are open. And yes, it's a race for who can get out of the wind and in through the doors first. "I'll beat you two," and with that the three of us transform into silly girls attempting to squeeze through all at once; we fail miserably at appearing mature. Now giggling and happy to be out of the biting wind we gather our composure (in other words, starting to behave more adult-like) and are about ready to sit down at the nearest table when we hear, "Good morning," and then, "We aren't open yet, but go ahead and take a seat." They take pity on us, understandably, upon seeing what the wind just blew in. And right now? Pity is just fine with us. "We are so sorry. But thanks for letting us stay. Are you sure? We truly appreciate this. Thank you." We can't emphasize to them how grateful we are to be inside rather than out in the brutal wind.

"Nae bother" sounds so lovely in a Scottish accent. Nevertheless, we very much appreciate these three young male employees letting us bother them. Then again, we are the only customers. But still, they are sincere. "Do you have everything you need? All good?" Such kindness. And then we see just how truly kind they are when one employee hands off a bag of food to the other employee who is sweeping. He in turn hands it off to a poorly-clothed homeless man. Be still, our hearts.

For years, Mom drove a school bus, and from the high school kids to kindergartners, she knew them all. So it confused Mom when I told her one of my fifth-grade classmates never had any lunch to eat.

"Lizzie, are you sure because she carries a lunch box every day."

"She carries a lunch box, Mommy, but there is nothing in it." She suddenly realized my little friend, one of eleven siblings, only carried a lunch box so it appeared to the rest of our classmates that she had food in her lunch pail. Besides, this avoided any chance of her being asked each day, "Where is your lunch?" And though we had little, we had more than nothing. From that day on, our thoughtful Mom packed extra food in my box for my classmate, which I would covertly slide over to her.

This was the same family that Mom made sure had Christmas the year their drunk dad landed in jail; Mom paid attention and listened with her mommy ears as she drove the bus. That Christmas Eve, Mom found a free tree in an abandoned Christmas tree lot. Next, she headed over to Pick and Save (the same source of our Christmas gifts) and bought a few new things. She instructed us to go through our things and choose one item to give. She then wrapped up everything and we delivered our surprise to an extremely grateful family that night. Mom made it very clear to her young brood. "You don't go telling your friends what we have done. We don't ever want to embarrass the family." More than one lesson was learned that day, as well as each time she helped others.

Although she has always been an advocate for the underdog, mom could be and sometimes still is a real conundrum for her children. So often her choice of words fails her. As though she does not know how to line them up in the correct sequence, and then her words do not convey what was intended. It's as though her tongue hobbles her meaning. Because of this, her children have often struggled to reconcile her words against her caring and thoughtful actions toward others, she whose heart is so full of innate empathy and caring for those who have less. At ninety, her heart remains the same.

After the homeless man leaves with his bag of food, the two Scottish lads look at us as if they must justify giving food free of charge. I speak up, "There is no need to explain. Thanks for taking care of him." Echoed by both Les and Rie's, "Yes, thanks so much for caring." The actions of the young lads speak volumes of grace and thoughtfulness, and it was heartwarming to watch it all unfold in front of us, on this early, cold, and very blustery Scottish morning.

After finishing our breakfast, we depart with our hearts stuffed with gratitude. It's good to have a reminder to stop right where we stand and whisper a "Thank You" out to the Universe.

Rie chooses well for this tour; let's say better than my choice in Ireland. No over-sized passenger bus tour this time, but an eight-passenger van. Any straggler problems are now solved. This is going to be a much better choice.

Everyone takes a seat and then we wait. We wait. We wait. Oh boy, this is starting to feel all too familiar as we wait for that one person who seems quite comfortable making everyone else wait. (Again, why aren't these people just left behind? I get it: paying customers; poor ratings on social media; whatever.) Guest #8 finally boards the van, albeit casually. She experiences no love from any of us. She doesn't deserve it.

We are off and while doing his best to include some schtick in his monologue, our driver/guide is best just driving and sticking to the facts. No matter. I simply tune him out and let the stunning countryside tell its own story as we head into the highlands.

But first, the Scottish Lowlands. While they are beautiful in their own right, our driver shares how such views are best appreciated with a bit of freshly baked shortbread. He pulls up to a small bakery. Well, when in Rome.

Taking my order is a young girl wearing a t-shirt covered with extra-large print and in capital letters, the words COACHELLA. Seeing a familiar name on her t-shirt thousands of miles from that location, I cannot resist. I must ask. "Have you been?" She shakes her head back and forth. Then she continues, "No, but I sure hope to someday. Have you ever been," she inquires with hope in her eyes.

I have two ways to respond to her question. Have I been to Coachella Valley, the location of Coachella? Yes. I've passed through Coachella Valley more than visited. Have I been to the Coachella splayed across her t-shirt? No. I haven't been to the wildly popular music festival

Coachella, and I know this is what I am being asked. "No, but I happen to live just a few hours north of where the festival is held." Her eyes get big and then wistfully she responds with, "I'm so jealous. You're so lucky." I sense a delicate balance between her dreams and her reality, and I confirm what she believes about me in almost a whisper, "Yes, I guess I am lucky." Yet how I see this and how she sees it are from two very different lenses. Before I leave, I encourage her to never give up her dream of going to Coachella. After all, I am visiting her country from so very far away. Certainly she can visit mine.

Back on the road again, coming into our view is the fourteenth century Castle Doune. A stronghold in its day, to be sure, but in recent years serves as the shooting location for the filming of "Monty Python," later "Game of Thrones," and "Outlander." The latter being my favorite, having read the first four of Diana Gabaldon's books as well as watching the television series. I explore the inside of the castle and then enjoy walking about the castle grounds as I imagine the different scenes that play out in each area. It's a beautiful location. It's as though I can't take it all in, and then the irony hits me. The young girl with "Coachella" on her t-shirt? I see her as lucky to have all of this in her backyard. As is with everything else, being lucky is quite subjective.

Underway in the small van once again, we come into the very small village of Inveraray, and the first thing to come into view is a castle. With turrets, towers, and the family crest flying from the highest point of the roof, fairy tales were no doubt inspired by this magical-looking castle. And while Rie and I have seen our share of castles, Inveraray is now at the top of our list of favorites. Les is equally impressed. "It's probably my favorite." I look at Rie; we try to stifle our laughter. Rie looks at Les and says, "And how many castles have you seen?" I start to list them for her. "There's that medieval castle in downtown Dublin. That's one. And let's not forget Buckingham, but then again that's a palace. Wait, Windsor Castle. Oh, right, we can only imagine what it looks like because of our second trip to Wimbledon. But it's all water under the bridge now—or should this be moat?" We are feeling lighthearted on this tour, enjoying each other's company as we do so often. Most of the time. Right now? This many days into our journey, we are doing great.

Our tour guide pulls into the parking lot of the castle then turns around to address his eight passengers. "If you are going to explore the castle, you are to be back here in two hours, exactly. I'll be parked right here." My thoughts? *Wow. Taking a big risk here, bud. I mean no hand gestures, no finger-pointing at the watch? It appears he didn't go to the same tour guide school as Jack, our guide in Ireland. Well, let's see how this plays out.* Then he goes on to explain further. "For those who want to do something else, the other option is to explore the local village of Callander. It's known as the Gateway to the Highlands." The three of us are tour rebels, so we choose Callander over Castle. We've seen castles, but not this village. Besides, we enjoy breaking away from the rest of the group, this time, all five of them.

With a population of a little over 2,000, Callander comes with a very abbreviated main street, yet we are content walking through the few shops, admiring the old buildings, and stopping for lunch where I enjoy Fish and Chips while my sisters prefer to eat salad. And yes, as a matter of fact, I am still keeping track. And yes, I do believe Rie and I are now neck-in-neck in the eating contest in which she remains an unwitting participant. Her not knowing works in my favor. I am of the strong conviction this provides me a competitive edge. I am now certain that the best way for me to win is to delay mentioning this whole eating contest thing to her. I'll get around to it. The flight home works for me.

All of us are back in the van (so easy). Okay, a few are late, but not Ireland late. We are now making our way to Loch Lomond, only second in size to the famed Loch Ness. Together they make up the two largest lakes in Great Britain.

Even with it now sprinkling off and on (of course), we still head down to the lake, sans umbrellas (we might as well be locals), to dip our toes in the beautiful water. Sure, the legend of Nessie of Loch Ness is perhaps one of the more famous stories coming out of this country, yet we come to learn Loch Lomond also carries a legend in the song, "The Bonnie Banks o' Loch Lomond." Here, in brief, is how our driver explained it:

With the Jacobite Rebellion raging on, two brothers are serving alongside each other in the Scottish army. Captured by their enemies, both brothers are imprisoned but only one will be executed while the other one will return to freedom. The caveat? These two brothers must decide between themselves which one is to be executed. The younger tells the older to go home and be with his wife and children. The older tells the younger he needs to have the chance to experience a wife and children and he has so much more life ahead of him. In the morning the younger tells his captors he will be the one executed. Instead, he is told to go home as his older brother was executed earlier that morning. So the younger takes the high (earthly) road home while the older the low road (death). They will meet once again back home, one still alive and the other in spirit.

Deeper research and broader tales of this legend reveal a plethora of interpretations. What the Scots do agree upon though is that it is a very sad song, yet they sing it at all kinds of gatherings, including wedding receptions, because this sad song becomes one of appreciating togetherness. Ah yes, togetherness, something we are familiar with. And because it is a life-long habit, the three of us begin softly singing this song (because we know this song), as we make our way down to the loch.

It was when traveling in our 1961 green and white VW van that the seven of us sang together, harmonizing. Our catalog of music was wide and varied thanks to our parents. We also learned from Camp Rangers. Years ago, campgrounds included nightly gatherings around anything from an amphitheater to smaller gatherings where campers sat on fallen trees around a big campfire to all kinds of settings in between. The songs we learned from Camp Rangers (a camp classic, "You Can Plant a Watermelon Right Above My Grave"), along with others that remain in the collective memory of the Moore kids. We also participated in the co-ed SDA Pathfinders Club (think Boy Scouts/Girl Scouts scouting together.) With the Pathfinders, we learned many things to earn badges, and here too we sang many hiking and camping songs. So, of course, we were familiar with the lyrics of Loch Lomond: "You take the high road, and I'll take the low road" because we sang it as we hiked.

Next stop, the Argyll Forest, where our van traverses up a very steep and narrow road. It's when we reach the top of the mountain that we appreciate the location and view from this spot, which is known as "Rest and be Thankful." (Yes, this is the real name.) From the information posted on this site,

"This is where English soldiers built a military road in the 1740s... [making] it easier for them to move from place to place and suppress anti-government revolts." In other words, preventing tribal Highlanders from living their life according to their rituals and traditions, including wearing their clan tartans, kilts, and playing bagpipes, all of which were considered to be an act of war.

After spending some time at this stunning location, our driver lets us know we are on our way back to Edinburgh. Zipping along, our guide announces in a loud voice, "Keep an eye out on the right side of the highway because you will see two horse heads that appear out of nowhere." I turn to Les and Rie. "He said 'two horse heads' right?'" And before we can make sense out of this sure enough we see two horse head sculptures of monstrous proportions. With extremely tall necks (ten stories high) jutting out of the earth, this pair lords over all for several miles. When we pass by, it is 5:30 p.m. Thanks to the August sun still high in the sky and canals of water below, the artistry of Andy Scott's magnificent creatures explodes in a glimmering brilliance.

Our driver explains the horse heads represent the mythological creatures known as Kelpies. It seems the kelpies are water spirits, shape-shifters (changers) that haunt lochs, rivers, and streams of Scotland. As their myth goes, kelpies appear friendly and safe thus making children want to enter the water and climb on for a ride. Unfortunately, once they are on what appears to be a tame horse it turns into a malevolent spirit and children cannot get off because the once smooth skin is now very sticky. The kelpie takes full advantage of this opportunity by dragging the child underwater until it drowns, then proceeds to eat the little one. Well then, this is a lovely bedtime story to share with a toddler before drifting off to sleep. "Sleep tight, little babe. Close your eyes. There is no need to be afraid of the dark." Maybe not for them, but I do believe I will be seeing creepy Kelpies tonight in my dreams, I mean nightmares.

Of course, the purpose of such tales is to teach lessons. My interpretation is to remember not everything or everyone is how they project themselves to others. Perhaps trusting any man who appears to be a local? (In all fairness, not one of them entices us to enter any body of water.)

Arriving back in town, the weather is a repeat of this morning, sort of. Once we've disembarked, Les, her voice quivering, wonders aloud, speaking for her two sisters as well, "How is it possible the wind is even colder and stronger than this morning?"

"It's freezing," comes from Rie and then I follow up with "I don't mind the cold at all, but that dang wind!" The wind. It's always the wind for us and now it fights back at us as we push forward to catch 41 back to Fair-A-Far.

Stuffed in the bus with mostly locals heading home after work, I watch the now familiar scenery and feel a twinge of sadness knowing our rides on bus 41 are coming to an end.

27

ENVELOPE & BACON

LOCATED NEXT TO OUR MARKET ARE TWO BUSINESSES SHARING A VERY SMALL space, Envelope and Bacon. In need of fresh-brewed coffee along with delicious baked goods or breakfast food? Upon entering the only door, veer ever so slightly to your right. The owner and her one-person staff are welcoming and chatty and their product is delish.

Postal needs? Walk straight in from the door toward the counter, all of about four feet if that. The Postmaster is an older gentleman with a stern countenance. It takes him a good while to crack a smile, yet he isn't gruff or off-putting, it's just who knew post mastering to be such a serious task?

There are no posted warning signs of the difficulty one must face while standing in line anytime between 8 a.m. and noon on the Envelope side. The smell of baked goods/breakfast foods wafting through the air a mere two feet away forces a customer to shift allegiance and move over to the Bacon line. Today though, we are outsmarting Bacon and showing up at Envelope in the late afternoon when the ever-tempting olfactory draw from Bacon has finally ceased.

Growing more travel-savvy as each day passes, the three of us have been chatting the last day or so about mailing some things home, you know, to avoid paying extra for our heavy bags. Okay, my suitcase is the one getting heavy. "Just so you guys know, when Dave and I shipped items home from Denmark last year, it was around $125.00, so you should be prepared for anything."

Les, yes Les, expresses a true lack of concern. This is rather odd until she volunteers, "I was talking with Greg. He knows it might be expensive to ship things, but he told me to just relax and not worry about it. I need to spend what's necessary to mail things to my kids in Kansas." Okay, Les. Duly noted. Rie and I give each other a side glance filled with some disbelief, yet because Les sounds (so incredibly) comfortable with an undetermined outlay of cash, then so are we.

Rie is sending clothes home, as am I so ours might cost a little bit more than what Les has to spend. And by the way, with Scotland closer to the States than Denmark, I can't imagine it being as expensive. Either way, we are prepared to pay for the shipping rather than paying for heavier luggage.

Standing in line at Envelope, we each wait patiently for the non-effervescent Postmaster to call us to approach his counter much like a king extending his royal scepter. With his monotone voice in a very thick Scottish accent, we must ask more than once, "Excuse me?" Today though, we are hoping for something different. Fewer words, fewer things lost in translation. Each Moore sister now awaits her summons to approach the counter.

"Next." Rie is ahead of me and places her package on the counter. She hears the shipping price, then, Postmaster (PM): "Do you want to insure your package?"

Rie: "How much?"

PM: "That'll be additional 9.30-pound sterling, Miss.

Rie: "Yes. Thank you." Easy decision. Done.

PM: "Next." My turn. I step up and place my package on the counter, which he weighs. I learn what the shipping expense will be, and then he asks me the same question as Rie:

PM: "Do you want to insure your package?"

Liz: "Yes, thanks. How much do I owe you?"

PM: "That'll be 9.50-pound sterling, Miss." I gladly pay. Easy decision. Done.

PM: "Next." It's Les' turn. She follows suit—package on the counter (check), he weighs it (check), and then asks her, "Do you want to insure your package?"

Les: "Hmmm. I'm not sure. How much is this going to cost to insure it?"

PM: "Yours will be 11.47-pound sterling, Miss."

Not an easy decision for this sister. Not anywhere near done deciding. Rie and I observe as Les struggles to respond to the elderly Postmaster. He just might not outlive our older sis as she stands firmly in place while thinking about having to part with her cash. Then, she says to the Postmaster. "Hmmm. Let me see. Oh, that is $16.00. This is your mail service, so don't you pretty much guarantee it will get there? Should I worry about that?" I am now thinking to myself, What happened to Miss "Spend what I need?" Poof! She is gone at the sound of having to part with some of her coins. I now slide up next to her and gently chide as I whisper near her right ear. "Les, remember you said you were going to spend what you needed?" And her reply to me? Both predictable and priceless while not in a completely soft voice. "I know, but 16.00 American dollars? Don't you think that's a bit much when the shipping is already $34.00?" We do love her so very much. She makes it easy for us to laugh, joke, and tease--with/at her.

I turn to Rie. We both begin shaking our heads. Here come our matching smiles. This isn't good because we know what comes next:

poor attempts at stifling our laughter. We can only hold this in for so long. So I take a deep breath and leave Les with only one word, spoken not entirely in a whisper, yet in a sing-songy tone. "Ohhhkay." And as I turn away from her my whisper now a bit louder, "Mercy, Leslie Anne." And with this Rie and I step outside, shake our heads, and we burst out laughing. Just when we thought Les was going to surprise us; that close.

It's only now on this trip that we learn how that first husband of Les' held her accountable for every damn dime. Even after grocery shopping, he demanded to see the receipt. All of this he put on her while time after time he bought what he wanted for himself, including various automobiles. All he demanded those years ago never left her. Stitch this together with her innate frugality, and well, this is just who she is when it comes to matters of money.

But now for the rest of the shipping story, because it is so worth sharing. We've been home a few days when Rie's package arrives; it has been less than a week. Mine arrives a couple of days later. It takes Les' package just shy of a month to finally reach her family in Kansas. Until this occurs, Rie and I are going back-and-forth with each other, pretty much each day laughing, yes, absolutely at the expense of our older sister, as we imagine Les' treasures taking the oceanic route around the Cape of Africa. Perhaps China? Rie and I even joke about Oz as a possible route for her package, dropping from the sky above Kansas. I call Les, often, okay, every other day because I can't help myself (besides, Rie won't do it). I can't resist asking her, "So, any news about your package arriving yet?"

"No! Not yet, but I know it will be any day now. I'll let you know." Oh, any day now? How does she know this? Following phone calls with the oldest sis, this mischievous middle sis calls the equally mischievous little sis with the daily shipping news. By the way, later we share with Les that she is the source of much laughter for her two younger sisters. She gets it. She laughs too. I know, I know. Some might be thinking poor Les, but come on, she brings it on herself when some peace of mind comes for a mere $16.00, which she had in her wallet. Anyway, once she receives word the package arrives, Les shares, "I knew it would be okay." Rie and I agree she had not been one-hundred percent sure.

This evening as I write in my travel journal, now burgeoning with our escapades, I reflect upon our time in Scotland. There is no doubt we look forward to heading home; nevertheless, each of us is projecting a bit of hesitation as we conclude our remarkable journey. This has been something that we never, ever imagined for ourselves. Scotland proved to be a great place for us to unwind. And lucky for the three Moore sisters, no Kelpie shape-shifters among us. We continue to learn to navigate the waters around each other, willing to save, if need be, each other, from any possible emotional drowning. We've done well in this stunning land.

Farewell, Scotland: Mar shin lat Scotland.

Her majesty, 'The Castle of the Maidens.'
(Edingburgh, Scotland)

Another Day, another adventure for the Moore sisters.
(Fair-A-Far; Cramond, Scotland)

In the Scottish Highlands at 'Rest and Be Thankful.'
(Cairndow, Scotland)

Sculpted by Andy Scott, giant horse heads jutting out of the ground.
(Falkirk, Scotland)

28

FOURTH TIME'S A CHARM FOR THE THREE OF US

OH SURE, IT WAS ALL GOING SO WELL CHECKING INTO THE EDINBURGH International Airport for our flight back to Ireland. That is until we locate our terminal and Les glances out the window and spies an Aer Lingus prop plane. This is when things start to fall apart. Specifically Les. Much to her chagrin, it's a much smaller plane from what we have been flying. Her displeasure (another word for fear), is discernible in her voice when she points at the plane on the tarmac. "Is that the plane we are taking back to Ireland?" This followed by a very clear announcement: "I'm NOT getting on that small plane. No sir-ee. Liz, just tell me that's not our plane."

"Uhm, yes it is. You'll be fine. It's only a half-hour flight. No big deal, sis. We'll be in the air at a low altitude because as soon as we take off we will be preparing for landing." But Les isn't thoroughly convinced, if even at all. Her mindset quickly changes though when we tell her we will see her in Ireland once she figures out alternative transportation for herself. "Les, all you have to do is get on the plane, buckle yourself in, and close your eyes. Before you know it, we'll be landing in Ireland. It's up, levels off, it's down. Easy-peasy." I'm on the receiving end of a look that clearly conveys her total disbelief in me.

Upon landing, Les can't get out the rear exit door fast enough. She is walking quite fast; I'd even categorize her stride as a sprint. But the story here is that she is leading. Rie and I cannot believe this phenomenon occurring right before our eyes. It is indeed a rare sighting, so rare that I can't resist taking a picture. She continues in full stride inside the terminal, and we have to call after her. "Les. Where are you going so fast?" Rie and I are cracking up at her. When we get Les to stop, she says, "I couldn't get off that darn plane fast enough."

"Do you think?" I ask. Then I turn to Rie; she is as dumfounded as I am. Then we show Les her the photo that encapsulates such a larger story as walking is the norm but Les leading is not. Yet here she is, finally, at the end of our journey leading. It still counts, we reassure her. And with that, we three stand in the middle of the terminal sharing a tired, silly, uproarious laugh. At this point, who cares who gives us a sideways glance? Then, we decide this funny start is a good omen as we finally turn for home. Just one more day. We hail a taxi and head for our hotel, The Maldron.

Because we are back in Ireland, the responsibility landed on me to book a hotel room. We wanted to stay close to the airport and "The Maldron" is just one street away from the airport, perfect for my airport anxiety. When we walk inside we see it's a good decision: It's clean. It's modern. It serves food. Our room is ready. And upon receiving our room key we hear. "Just take the lift down to the lower floor." (Cue choir of angels singing; at this point, why not?) Did she just say the 'L' word? And looking over we see it: the lift. (First of all, there is one. Second, no evidence of yellow tape, and no typed note across the doors.) For the Moore sisters, the fourth time's a charm.

And when we enter our room? Three single beds. All in a row. All close together. But this time, they look extremely comfy, and they are. Do we give Les her choice of beds? Does it truly matter at this point?

Travel isn't always pretty. It isn't always comfortable.

Sometimes it hurts . . . But that's okay.

The journey changes you; it should change you.

It leaves marks on your memory, on your consciousness, on your heart.

–Anthony Bourdain

PART FOUR * HOMEWARD, TOGETHER

29

PATIENTLY IMPATIENT

READY FOR OUR LONG FLIGHT HOME AFTER A GREAT NIGHT'S SLEEP, WE ARE sure to pose for our last sister selfie in the doorway of our hotel room. This has been a journey made up of one photo at a time and one step at a time.

Boarding passes in hand, we make our way to Security when just as quickly Les and her bag are in secondary check. I know she is nervous, yet she is good at hiding it until this happens with her suitcase. Her frustration is easy to detect, she leans into me and whispers, "Why am I always singled out?" I must reassure her, again, it's random, and to cool it, otherwise, they might become suspicious of her when there's nothing to be suspicious about.

Once inside the terminal, we find the digital board Customs uses to show assigned numbers to enter. Now, we wait for ours to appear.

As it so happens, the Dublin Airport is only one of the handfuls of European airports to offer a U.S. Customs preclearance for departing flights back to the U.S. This means having to arrive even earlier because of Customs, but it also means that after flying eleven hours, we will land at LAX as a domestic flight; we go directly to Baggage Claim. It's a great benefit, especially after a long flight.

We aren't there yet. Back to the digital board. The purpose of assigning numbers is to stagger the number of travelers entering the line at Customs. Because I require further clarification, I ask an Aer Lingus employee. The response given is too nonchalant. I refuse to trust her advice: "Oh, just wait until 12:45 p.m. Then, go on ahead through the process. This way you don't have to worry about the number." What? She is advising we wait until almost 1:00 p.m. for a 2:55 p.m. international flight? I need to make sure I get this right for us and right now this doesn't feel right at all. It feels too much like the advice given to us at the Belfast train station all over again: "Sit in that small waiting room there with all of the others waiting to board. Your train will stop here. You will hear the call to board." No, one close call is enough, and it's not happening a second time, especially with our flight home. This time, we will take things into our own hands. More specifically, I will take into my own hands by placing my faith in something much more trustworthy: Google. The advice is a three-hour early arrival to avoid a long line. We are right on time! It's almost noon when I engage in a serious stare-down with the electronic board as I watch for our numbers. I worry I might miss something, starting with our three numbers. Remember, worrying is my job, and right now I'm oh so great at it.

Numbers to queue up for Customs appear and disappear, well, all numbers except for ours. And now a new set of numbers flash. Yes. No. Not us.

Daring a brief break away from the board, I swing around to take a look back at my two sisters. I think of our collection of sister selfies, other photos, and steps, reaching almost 220,000 in total, walking nearly 100 miles. Yet just look at those two relaxing away in their airport chairs. Talking, laughing, playing some ridiculous word game on their iPhones. Not a worry or a care in the world. Well, it's a good thing I know how to properly worry because those two certainly do not. We'd miss our flight if I left it up to one of them. I feel better being the one keeping watch for our numbers. Whatever. I turn my attention back to the board when I see our group numbers appear:

"Les, Rie—hey you two, let's go!" I am happy to see them respond quickly. I'd hate to start yelling at both of them so very late in our trip, yet, if I must.

First a long hallway, then a long stairway, and then an extremely long queue. This is why it's worth following the advice of many travelers who have flown this route: "Get there early. The lines are long and oftentimes very slow." Right they are because we now stand at the end of a very long line that serpentines forever, and with so many people it does not appear to have a beginning. We soon come to learn this is not the line for Customs but a secondary security check. Rie and I turn to Les. We just look at her. Nothing more. But from her, we hear, "I saw that look from you two. Just remember, I've had my turn already, now it's time for one of you."

With so many people standing in line, many of us start talking with each other. The friendly banter helps everyone to focus more on the conversation and less on standing. Security is giving a very thorough check of everyone's bags, not just Les'. Security over, we now move on to the next queue—Customs. We are this close to home and right now the three of us work diligently at not falling apart, separately and together. Feeling both exhaustion and excitement as we prepare for our eleven-hour flight home, we all take a minute to calm ourselves down. We decide to focus on the last twenty days and revel in what we've accomplished together.

Customs is nothing new to Rie; she is calm. My airport stress long gone, Customs is not new to me either, yet we suspect Les is still nervous. We ask how she is doing and she quietly confides she is getting nervous. (Just look at her sharing.) Yet to experience U.S. Customs, she asks what she needs to say. Rie advises her to just relax. I believe Les expects me to give her a few smart-ass quips, yet even I know this is not the time to do so. So I suggest to her "Just stand kind of behind me, a little off to the side. Okay?" She likes this idea; it calms her down. The truth is Les will realize soon enough there is no hiding and she must speak on her behalf but why tell her this now? I'll just let it unfold organically. She will do fine.

The three weary Moore sisters step forward for face recognition. A Customs Officer calls us to his open station, and yes, Les is doing her best version of semi-hiding behind me. Because the officer projects a casual demeanor, I can sense Les relaxing. I know this because she bravely moves to stand next to me.

"Ladies, hello. Passports, please." He takes them one at a time, slowing down the process. He then proceeds with his questions. "How long have you been gone?"

"Three weeks." We all chime in with that one.

"What countries did you visit?" Rie shares, "Ireland, England, Scotland, and now back to Ireland." And Les, suddenly calm and confident, offers up (atta, girl), "We are three sisters on our first big trip together." She is proud of the three of us. It can be heard in her voice. This stops the Agent. "What? You three survived each other for three weeks? Wow. Good for you." We tell him how during this entire trip people wonder the same when they learn we are sisters. The typical response? "Really. Sisters traveling together for this length of time?" We seemed to be a mental puzzle that required solving; disbelief telegraphed in one of two ways: the sideways shake of the head, or the dropping of the lower jaw. But we just smiled back at them with our mischievous grins, much like the Cheshire cat in Alice in Wonderland, leaving others to figure it out for themselves. I tell our friendly Customs Agent, "Yes, three sisters traveling for three weeks, visiting three countries, and hey, we are still talking!" He responds with a chuckle, then says, "I like how that sounds. Way to go, ladies." And with that, he sends us on our way. Gate 401 is nearby.

Soraidh slari, Ireland. Farewell Ireland, once again.

Our last Sister Selfie, at least for this trip.
(Cloghran, Ireland)

30

THE SURVIVAL OF OUR SISTER TENT

Lifting off from Ireland at 2:55 p.m., our plane lands in California at 5:55 p.m. Although it appears we complete the trans-Atlantic flight in just three hours, the truth is we end up flying those mighty long hours again, covering over thousands of direct miles (5,594, according to the in-flight screen). Upon arrival, we are more than ready to be back on the ground. That being said, we are also more than ready to take a break from our daily walks, always consisting of several miles. But right now, we have no choice but to add a few more steps to our already one hundred miles of walking to reach Baggage Claim. This involves some prodding and begging on our part as we must convince our weary feet to go just a few steps farther. They begrudgingly carry us down a long corridor then down a flight of stairs to where we wait for the arrival of our luggage alongside our fellow travelers.

It's also here where most are greeted by family, friends, lovers, or whomever, well, in most cases but not me. I already know ahead of time Dave must stay home with our pup Sully, so my brothers-in-law serve as Dave's stand-in. Tim and Greg are happy the three sisters arrive safely, and together. This means two things: One, the plane did not crash as our elderly mother feared, despite her words "I trust God to keep the plane in the air." And two, that I have not left either one of my two sisters forever in a Scottish bog. In other words, this middle sister did not have to activate a backup plan.

Even so, at this particular moment, I am feeling left out. While I have no doubt Dave misses me something fierce (this is me putting words in his mouth), my annoyance level grows stronger by the minute as I am missing out on my husband's greeting. And just as quickly as my petulance arrives, it just as quickly vanishes. This is a happy time for us all and besides, someone has to watch out for our luggage. (I somehow end up being "someone.") Funny, I don't remember deciding to be the one to do this but no matter. However, what does matter to me is how other travel-weary passengers are trying their best to covertly nudge me out of my prime location next to the luggage carousel. It's been three weeks. I am ready for my bed. I. Am. Not. Budging. And then thankfully, the carousel bell rings and the red light flashes to signal the arrival of luggage. All of it starts tumbling down the slippery silvery chute, much like misbehaving children bumping and pushing one or the other out of their way. It appears as if each piece is vying to be first, just like their human counterparts wanting to escape after such a long flight.

As we gather up our luggage and head for the parking structure, we will once again ease back into our own lives, our pillows, and everything else our own. It's as if our journey has gone by much too quickly.

Reaching our cars, I just can't resist. I am after all the one who creates memories through photos, "How about one last sister photo at the airport to book-end our first photo when we arrived at LAX?" And just like that, we are huddled next to each other. Although not a selfie, we trust the task to Greg and Tim. The two of them capture the three of us in one remarkable last picture. When the Moore sisters look at it together, we can't help but marvel at ourselves, which leaves me to wonder aloud. "How many other sisters could pull off such a trip while also being joined at the hip? Really. Come on, how many? And look at us wearing the same matching smiles as when we posed before leaving." These are the smiles of three sisters who have persevered and, through most all of it, have also laughed. Our sister tent has remained intact even though there are tatters and tears here and there. After all, it took quite a beating weathering the storms we brought upon ourselves. Then I ask both of my sisters: "Remember my concern about this trip possibly destroying us, and if so how would we deal with any fallout? Well, this last photo says it all." There we are, standing in our birth order, naturally, while leaning into each other, arms casually and comfortably around our shoulders, around waists. This priceless photo further emphasizes how opening ourselves up to vulnerability paid off. And then the three of us give ourselves a group hug and say our goodbyes.

I catch a ride home with Rie and Tim, and soon my weary self slides into a slouching position in the back seat. I wish my mind to slow down, but all thoughts keep bringing me back to our sisterhood and how for too long we let ourselves settle into believing we knew each other well. Fortunately, over these past few week we've dismantled these beliefs. We have also come full circle with Margaret Meade's observation about grown sisters and creating a stronger bond. This might not be true for all sisters, but for the unique Moore sisters we have a deeper under-standing and appreciation for our uniqueness. We have a sisterhood worth protecting.

This photo says it all!
LAX; Los Angeles, California

A sister is a kind of friend you'd travel far to find,

only she's been standing right beside you all along.

-Leigh- Standley

PART FIVE * POST-JOURNEY

31

SOME 'MOORE' TOGETHERNESS

IT IS ONLY A FEW DAYS LATER BEFORE THE THREE OF US ARE ON THE PHONE WITH each other, reliving experiences, laughing at ourselves. While we can't help but marvel when reminiscing about our journey, it's the wonderment of this whole new equilibrium we are coming to enjoy with each other; it's palpable. Before our trip when we brushed up against each other we would typically stomp off if necessary; we were unsure of ourselves so why would our sisters be sure of us? Yet now, we've come to trust ourselves and our sisterhood. It's our new 'normal' and it feels comfortable and secure. The knowledge we have gained about each other on our journey generated greater understanding and compassion, which, in the process removed subconscious tension and erased our emotional distance. In its place, a new path spreads out before us, one we are appreciating together.

Months later, and we are still talking. In fact, I reached out to my sisters with a proposal. "Are you interested in spending a long weekend together in Mammoth?" I hear the same response from both sisters, "Yes. Why not?" Look at us. Even following our three-week trip together that included some rough spots, where others would have dismantled their tent and called it quits, the response from the Moore sisters is still Why not? when it comes to spending time together, not Why?

"Let's invite the husbands too. It's time for the six of us to have some quality time together, create new memories, right?" And so it's decided with no hesitation. And by the way, we don't consider how being together for more than three days might test us. True to form, we don't discuss it. We don't plan for it. We just pack.

While in the evenings, the six of us play cards and board games together, during the day the guys go off to do their things while the three of us do ours. At one point, I am driving and Les is in the front passenger seat with Rie in the back seat. Although there is no carry-on luggage this time, we just can't resist singing "Carry On Wayward Son," by Kansas of which we still fail at most of the lyrics. As might be expected, this conjures up so many memories from our trip, starting with pesto, treasure trash, and Les' jeans, always the first story for us to share with anyone who wants a good laugh. It does fascinate us how we all share the same experiences yet come away with different perspectives of these memories, which leads us to lively discussions and even light-hearted disagreements about who is right (this would be me, of course). We are enjoying being sisters together in Mammoth. It is this same Sierra Nevada mountain range that holds so many camping memories for the Moore family. This brings out the mischievousness in me. I offer up to Les and Rie about giving tent camping another try, "I know you two and your husbands are talking about getting travel trailers, but how about one more tent camping event for ol' time's sake?" Les is quick with her emphatic reply. "Are you kidding me? No! And who is going to help us up off the ground in the morning?" Great question. Then Rie interjects, "Oh my gosh! Can't you picture us as turtles on our backs? Forever stuck!" As we envision this we burst into laughter. Then, I confess how I too lack a desire to tent-camp. "Let me make it very clear just how unwilling I am to sleep in a tent again, if I can help it. I remember the first time I slept in a hotel, and from that moment on I was done with tent camping."

In the middle of the talking, singing, and laughing, Les says, "Mom asked if I'm up for another sister trip. I told her I would. What about you two?"

Rie's response is immediate, the length of travel time not a part of her mindset, not at all. "Sure! Of course. Where to this time?"

My reply? "Absolutely. A two and three-fourths week trip for the three of us sounds perfect!"

And with this, the three Moore sisters pick up where they often leave off—laughing.

Months later, and I'm having to prop Les up as the three of us continue to laugh together.
(Mammoth Lakes, California)

Traveling–it leaves you speechless,

then turns you into a storyteller.

–Ibn Battula, (1304-1368)

BOOK CLUB QUESTIONS

1. What did you make of the depiction of family and sibling dynamics in the story? What made it accurate or relatable for you, regardless of your family position/makeup?

2. When it came to taking this trip, the Moore sisters were, and still are, of the why not? mindset rather than why? If an opportunity for such a trip were to be made available, which would you be: why not? or why?

3. Which one of the three Moore sisters did you find yourself connecting with the most and for what reason did she draw you in?

4. Traveling through Ireland, England, and Scotland, explain which jaunt with the Moore sisters you enjoyed the most and why?

5. Which particular event did the author recount that made you laugh, or cry?

6. How does the author's use of flashbacks serve to further enhance the experiences of the trip for you?

7. If there is anything that surprised you about these three sisters traveling together, what was it?

8. Since reading this book, how encouraged are you to start planning a trip (of at least three weeks) with others, and with whom would you travel? Who would you leave at home?

9. Even though the title reveals the Moore sisters are "still talking," nevertheless, did anything still surprise you at the end of their trip?

10. If you were to meet any of the Moore sisters, what question/s would you ask?

11. After reading, which of the three countries are you now the most curious about visiting?

12. Although this book is about the Moore sisters, what did you learn about yourself from reading this memoir?

CONTACT THE AUTHOR AT HER WEBSITE
ELIZABETHMOOREKRAUS.WEEBLY.COM

We Love Memoirs

Join me and other memoir authors and readers in the We Love Memoirs
Facebook group, the friendliest group on Facebook.

www.facebook.com/groups/welovememoirs/

Ways to Connect with Liz:
elizabethmoorekraus.weebly.com (Website)
@lizkrausauthor (Instagram)
@LizKraus8 (Twitter)
Liz Moore Kraus (Facebook)
elizabethmoore_kraus@yahoo.com (email)

ACKNOWLEDGEMENTS

It's not joy that makes us grateful; it is gratitude that makes us joyful.

- Brother David Steindl-Rast

TO THE COMMUNITY OF WOMEN INVOLVED IN MY WRITING PROCESS: THANKS! Claudia Brewer Michel. I knew I could trust my words with you just as I have trusted our 50 + years of friendship. Kathy Milleman Mack. Your willingness to help read aloud the early manuscript was the encouragement I needed to continue. Erin Donnelly Kraus. My dearly loved daughter-in-law, I'm forever grateful for the heavy lifting you did with the early editing. You are both joy and inspiration to me and our family. Catherine Hillman Clark. My friend and former colleague, forever just down the hall from one another, I'm so grateful for your insight, editing, and assistance. Amy Madsen. Neighbor, once colleague, you helped by stepping in at the 'last hour' to marry my words with your ideas and words. Carol Soffietto. And then there was you (unexpectedly), and your willingness to read and critique. Leslie Moore Patch, Rie Moore Dekker. Thanks for your sisterly encouragement and laughter as I wrote my side of our story.

David Stuart Kraus. With your feet firmly planted on the ground and me spinning above you, you have always encouraged, supported, and accepted me; your love is expansive. I'm always looking forward to what our next chapter in life will bring. Brent-Stig Kraus. My son, you bring love, laughter, and joy to me. You are forever my champion, encouraging me in all that I attempt/do, including my storytelling. Thanks for always reminding me, "Stay the course, Ma."

Janice Miller Gish. Mom, you are honored and loved. Marji Adams. Sharon Allegra Ellis. Janet Evans Emery. Carol Soffietto. (Again). Individually: Bright. Well-read. Together: My dedicated community who read final proofs; forever grateful. Catherine Hillman Clark: Thanks for the beautiful web page. Jennifer Whitsitt. Thanks for the great headshots.